Human Resource Strategy

Human Resource Strategy

Towards a general theory of
Human Resource Management

Shaun Tyson

PITMAN
PUBLISHING

PITMAN PUBLISHING
128 Long Acre, London WC2E 9AN

A Division of Pearson Professional Limited

First published in Great Britain 1995

© Shaun Tyson 1995

British Library Cataloguing in Publication Data
A CIP catalogue record for this book can be obtained from the British Library

ISBN 0 273 60096 6

10 9 8 7 6 5 4 3

Typeset by Land & Unwin (Data Sciences) Limited
Printed and bound in Great Britain by Bell & Bain, Glasgow

The Publishers' policy is to use paper manufactured from sustainable forests.

I wish to dedicate this book to my mother and father,
and to Zoe, for their love and understanding

CONTENTS

PREFACE

This book was written in order to set out the role of human resource management as an interpretative, representative and determining force for management intentions at work. The book is intended for the thinking practitioner, and as such I hope will be of value to students and to managers alike. It was prompted by the view that, while technological progress hastens us towards ever more new products and services, advances in the way we manage ourselves seem painfully slow.

In spite of all the rhetoric about managing people, the task is as difficult now as it has always been. This may be because the trappings of modern life disguise the fundamental realities of our existence. Some may argue that the civilising influence of the last one hundred years has removed the worst excesses of the industrial revolution, but sweat shops still exist, there are still strikes, and structural unemployment is a plague throughout Europe. One could be forgiven for thinking that little or nothing has been learned about how to create cohesive societies, and that our social conscience has dwindled, not become stronger in defence of our liberties. In 1945 Beveridge wrote:

> 'Full employment, like social security must be won by a democracy, it cannot be forced on a democracy, or given to a democracy. It is not a thing to be promised or not promised by a government, to be given or withheld as from Olympian heights. It is something that the British democracy should direct its government to secure at all costs, save the surrender of essential liberties. Who can doubt that full employment is worth winning, at any cost less than the surrender of those liberties? If full employment is not won and kept, no liberties are secure, for to many they will not seem worthwhile.'
>
> (William Beveridge, *Full Employment in a Free Society*, Norton, New York (1945) p. 258.)

That our present democracy is so cynical, or alienated, that we have ceased demanding full employment as a fundamental right is perhaps not surprising. Punch-drunk from successive boom–bust economics, shell-shocked from experiencing change upon change, numbed from the everyday necessity to keep a job, pay the bills and maintain the dignity of basic relationships, the people of this democracy may wonder what human resource management has to do with them.

This book seeks to explain the strategic purpose of human resource management by reference to the practice in high-performing UK companies, and to show that there is a theoretical basis for the activity.

The theoretical basis turns on the capacity of HRM to mobilise the human resource through interpreting societal, organisational and sentient influences into a coherent management philosophy, by using the symbolic order. Organisational performance is contingent upon the use made of the human as well as the capital assets of the business. By mobilising the human resource in pursuit of strategic goals, human resource management contributes directly to business success. What we have learned over the last twenty years is that without business success, translated into work opportunities, there can be no full employment; no reduction in the apocalyptic evils of Want, Sickness, Idleness and Ignorance; no democracy and, ultimately, no society. The hopes of future generations rest upon responsible employers and the way in which they use human resources strategically.

ACKNOWLEDGEMENTS

I wish gratefully to acknowledge the contribution of all those who were involved in the 'Different Routes to Excellence' Project which is reported in this book, in particular Noeleen Doherty, Michael Witcher, Dennis Henry, John Barnard and the 30 companies surveyed, whose senior staff were unstinting of their time. I wish to thank also Phil Rowlands, Penelope Frow, Philip Davies, Gwen Jones, Alison Mulcock, Karen Scott Evans and Belinda Mocatta for helping with the interviews.

I would also like to express my thanks to Professor Dr Karl Freidrick Ackermann of Stuttgart University for permission to reproduce his diagram, and to the President and Fellows of Harvard College for permission to use the diagram 'five phases of growth' from L E Greiner's article which appeared in the *Harvard Business Review*, July/August 1972.

I am also grateful to Ann Davies for all her work in the preparation of the manuscript and to Dr Penelope Woolf, the publisher, for her suggestions and for her patience. Any errors or omissions in the book remain my own.

CHAPTER 1

Corporate and business strategy

As the twentieth century comes to a close, the essentials of the human condition are more and more sharply revealed. Not, as was once feared, by the coming of a new dark age – some horrific nuclear winter, or devastating drought which returns mankind to a primitive existence, but rather because of the sophisticated and complex social, economic and political interrelationships which govern our lives.

Political and economic changes in Europe, added to new technology, demographic change and a felt need for softer values, have produced a sense of turbulence and uncertainty in business life. A world-wide recession and its effects on stock and currency markets have prevented organisations from settling back into an unchanged state. The adaptability of organisations has never been more important: 'adapt or die', is a Darwinian truism which underpins every mission statement. There has never been a more propitious time to study the way in which those who manage organisations seek to direct the efforts of their employees in support of their business objectives.

The way the human resource is used strategically to achieve business or organisational objectives is the subject of this book. First we should explore what is meant by strategy. Then the fundamental issues of what are business and human resource strategies, and how they fit together and influence each other will occupy the following chapters of the book.

DEFINING BUSINESS STRATEGY

For the moment, a working definition for business strategy may be used. Business or organisational strategy may be described as the attempt by those who control an organisation to find ways to position their business or organisational objectives so that they can exploit the planning environment and maximise the future use of the organisation's capital and human assets.

This definition is a little different from those found in most strategy textbooks, which usually define strategy as 'determining' long-term goals, and adopting courses of action and allocating resources to achieve long-term goals (Chandler 1962), or as the process of deciding the basic mission of the company (Hofer and Schendel 1978). The process is certainly significant but these definitions do not give enough emphasis to the planning environment. The planning environment, that is those variables which influence plans but which are outside the direct control of the organisation's management, is the setting which managers must exploit. Our working definition stresses the potential for making the most of the organisation's strengths, to survive and develop in that environment.

There are also difficulties when defining 'human resource management' and 'human resource strategies'. Furthermore, the issue of whether human resource management is an alternative phrase to 'personnel management' or whether it means something different has become a vexed question, still unresolved despite considerable research. Recent findings show that the title 'human resource manager' is still not commonly accepted within the UK, is used mainly within the head offices of larger corporations and is not associated with any coherent set of policies (Guest and Hoque 1993). In the chapters which follow, we will return to the question of whether the new phraseology does represent a significant movement in ideas. We will use the term 'human resource management' (HRM) as an equivalent to the term 'personnel management', whilst acknowledging HRM as a more modern title.

One further dimension to the semantic debate does concern us here. The terms 'policy', 'strategy' and 'practice' are used sometimes interchangeably. This confusion covers a deeper ambiguity. Within corporate strategy, the HRM element may well be a 'second order' strategy, or a set of policies designed to deliver against 'first order' strategy objectives (Purcell 1989). Policies are not always written down. They are changed, exceptions are made, and they are adapted to circumstances. In this sense they may be regarded as 'practices'. Even if we accept that HRM practices are designed to help achieve strategic corporate or business objectives, such practices may still be regarded as strategic because there are choices.

> 'The idea of strategy, however, does seem to imply an external force or forces which one must anticipate and try and come to terms with; strategic thinking arises from the need to cope with such pressures, not because they can be ignored. Lack of autonomy and strategic thinking are not mutually exclusive. To argue otherwise is to make the very common mistake of associating choice with freedom, and treating its opposite as determinism.'
>
> (Thurley and Wood 1983, p. 2.)

We will therefore use the term 'HR strategy' to describe a set of ideas, policies and practices which management adopt in order to achieve a people-management objective.

The changing political and economic environment, and the most difficult business conditions since the 1930s are bringing change to all organisations. Human resource strategies are now frequently seen as the key to the achievement of business objectives, to keep companies competitive. This can be illustrated by reference to one or two examples drawn from the many that are available through the media. For example, Calor Gas has reduced its permanent workforce by one third, replacing permanent staff with temporary staff on lower rates, and has substituted lower regional rates of pay for national rates of pay.

> 'John Harris, operations and personnel director, said the Company needed to cut costs, increase productivity and change its culture.'
>
> (Pickard 1992, p. 1.)

London Underground's change programme, the 'Company Plan', anticipated a reduction of 5000 staff and was intended to change decision-making, pushing responsibility down and introducing a total quality management programme (Crofts 1992).

However, human resource strategy is not just a matter of change programmes. In his well-publicised description of Nissan in the UK, Wickens comments on human resource strategies:

> 'Companies such as Nissan, IBM, Pilkingtons, Eaton, Nabisco, Whitbread, Continental, Formica, Eldridge Pope, Kimberley Clarke, Hardy Spicer, Inmos, Norsk Hydro and many others have looked at the totality of the people part of the business and have determined how to get from "here" to "there". They have not imposed change, but have taken people with them.'
>
> (Wickens 1987, p. 189.)

We must therefore seek to explain what are the characteristic features of human resource strategies, how these connect to business strategies and what actual consequences for organisational performance flow from this strategic conjunction. Our starting point in this quest is to examine the frameworks which have been created to explain how different strategies operate.

CORPORATE STRATEGY AND TACTICS

The idea of following a strategy to achieve objectives has a military origin. There has always been some confusion over terminology. 'Stratagems' are sometimes perceived as clever ruses, wiles to outwit the opposition. In games, such as chess, strategies may be calculated risks such as opening gambits. In sport they may be seen as game plans, where the strengths and weaknesses of the opposition have been evaluated and teams selected and moves rehearsed to beat them.

In the nineteenth century, military theorists such as von Clausewitz and Moltke attempted to produce a 'scientific' account of warfare, just as FW Taylor attempted to propose a science of management half a century later. For von Clausewitz, tactics were quite different from strategy.

> 'Tactics, or the theory of fighting, is in reality the principal thing, partly because battles are decisive, partly because it comprises the most of what can be taught. Strategy or the theory of the combination of separate battles towards the objective of the campaign is a subject more of natural and matured power of judgement.'
>
> (Vol III, 1949, p. 179.)

Here, there is a distinction drawn between tactics: the operational, action-oriented day-by-day manoeuvring to achieve immediate objectives, and the broader planning of the whole campaign. Military terminology as a way of describing action has found a resonance with companies who are in competition with rivals. In sales management, for example, we happily speak of sales campaigns, of capturing territory from the opposition, and of market intelligence. Corporations have taken to corporate strategic planning, and the notion that, to achieve objectives, careful preparation and planning are necessary. The quotation from Clausewitz also suggests that tactics can be taught, whereas strategy cannot; an issue to which we will return later.

In the distinctions between strategy and tactics we can see the difference between corporate, long-range planning and tactical, day-by-day management. The process of creating strategies and adapting them to everyday use may produce a more complex relationship between tactics and strategy. The 'tactics' are the managerial processes: organising, coordinating, motivating and controlling (as we may suggest from Fayol's ideas). The speed of change, however, has made adjustment of policies and strategies essential for survival. Strategies can thus only be successful if there is a feedback process. IBM has only been able to survive because the senior management recognised that their product development was not as flexible as that of their smaller competitors. A rapid turnaround has been achieved, with a slimmer organisation and new products and new solutions.

The formation and reorganisation of companies is now so rapid that the tactical and strategic levels frequently merge. In 1992, the Hanson Group made a hostile bid for Rank Hovis McDougall. In its attempt to resist the bid, RHM reorganised into three divisions: a grocery business, a milling and bread business, and a cakes business. This demerger strategy was intended to raise the price of the acquisition, and may result in divisions floating off and being purchased by another company, so a company such as RHM would become a less attractive buy. ICI and Racal have also separated out parts of their businesses as a defence against takeover bids and fears (Hamilton, *Sunday Times*, 18 October 1992). Clearly, immediate concerns for survival may override 'strategic' planned considerations and the days of the sedate processes of careful long-range planning may be over for good. If a company does not survive in the short term, there will be no long term. Strategic processes are broad outline plans and objectives, which can be changed, albeit temporarily, if there are overwhelming tactical reasons for doing so.

This can be seen in the distinction which should be drawn between corporate and business strategy. This distinction is usually defined by the level of strategic action in an organisation. Corporate strategies are operated in large conglomerates or groups where the corporate strategy is concerned to determine the portfolio of businesses in which to invest. Such strategies would therefore concern strategic alliances, the search for synergies within existing businesses, acting as bankers for their businesses and future prospecting. Business-level strategies are concerned to find ways in which to compete within a particular type of business. Small, non-diversified organisations or those which only trade in one field may have an identity between their corporate and business strategies. Divisional or product strategies may more correctly be described as business strategies which seek to exploit the benefits of a particular business, and which seek to meet the needs of their markets.

The clearest explanations have come from academics who have taken the old notions of corporate planning and have moved these forward to delve into the reality and the interpersonal processes where strategies are created. We can divide these explanations under three headings: strategy classification frameworks; process theories; and contingency approaches.

CLASSIFICATIONS OF STRATEGIES

Numerous academics have proposed taxonomies of business strategies. Amongst the most quoted, and perhaps misunderstood, Michael Porter's three generic strategies have prompted a debate about potential conflicts between business strategies (Porter 1980).

Porter argues that there are three main strategies which organisations can follow with success:

1 'Cost leadership strategies' aim to combine the lowest costs with average prices in an industry.
2 'Differentiation strategies' seek to innovate and to differentiate products and services in the market-place.
3 The third generic strategy applies a focus on either cost leadership or differentiation, within a narrow segment of the market; a form of niche marketing.

The greatest danger, according to this analysis, is to be 'stuck in the middle' – that is to move between the three generic strategies, failing to concentrate the organisation's resources on one or other strategic choice, and therefore failing to compete on favourable terms.

From the various critiques there is doubt that organisations do regard the generic strategies as mutually exclusive (Miller and Friesen 1986, Murray 1988). There is doubt whether companies compete consistently on price, or on costs. Issues such as market share, and differentiation on service, quality and product types may be equally important. In his analysis of Porter's generic strategies, Bowman (1992) has shown how much confusion exists between terms such as 'cost and price' and phrases like 'cost leadership and market segmentation'. Bowman goes on to describe a small research project which demonstrated that managers see four main strategic competitive directions: price; cost control; unique products or services; and product or service development.

Most authors seem able to agree that marketing differentiation is an appropriate strategic approach in highly competitive markets. For many companies, keeping one step ahead of the market is an almost impossible task, because the cost of entry to their markets is low, and because the products or services can easily be replicated. In these situations, companies may try to capture a particular niche. For example, for a small business to survive it has to have some unique selling benefit or be able to capture a particular niche.

Innovation strategies are similarly designed to put companies one step ahead, and most pharmaceutical, high-technology companies will seek to achieve a competitive advantage by investing heavily in research and development. Competition on cost or on price is also clearly a strategy which can be effective if economies of scale can be achieved. This is best suited where mass production products, or the equivalent in service, are possible.

Spectacular new technology developments have brought the possibility of competition through all the main strategies described:

innovation with consumer products has now outstripped demand. One has only to think of the range of televisual, audio and telephonic devices for which the innovation itself has created the market, to realise how significant research and product development can be. For example, no one could really have thought of buying a video or a compact disc until the product was invented. New technology also has enabled companies to differentiate products and services, and to add value, from aircraft to cooker manufacturers and from banking to travel services. Equally significant are the possibilities for flexible specialisation which allow companies to produce highly specialised, tailored goods in large numbers, cheaply, by computer-aided design and manufacturing techniques.

Attempts to classify strategic direction for a company are likely to be so oversimplified as to offer only a very rough analysis. While one or more of these strategic directions may be chosen to enhance the competitiveness of a product or service, there may indeed be different and apparently contradictory strategies pursued for different products, within the same business or for different businesses within the same corporation. Strategic direction may also change. While following an innovative strategy to begin with, a business may move towards cost reductions, through standardisation and mechanisation so that the product or service can compete on price. As Bowman has suggested, companies may well wish to compete on price but simultaneously to differentiate on, for example, service quality or speed and flexibility of response to customers.

We might anticipate different human resource approaches according to the critical variables on which the company seeks to compete. One major study illustrates the extent to which we can see a direct relationship between particular human resource management policies and organisational strategies (Schuler and Jackson 1987). The strategies identified were:

- 'dynamic growth stra _egy' (an expansionist, innovative strategy);
- the 'extract profit strategy' (which equates to competition on price through economies of scale); and
- 'turnaround strategy' (here the emphasis is on survival in the short term, through cost cutting and rationalisation of operations).

Schuler and Jackson go on to examine these through surveys of 150 line managers and 304 human resource managers, who were asked questions about job knowledge, careers, performance appraisal and compensation. From the survey evidence, there is some justification for suggesting that human resource practices in these areas vary according to the three strategies pursued. The results of this survey are difficult to assess because not all the responses are reported, and the differences between the different company strategies are not consistently reflected in human resource practices. For example, growth strategies create uncertainty in the nature of jobs, and result in different approaches to the appraisal process, which is reported paradoxically as using appraisal for developmental purposes whilst training is focused on the present. These conclusions raise questions about how one can interpret survey data in a field where the context is so important. Other contradictions include the puzzle of why under the strategy of growth should there be fewer opportunities for promotion, as the results indicate? The compensation practices do not appear to be differentiated according to the three business strategies, whereas the training and development practices seem most sensitive to different strategies.

There are therefore a number of problems with this approach to understanding the relationship between human resource and business strategies. First there is often a coherence between different human resource policies, which are mutually reinforcing. These are not necessarily related individually to particular business strategies. Second, business strategies as represented by the kinds of categories described by Porter's or Schuler's version are defined too broadly to evoke particular human resource responses, and are too vague, and not mutually exclusive. Finally, this research into human resource strategies failed to take account of external factors such as the labour market. This partially explains why compensation policies were not seen as oriented towards business strategies in a simplistic, direct relationship. Instead, they must have been at least partially responsive to external conditions.

PROCESS THEORIES

Strategy formation is studied from a different perspective by those academics who have seen the significance of interpersonal processes in the creation of business strategies. In this school of thought, the subjective, emergent and changing nature of strategy are emphasised.

Process theorists look at strategy as one outcome from the interpersonal relationships, the mix of personalities and cognitive styles which are found in the top team, and in various sub-groups of managers who can influence strategy. Those who believe in ideological or belief systems creating organisation cultures would also belong within this category. What is of critical importance to these researchers are the processes which result in strategy development. Implicit here is the notion that if one could influence the process, the strategy also would be affected. There are two distinct approaches: there are students of the cognitive processes, and there are those who study the influencing interpersonal processes – the 'political' perspective on strategy formation processes.

The actions of senior managers are influential in deciding the strategic direction an organisation should take. Clearly, their belief systems, their thought processes (as George Kelly would have put it, the way they construe the world), are of paramount importance in the creation of strategy.

The choices faced by senior managers are frequently understood by them as 'dilemmas', according to Hampden-Turner (1990). He argues that values are 'reconciled' into products or services; that is, companies offer combinations of choices to their consumers, and the apparent dilemmas faced when deciding on product development or strategic direction are best resolved by 'combining values' – finding super-ordinate constructs which subsume the opposing values, or connecting the 'alternative' ideas in some way. Such dilemmas typically include how to coordinate people working under the principles of the division of labour, how to aim for a mass market, but also to conquer and defend market niches, and how to use the labour market whilst allowing workers to feel 'justly treated and consulted' (p. 25).

One of the chief benefits of this type of analysis is that it shows strategic issues are as much a function of the mind sets which produce them as an outcome of some form of objective reality. This approach has also resulted in explanations about how strategies develop in organisations. Drawing on studies in decision-making, and acknow-ledging the distinction between intended and actual strategies, there are a number of insights possible when adopting psychologistic explanations of strategy formation.

A study by Bailey and Johnson (1992) reports the discovery of managerial perceptions of the processes of strategy formulation within their organisations, which the authors classify under six headings: logical incrementalism, planning, natural selection, visionary, cultural and political processes. The tendency towards any mix of these through a consensus is seen to explain the prevailing decision-making profile of any organisation.

These offered process categories have the benefit that we can see whether particular processes associate with measurable outcomes. There is also an acceptance that strategy formation is not a mechanistic process, and that there are a variety of interpersonal processes at work. As the authors point out:

'The influence of the process of strategy formulation on the organisations generally and particularly the relationship with organisational performance requires further attention.'

(p. 176)

The problems we are left with when we see strategy as process are that, since there is no real difference between senior managerial decision-making and other forms of decision-making within groups, what we learn from examining the process could be discovered from any similar group decision-making observation. There is nothing specifically strategic about the process.

From the human resource management perspective the process issues are critical to the understanding of how the function may contribute. Whilst management style and the involvement of human resource specialists in change management are significant, we also need to think about other processes. Employee involvement, communication strategy and managing cultural transformations are more important process matters. To study the process strategies we would thus need to research employee relations policies, and the processes by which organisations adapt and change in response to organisational strategies. It seems unlikely that we will discover the complex interrelationships between the factors which influence strategy by concentrating on process alone, although there is likely to be a coming together of these factors within the top team's working.

CONTINGENCY APPROACHES

If classification strategies are typically described without reference to the structure, size and technology of organisations, and process views of strategy concentrate on individuals and groups, there is clearly a value to be found in moving to the organisational level of analysis.

Chandler's famous axiom, that structure follows an organisation's growth strategy, was based on studies in 70 large companies in the USA (Chandler 1962). He showed how diversification in companies such as Du Pont and General Motors was followed by the emergence of the multi-divisional form. This seminal work has since been built upon by sociologists and economists within the broader organisation theory field.

Following on from these design perspectives, there have been several attempts at producing integrative typologies bringing together strategies and organisation types in one classification scheme. Miles and Snow (1978) proposed four strategic types:

1 **Defender organisations** produce products or services for a small niche market which they defend by pricing policies or by the quality of their products.
2 **Prospector organisations** use innovation strategies, moving quickly into new markets and moving out of such markets when others are able to compete equally. Flexibility and decentralisation are characteristics of this organisation type.
3 **Analyser organisations** wait for others to innovate, and reduce their risks by only entering new markets when they have been proved to be profitable. Large and small organisations follow this approach, but emphasise efficiency and stability, with mass production and separate, more responsive departments such as marketing, or sub-units with high degrees of flexibility and responsiveness.
4 **Reactor organisations** are those whose reactions are not consistent – they often do not follow a clear strategy, and tend only to react to short-term pressures. This strategic approach is reminiscent of Porter's 'stuck in the middle' category, and is given a negative connotation by Miles and Snow.

The implication here is that the business strategy and the company's operations are so intertwined that the organisation structure and the policies within the human resource and marketing functions are all mutually dependent, so the organisation as a whole may be typified within the classification. Taking this approach a step further, Goold and Campbell (1986) produced a company model taxonomy which sets out three ways in which companies manage their portfolios of businesses:

- 'Strategic planning' companies have long-term planning horizons, and balance performance amongst their divisions, allowing under-performance in the short term.
- 'Financial control' companies manage each strategic business unit (SBU) against tight, short-term financial performance criteria, but each SBU is given autonomy to achieve the results.
- 'Strategic control' companies, on the other hand, are more concerned with long-term performance, but will use financial performance as an important guide, seeking to balance their asset portfolio even if this means tolerating some SBU underperformance.

There are rich human resource management applications from these organisation-level approaches. At this level it is possible to try to isolate the variables which influence business strategy, and to establish which of those we may regard as part of human resource management, that is those which are independent or dependent variables.

Attempts to establish these contingencies include Miles and Snow's own effort to relate their typology of organisational and managerial characteristics to human resource management systems – such as recruitment, selection, staff planning, training, development, appraisal and compensation systems (Miles and Snow 1984). This was taken a stage further by research into 80 German and Austrian companies in which a contingency model of human resource strategies was tested and applied to the fourfold typology of Miles and Snow, including a fifth category of 'hybrid' strategic types (Ackermann 1986).

The conclusions from these and other similar studies will occupy the following chapter, where we will look at how a general theory of human resource management may be developed. However, it is useful here to report the conclusions to Ackermann's study: 'The research findings support the basic thesis that companies *have* HRM strategies. It is shown how HRM strategies are identified and measured, and also how they vary with the business strategies pursued.'(p. 81.)

The typology approaches, even if contingency theory is used, suffer from the weaknesses one expects to find in any classification scheme – the oversimplification, the overlap in strategies, and the failure to connect human resource strategies with the external market conditions in terms of variability, change and the full range of internal and external factors which produce business strategies. In part, this is a consequence of the survey methodology employed. In order to find statistical relationships, strategies need to be reduced to indices and correlations are sought irrespective of the context.

One major problem is the number of cases required to isolate causal relationships in such areas as organisation structure, size, environment, industry type and the mix of strategies. Many of these difficulties can be overcome by adopting a more qualitative approach, as we shall see. Ackermann's conclusion is encouraging:

'Our conclusion is that HRM strategies are dominated by the business strategies which fit specific environments and are supported by suitable company sizes and structures.'

(p. 79.)

We will try in the following chapters to determine what 'suitable' means; what is a fit between human resource and business strategy.

HUMAN RESOURCE STRATEGIES

The literature briefly reviewed in this chapter has shown that, whatever approach is taken to analysing business strategies, there are clear and perhaps provable human resource consequences and influences. However, these statements beg the important question: 'What constitutes the general theory of human resource management on which any proof can be based?' Without such a theory, all our descriptive models and behavioural assumptions cannot be connected to business performance. This must be the central problem to which we now turn.

BIBLIOGRAPHY

Ackermann, K-F. (1986) 'A contingency model of HRM strategy. Empirical research findings reconsidered', *Management Forum*, Band 6, pp. 65–83.

Bailey, A. and Johnson, G. (1992) 'How strategies develop in organisations' in Faulkner, D. and Johnson, G. (Eds) (1992) *The Challenge of Strategic Management*, pp. 147–78, London: Kogan Page.

Bowman, C. (1992) 'Interpreting competitive strategy' in Faulkner, D. and Johnson, G. (1992) *q.v.* pp. 64–78, London: Kogan Page.

Chandler, A. D. Jr. (1962) *Strategy and Structure: Chapters in the History of the Industrial Enterprise*, Cambridge, Mass.: MIT Press.

Crofts, P. (1992) 'New direction for London Underground', *Personnel Management Plus*, Vol. 3, No. 8, August.

Faulkner, D. and Johnson, G. (Eds) (1992) *The Challenge of Strategic Management*, London: Kogan Page.

Goold, M. and Campbell, A. (1986) *Strategies and Styles: The Role of the Centre in Managing Diversified Corporations*, Oxford: Blackwell.

Guest, D. and Hoque, K. (1993) 'The Mystery of the Missing Human Resource Manager', *Personnel Management*, June, pp. 40–1.

Hamilton, K. (1992) 'RHM bakes a new cake to fight bid', *Sunday Times*, 18 October, p. 5.

Hampden-Turner, C. (1990) *Charting the Corporate Mind*, New York/London: The Free Press/Collier Macmillan.

Hofer, C. and Schendel, D. (1978) *Strategy Formulation: Analytical Concepts*, St. Paul: West Publishing.

Miles, R. E. and Snow, C.C. (1978) *Organizational Strategy, Structure and Process*, New York: McGraw-Hill.

Miles, R. E. and Snow, C.C. (1984) 'Designing Strategic Human Resource Systems', *Organizational Dynamics*, pp. 36–52.

Miller, D. and Friesen, P. H. (1986) 'Porter's (1980) Generic Strategies and Performance: An Empirical Examination with American Data. Part 1 Testing Porter', *Organizational Studies*, Vol. 7, No. 1, pp. 37–55, and 'Part 2 Performance implications', *Organizational Studies*, Vol. 7, No. 3, pp. 255–61.

Murray, A. I. (1988) 'A contingency view of Porter's Generic Strategies', *Academy of Management Review*, Vol. 13, No. 3, pp. 390–400.

Pickard, J. (1992) 'We've had the bottle to change, says Calor Gas', *Personnel Management Plus*, Vol. 3, No. 9, September.

Porter, M. (1980) *Competitive Strategy*, New York: The Free Press/Macmillan.

Purcell, J. (1989) 'The impact of corporate strategy on human resource management' in Storey, J. (Ed) *New Perspectives on Human Resource Management*, London: Routledge.

Schuler, R. S. and Jackson, S. E. (1987) 'Organizational strategy and organizational level as determinants of Human Resource Management practice', *Human Resource Planning*, Vol. 10, No. 3, pp. 125–41.

Thurley, K. and Wood, S. (Eds) (1983) *Industrial Relations and Management Strategy*, Cambridge: Cambridge University Press.

von Clausewitz, C. (1949) *On War*, Vol. III, London: Routledge & Kegan Paul.

Wickens, P. (1987) *The Road to Nissan. Flexibility, Quality, Teamwork*, Basingstoke: Macmillan.

CHAPTER 2

The academic debate on human resource management

In this chapter, it is argued that what we should seek to understand about HRM is its place in establishing the symbolic order. From such an understanding we will see how managers use the symbolic order within organisations both to legitimate their authority and to fulfil their managerial roles. Such roles are typically concerned with achieving goals which require changing ideas and relationships and with causing actions. The management process is centred on change, as part of its *raison d'être*.

Thus, although one such set of changes may represent a fundamental shift in ideas, so that we may describe it as a shift in the paradigm of management, we are not moving from one steady state called 'personnel management' to another steady state called 'human resource management'. Without doubt, paradigmatic shifts do occur, but the models of personnel management have always been changing, driven by the problematics of the employment relationship. These unresolvable tensions are so old, so well established, that traditions within personnel management have grown up around them. These unresolvable tensions are a constant source of change. The management process consists of finding ways which enable the tensions to be resolved to a point of compromise where managerial action is possible. What is important about 'human resource management' as representative of a new paradigm is therefore the compromises and accommodations reached within these traditions which allow the management process to continue.

The management of labour is a fundamental process within any society because it creates the kind of society in which people live. Relationships in society are a consequence of the relationships people sustain in their working lives and the life-chances their income provides. This is therefore the main reason why so much attention is paid to what is now called 'human resource management'. The importance of the employment relationship is revealed by the way the State has become involved whenever a crisis has been threatened within national affairs:

the direction of labour in wartime, the 1980s' changes to employment law in attempts to further competitiveness and to strengthen market forces, and the debates over the European Community's Social Charter all exemplify this political dimension.

The miners' strikes of 1974 and 1984, and the public outcry over proposed pit closures in 1992, neatly demonstrate how working relationships come to reflect societal issues. In 1974 the confrontation with the Heath Government, which resulted in a three-day working week, brought disapproval on the Government for allowing the challenge to affect vital economic interests. In 1984 the challenge over pit closures also divided the nation, but this time there was a felt need for change, an acceptance that the public at large should no longer support a working-class attack on a government which had a political mandate to modernise institutions and to change attitudes. By 1992, when more pit closures were proposed, a further shift in values had occurred: unemployment and the apparent carelessness with which thirty thousand people were to be made redundant produced a strong public reaction of 'this far, but no further'. This represented a shift to the point where the value of work in society was regarded as being of greater significance than narrow definitions of efficiency.

At the organisational level of analysis, there are numerous small signs which are evidence of the importance we all attach to managing people: the joking relationship which so often is found in the managerial hierarchy over the work of the personnel function, for example, is conventionally a way of coping with sensitive relationships to prevent potential hostility (Radcliffe-Brown 1952). There are also those reported statements from Chief Executives that 'personnel' is too important to be left to the personnel department.

Deep issues revealed by employment relationships bring to the fore broad ideological questions. The politics of conviction in the 1980s have given way to the politics of consent in the 1990s. The status groupings which arise from employment relationships are not just a function of reward policies. Rewards also include the sense of worth which employees obtain from their work, the challenge they find in their jobs, and their sense of success as human beings (Herzberg, Mausner and Snyderman 1959, Gowler and Legge 1982). Work is a social activity which confers these attributes on those who take part.

The sociological aspects we find in employment relationships have perhaps been overshadowed recently by questions about contribution and business competitiveness. This reflects immediate economic concerns rather than long-term questions about the way society is developing. Whatever the point in the economic cycle, the employment relationship underpins the political, social and personal concerns of institutions, employers and individuals.

THE ORIGINS OF PERSONNEL MANAGEMENT

We can trace the origins of the specialist occupations which have been given various titles over the years – including 'employment officer', 'labour manager', 'personnel officer' or 'personnel manager' and now 'human resource manager' – back to four main traditions. These traditions have formed around the fundamental problems in managing the employment relationship. They are the welfare, industrial relations, employment management and professional traditions (Tyson 1979, Tyson and Fell 1986). The frequent job title changes are in themselves signs of the changing priorities that managers associate with managing the employment relationship. However, the author believes the four traditions are current today, and have sufficient permanence to be sources of demands and of unresolvable problems for managers, to which they are responding. Although these traditions are a source of difficulty for managers, they are also the areas where specialists can contribute to the managerial task. Each of the traditions will be examined in turn.

It was within the potential conflicts between capital and labour that the specialist personnel function emerged. Welfare workers in the late nineteenth century were the occupational forebears of 'human resource' specialists, and were ideologically a product of the industrial betterment movement, which embraced a range of responses to the worst excesses of *laissez-faire* capitalism. Although only working originally in a minority of companies such as those with Quaker founders, there is no doubt that welfare workers quickly realised there was conflict between their objectives and those of their line manager colleagues (Niven 1967, Child 1974). These early pioneers, for example the Misses Wood and Kelly, wrote of 'doing good by stealth', of trying to find ways to influence rogue supervisors and foremen to ensure fairness of treatment. Sexual harassment, unfair dismissals and victimisation are as old as work itself. The normative tradition within personnel management is based on a need to ameliorate the worst aspects of domination in the employment relationship. Frequently the welfare tradition represents a unitarist solution to this problem (Fox 1974). By contrast the industrial relations tradition offers pluralist solutions, through procedures and joint consultation.

The set piece conflicts, such as the transport strikes, the famous match girls' strike at Bryant and May, the transport strikes and the discontent which spilled over into riots in Trafalgar Square in 1887, were quite clearly class conflicts. It may be that there has always been a socialist fundamentalism in British society which has, at various times been coerced, bought-off, marginalised or subsumed into a broader cause. Only occasionally has the underclass found an opportunity to express dissent, as in the eighteenth-century mobs fighting in bread riots, the nineteenth-century Chartists, and the general unions' political strikes in the first part of the twentieth century (Hobsbawm 1964). There are still arguments concerning the rules of work in which personnel specialists are caught-up: struggles with workers over the boundaries of control are essential ingredients in the personnel role, so any changes to these boundaries are perceived to be significant. This helps to explain why in the 1980s the 'new industrial relations' was hailed as a breakthrough, and commentators have argued since over whether the shift is permanent (Bassett 1986). If, of course, this were proved to be the case, with managerial prerogatives firmly in place in all the main strategic aspects of the employment relationship, the need for human resource specialists would be removed. Fortunately, in spite of reports to the contrary, the struggle for control over one's own destiny is eternal.

The emergence of large, impersonal organisations with management separated from ownership means there will always be a need for working rules and policies. These are at the heart of the problem of how to ensure compliance, which the employment management tradition seeks to resolve. Mergers and acquisitions, such as the amalgamations which created ICI in 1926 (Reader 1975), make it necessary for managers to produce guides for action, and to write down policies in such fields as recruitment, rewards, training, promotion, discipline, and the like. Maintaining the rules in a bureaucracy is also a way to preserve the legitimacy of an organisation (Weber 1947). Actions must be supported by rules, and can only be questioned if they are not in accord with the rules (Crozier 1964). Managing employment has always meant controlling budgets, headcount and the rules which influence costs such as appointments, promotions, salary increases, overtime, etc. This bureaucratic employment management tradition is also surprisingly resilient. While it may not seem to accord with modern, flexible organisations, there are logics in people management which cannot be denied. Setting performance standards, developing and educating people, rewarding and motivating people, all require some basic frameworks of jobs, established performance criteria, position descriptions and mechanisms for evaluating work.

Legitimacy can also be based on expertise. In the professional tradition, the problems of managing people are thought to be resolvable. The search for a science which will enable managers to predict and to influence behaviour at work has continued throughout this century, from the attempts by F W Taylor to propose a 'science of management', through to attempts to convert industrial sociology and psychology into managerial tools, which continue today (Silverman 1970, Tyson and Jackson 1992). Along with the search for organisational behaviour nostrums have come some immediately helpful insights drawn from labour economics, statistics, and a burgeoning range of 'techniques' which apply these various disciplines to managerial problems. A considerable boost to professional claims in the UK has come from employment law. Nevertheless, it is its inexactness as a science that makes the human resource management occupation worth the continuing effort: it is not that the problems change, but that the solutions offered are never quite or totally satisfactory.

Commentators have already explored the ambiguity inherent in the personnel occupation (Tyson 1979, Ritzer and Trice 1969, Watson 1977). This arises from its powerlessness, its unclear goals, its position at the nexus of competing value systems, and its need not to be closely identified with individual members of the top team. Personnel people are organisation people. The claim to professional status (a largely British characteristic) is set against the ambiguous, shifting sands of this role, a role which seeks to represent organisational interests and to take advantage of the ambiguity of the function's organisational position in order to assist change, to provide a consultancy service, or to derive whatever advantage is possible in order to create new realities (Tyson 1980).

While the general description of these traditions offers a guide to the origins of this range of work, this does not explain what happens in organisations and why. These traditions may be present to a greater or lesser extent, but without a more detailed description of how organisational influences affect or create the function at the organisational level of analysis, we will not be able to understand how the management of people contributes to business performance.

MODELS OF HUMAN RESOURCE MANAGEMENT

One way to advance our knowledge of what happens in organisations is to create 'models' of the varieties of personnel functions, such as behaviours, actions, roles and relationships, which will permit us to understand how changes affect these variables. Models may be 'ideal types' in Weber's (1947) sense or may be constructed according to some dynamic principle, so that we can understand how changes to one variable will affect other variables. Econometric models, although well established, have not so far produced any dramatically accurate predictions about the economy. Nor is it likely that models of human behaviour, actions, roles and relationships can be formulated which will capture all the variants of these human attributes. The greatest value from models in this sphere is therefore the ordering of knowledge and the juxtaposition of the model's characteristics which help us to understand what is happening and why.

Models therefore should follow three design principles (Winter 1966). The principle of unification requires that they describe a distinct phenomenon, or address a particular question. They require also a dynamic structure, so that a model can be articulated, to show how it would change under different circumstances, or with a change from a variable. Models also require some ordering principle, so that the information they contain is internally related in a consistent way, allowing comparisons with different realities.

There are benefits to be gained from descriptive, analytical and normative models of human resource management. Each type of model examines human resources at a different level of analysis. Table 1 shows how human resource management may be seen from the perspective of different models.

In the pages that follow, the examples quoted will be described in detail to show how each contributes to our understanding of this field.

From contingency theory we know that what happens in organisations is dependent upon a range of variables, including the history of the enterprise, the values of the company's founder, the markets in which it operates, the technology used, the size and structure of the organisation, and the industrial relations traditions within which decisions about employees are made (Woodward 1958; Pugh, Hickson and Hinings 1969). We also know from the seminal work of Legge how significant these contingencies can be in determining what is the prevailing approach to personnel management (Legge 1978). She poses two archetypal responses to the contingencies which managers face:

- a convergent innovation approach, where personnel managers work within the prevailing value systems to respond to change, and
- a divergent innovation approach, where personnel managers act as the grit in the oyster, seeking to change the values by taking up a different ideological position from the one adopted by managers who are stuck with their current attitudes and values. There are indeed echoes here

Table 1: HRM seen from the perspective of different models

	Principle of unification		
	Descriptions of HR work	Analytical of HR causes	Normative content/purpose
Dynamic structure	How work changes with different settings and contexts	How HR people are able to perform a role and why	What HR people should do
Ordering principle			
1 Level of analysis	Organisation	Organisation and society	Company management
2 Activities described	Work of HR people	Reasons for the work	Contribution of HR to organisations
3 Purpose	To elucidate what happens	To discover why HR work occurs and how it interacts	To improve organisational performance and to help management
Examples	Tyson and Fell (1986)	Ackermann (1986)	Armstrong (1992)

of the old welfare workers, either seeking to do good by stealth, or standing up to managers in order to make them change their views.

The recognition of the benefits that flow from studying human resource management at the organisational level is now well established (Tyson 1983, Tyson and Fell 1986). The problem which this brings is how to research at this level, and how to create any theory which would permit generalisation from one or two companies to many organisations.

DESCRIPTIVE MODELS

One attempt to solve this problem has been to search for descriptive models at the organisation level which typify distinctive overall approaches to personnel management (Tyson and Fell 1986). Our research sought to discover whether there were any general principles in the way personnel work was done. We started from the premise that our experience had shown us a wide variety of approaches, but we needed to verify this. In particular, we wished to use a contingency theory approach to discover the variables which influenced personnel management. We examined the personnel function according to the policies adopted, the authority and controls used, the systems, planning role, specialist career path, reporting relationships and 'political' position adopted – that is the personnel specialists' access to power.

From the case studies we examined we could see three distinct models which emerged because the activities of those in personnel departments clustered together commonly on these dimensions. These ranged from a basic administrative model (we termed a 'clerk of works'), to a sophisticated, industrial-relations oriented, systems model (we called the 'contracts manager') and a business-oriented, strategically aware function, which designed the employment relationship (which we called 'the architect'). The construction industry metaphor was used to denote the different client relationships which obtained, and also the underlying purposes of personnel management to maintain, or sometimes construct, organisational life (Crichton 1968). Although these findings were a product of the 1980s, there is evidence that the models still accurately reflect personnel practice, but that there may also be new models emerging (Monks 1993).

A number of conclusions followed on from this. Firstly, there is clearly no one correct model – the key issue is the appropriateness of the model for the organisation. Secondly, models can change. Conflict over inappropriate models is inevitable, and may lead to change. One situation we find is most easily recognised is when a new 'Human Resource' Director is recruited to change the model. At least for a time there may be different models existing in the same organisation. Finally, the location of the personnel function, within the organisational structure, and the extent to which there are divisional or business units will be likely to influence the model.

One emergent issue from the research is to what extent personnel management is allowed to take on a strategic role. The study described in this book is a rational outcome from the earlier research. If the appropriateness of the model to the organisation is critical, then we need to be aware of what constitutes a fit between organisational needs or strategies and the human resource or personnel models.

ANALYTICAL MODELS

The contingency approach to studying personnel management, since the work of Legge (1978), has seemed to offer the most fruitful line of enquiry. From the bewildering array of theories which could be chosen, it does present the possibility that one may attach contingency research into human resource management to other research, in such fields as business strategy, organisation design, and structure. The theoretical idea of contingencies affecting action is also relatively easy to turn into research questions which will be understood by people working in organisations.

There are, however, more fundamental reasons for choosing a contingency approach. This connects to a general concern to explore and to explain the differences in human resource management between organisations, and is a long-standing research interest. This is born out by the discussion in Tyson (1979) and Tyson and Fell (1986) that there are significant differences in the way human resource management is performed, according to the organisational context. Above all, a contingency approach should reveal important aspects of the symbolic order. Symbols depend for their meaning upon the context in which they are used. For example, the particular symbolic values employees attach to rewards are dependent upon whether there are changes in the relativities between the various occupational groups in the pay structure, when general pay rises are granted. In studying organisations, the researcher is looking for systems of symbols which are interpreted as much by the employees concerned as by management.

A more detailed description of the research conducted in the 1980s by Karl Freidrick Ackermann, briefly alluded to in the first chapter of this book, will help to illustrate the benefits of this approach. Ackermann's 1986 study is the most thorough account to date, in which he uses a carefully-tested contingency model to look at five influencing determinants on human resource strategies. These five determinants are: business strategies, environment, organisational structure, company size and the availability of resources. Ackermann then sets out a 'model' or framework for HRM strategies, in which he shows the interactions between the five determinants (*see* Fig. 1).

Ackermann's definition of HR strategy being 'a pattern in a constant stream of human resource management decisions' (p. 67), his research takes the form of enquiring, through a questionnaire with 116 items measuring the decision variables of HRM, which were to be related by respondents to defined business strategies. He was able to define 25 variables describing personnel policy decisions, which he then reduced to four factors. These showed a characteristic pattern of individual decision variables, which he interpreted as four factor-analytical types of HRM strategies:

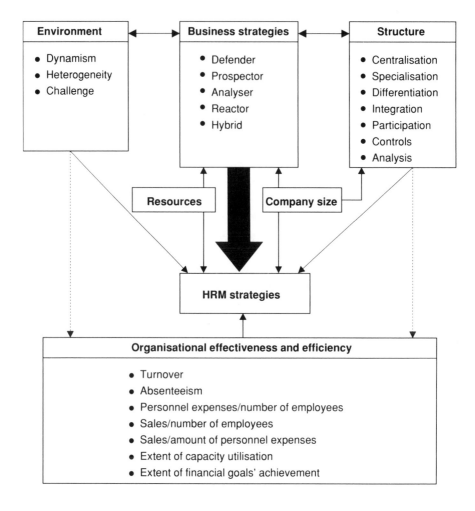

Fig. 1 A contingency model for HRM strategies
(K-F Ackermann's 1986 model)

1 Development strategy: emphasises training, long-term planning, internal hiring.
2 Control strategy: emphasises performance appraisal, performance-based rewards; no job evaluation.
3 Administrative strategy: short-term manpower planning, external hiring, low level HR.
4 Scanning strategy: emphasis on labour market scanning, attitude surveys, money incentives.

The research then looks at how these HRM strategies can be associated with the business strategies categorised by Miles and Snow.

Ackermann concluded that: HR strategies follow business strategies; they tend to be independent of environmental pressures up to a certain point, when the challenge forces a change; they are independent of company size and resource availability (except the development strategy) but they do vary with organisation structures.

One could not conclude overall, therefore, that the model proposed was proved to be accurate. What is most valuable from this study, however, is the identification of those areas which do change. The model may have been too static a representation of the variety and dynamic of organisations, but even this model has revealed that company size, structure and, in some cases, resource availability change with strategy. The other achievement from this study was the attempt (following Wächter 1973) to relate particular policy decisions to the dynamic of organisations by showing how policies might change with the business strategy. The limitations were in the research design itself which, by using the survey approach, could not show how strategies were connected to the business context and, unlike Storey's (1992) research, could not describe how changes to HR policies took place over time within a particular organisation.

The important learning from this research is that the way organisations use their human resource strategies does vary with their business strategies.

Table 2: Comparing business and HR strategies
(drawn from Ackermann 1986, p. 76)

	Defenders	*Prospectors*	*Analysers*	*Hybrids*
	Miles and Snow's Business Strategy Classifications			
No. of organisations	20	13	38	8
HRM strategies				
Development			✓	✓
Control				
Administrative	✓			
Scanning		✓		✓

No significant correlations between the control strategy and any of the business strategies were found. There was only one company which pursued a reactor strategy. As we do not know the details of the organisational contexts where these business strategies were pursued, we can only speculate on the reasons why the companies adopted particular business strategies.

The way the organisation uses the symbolic order is subject to change and the personnel policy decisions, whilst remaining much the same, can be used in different ways. This helps to explain the apparent contradictions. For example, job descriptions were seen to be about the 'control' strategy, yet this strategy concentrated on performance appraisal, linking it to pay determination. What seems most likely is that organisations adopting this strategy were using job descriptions in different ways, for example by concentrating on objectives and key tasks rather than a description of duties or activities. Similarly, the emphasis on 'development' as a strategy may not always have been so comprehensive in the organisations which adopted other strategies, but could, for example in the 'scanning' organisations, have been adopted for the more senior staff.

There are similarities between Ackermann's findings and those of Tyson and Fell, discussed earlier. The 'administrative' strategy equates to the 'clerk of works' model, the 'control' strategy equates to the 'contracts manager' and the 'development' strategy and the 'scanning strategy' could both be found in the architect model. Ackermann's study takes the debate a stage further however. He shows that clusters of personnel decisions ('HR strategies') are associated with specific business strategies, but that these HR strategies do not vary directly with the business strategies. One explanation of this offered in this book is that the symbols are being used differently, according to changes external and internal to the organisation. Ackermann has also shown that certain contingent variables (size, structure, and the amount of change) affect HR strategies. The limitations within the research design prevent more from being revealed on this point, but the conclusions do support the view that there are contingent variables which influence HR strategies.

Similar results were achieved by Schuler and Jackson (1987), when they researched HRM 'practices' in 304 business units to determine whether organisations adopted HR practices to support their business strategies. These were to be categorised under the headings: dynamic growth strategies, extract profit strategies or turnaround strategies. The further variables of organisational level and product life-cycle stage were included to seek explanations of the reasons for variation in human resource practices. They reported that the results did suggest predictable relationships between organisational strategy and human resource management practices. They also showed significant differences in the human resource practices adopted towards managerial and non-managerial employees, and they confirmed that the product life-cycle stage is an important variable in accounting for business strategy.

Perhaps the most significant result from this study, however, is in the explanations they offered as to why 'the results do not prove that organisations systematically selected particular practices to match their strategy' (p. 139). The rapidity with which companies change their strategies, the variety of practices and the differences between industry sectors all make predicting any precise relationship between business strategies and human resource practices awkward to achieve. However, the linkage between organisational contingencies and human resource practices is established. In the more complete report on the same study, Jackson, Schuler and Rivero (1989) indicate that 'the data provide evidence that personnel practices are related to several organisational characteristics, including the importance of innovation, as an aspect of the organisation's competitive strategy, the sector of the economy within which the organisation operates, the nature of the manufacturing technology used, the organisation's structure and size, and whether a union is present' (p. 772).

From the evidence of these German/Austrian and USA studies the conclusion we may draw is that linkages can be made between some of the formal characteristics within any organisation and the HR practices found there. What has so far proved difficult in survey-type research is to forge the link into the business strategies. The reason for seeking to make this final link is because the business strategies provide the dynamic for the HR practices, and give meaning to the symbolic acts by managers performing these practices. Clearly there is some benefit to be gained by looking at organisational structure and HR practices. The linkage between strategy and structure may reveal consequential linkages back to HR practices. For example, we may see how HR practices in the field of employee relations vary at different levels within the organisation, by inferring the behaviours we believe are required under different strategic choices.

The survey-type methodology always leaves us with the problem of not being able to contextualise the responses, and therefore makes us unsure of the direction of any causation. Do certain HR strategies result in particular business strategy choices being made? Does the climate of employee relations, for example on greenfield sites, encourage certain styles of governance, and hence result in strategies which reinforce and continue that style? Perhaps the most important question we are left with is what do these activities, such as recruitment, development, appraisal, reward and communications, mean in these organisations? If they mean different things in different contexts, we may need to re-evaluate the results.

NORMATIVE MODELS

Normative versions of HRM are frequently found in textbooks and in practitioners' articles. Both are aimed at selling ideas about either the relationship between management's people values and corporate performance, or the espoused values of a particular corporation. There are famous cases where mission or value statements incorporate beliefs about employees which are often quoted as evidence of the significance attached to the people who work for these organisations. Organisations which have achieved success, such as IBM, Johnson and Johnson, Marks & Spencer and the John Lewis Partnership, are quoted as evidence that these values have contributed to their continuing success. What has yet to be established is the actual contribution these strong, normative models make to business performance.

It is not surprising, of course, that senior managers have a view on what the HRM component is in the success of their businesses. If asked, 'What do your employees contribute to overall business performance?', the CEO can hardly respond by saying, 'I've no idea'. When attempting to answer such questions, the values of the respondents are likely to be revealed. Mission statements may be a bland representation of espoused rather than operational policies, but they do provide management with an officially sanctioned version of the company's position (Brewster, Gill and Richbell 1983). Whilst normative positions may be expressed in good faith, this does raise the question of how these views are formed.

Generations of managers have been brought up in the 'human relations' school of thought and have come to regard themselves as leaders of teams who will obtain support from their followers by paying attention to their employees' social and human needs. The admixture of entrepreneurial academics such as Herzberg and the British tradition – epitomised by the National Institute for Industrial Psychology, with its interest in relieving stress, boredom, and fatigue in the workplace as an aid to productivity – lead to managerial social science. The notion of 'expressive supervision' and eventually the alignment of social and technical systems in order to reduce conflict and to make the most of the social nature of work, were added to the growing body of theories about behaviour in organisations oriented towards managerial goals (Silverman 1970).

Optimism, even after the first flush of research into the psychology and the sociology of organisations, remained high. George C Homans considered that industrial harmony was a goal of paramount importance, which could be achieved by paying attention to nine basic prerequisites. He commented:

> 'In short the conditions for industrial harmony are the conditions of substantial justice, not justice in terms of what theoretically ought to be, but justice in terms of what is felt to be just by all sorts of persons here and now. Industrial harmony founded on justice is far more solid than that founded on 'good human relations' – if good human relations means at best being a 'good guy' and at worst being an 'operator'. I do not want a society based on nice and sensitive men. I want one based on just, responsible, and intelligent men.'
>
> (Homans 1954, p. 58.)

Few senior managers would dissent from that view, one assumes. But in the 1980s in the UK, and perhaps in the USA, industrial harmony ceased to be a superordinate goal. The industrial relations tradition was less in evidence as governments adopted Thatcherite and Reaganite policies towards employment. The early 1990s have been dominated by recession and unemployment, with the managerial emphasis shifting to labour-cost reduction and survival.

Management ideologies as much as political ideologies are belief systems and sustaining beliefs requires a rhetoric to which all can subscribe. Normative visions of HRM need to be based on the assumption that the values espoused are good for the business, if the vision is to be accepted by shareholders, management and customers. Normative visions must also be more than a gloss on management self-interest. The unitary frame of reference helps to reconcile these competing interests within one philosophy, which becomes the unquestioned mainstay of a management's ideology. Phrases such as 'team', 'mission', 'communications' and 'commitment' can then all form part of the rhetoric, and all will be understood to refer to working towards a common goal of efficiency and high performance levels. In this way the search for justice described by Homans can be reconciled with driving down wages for the sake of competitiveness.

FROM NORMATIVE MODEL TO PRESCRIPTION

One of the characteristics of the normative models of HRM is the tendency to slip into prescription. Managerial desires for 'golden rules' can be best explained as the search for a simple method of reinforcing management ideologies. The desire for a simple list of nostrums to live by can be found throughout human society, inculcated by religious belief and by socialisation processes. 'A guide to live by' quickly becomes a reason to live for, so strong is the need for certainty, to find meaning and to believe in what one is doing. Company managements may seek, therefore, to influence the organisational culture so that the conditions are created to entrench the golden rules as a part of the culture. This was the promise held out by the Peters and Waterman vision (1982).

The most thorough analysis of Peters' and Waterman's thesis appears in Guest's 1992 account of the 'in search of excellence' phenomenon. The argument that there are attributes within companies, which are found in successful businesses, has been heavily criticised on methodological grounds. This is because of the sampling frame, the uncertainty about how data was gathered and the research design, which concentrated solely on successful companies and failed therefore to provide comparative data. Guest also criticises the conceptual framework used, especially the failure to take into account the tangible conditions which influence company performance, such as technology, market share and government policies. It is perhaps the definitions of 'success' and 'excellence' which are most open to different interpretations, and therefore the subject of most debate. We will return to these issues in more detail in Chapter 4. The argument that Peters and Waterman are too simplistic in their explanations of good business practice is no doubt justified. However, as even Guest is prepared to admit, they were able to strike a powerful chord among managers. Their list of practical actions which could be described as applied strategies has become axiomatic. This is precisely the effect sought by those managements who promulgate a normative management philosophy, who would wish the whole style and culture of the organisation, 'the way we do things here', to be internalised by all employees.

Evidence for these assertions comes from such texts as Armstrong (1992) and Connock (1991). Armstrong states: 'HRM is a philosophy which provides guidance on how management should exercise its responsibility for managing people' (p. 202). He goes on to detail the main features of the HRM philosophy. These include 'strategic integration', a 'cohesive approach to policies', culture management', 'winning commitment', 'investment in the employee resource', 'flexible organisation', 'total quality', 'communications' and 'partnership with trade unions'. He does, however, go on to decry any packaged approach to HRM, and to stress that there are no quick fixes. Connock is similarly careful to avoid a simple prescription. He takes up the cudgels on behalf of HR as a main contributor to business success, through what he describes as 'HR vision'. This 'vision' will provide a cohesion to HR strategies in the business, have specific objectives and 'will be inspiring, aiming at excellence'; it will describe core organisation values and will provide 'a yardstick by which to judge the future performance of the organisation' (Connock 1991, p. 2). Both these accounts of HRM go on to describe ways that managers can practice HRM as defined, and are textbooks of 'best practice'.

Among the prescriptive texts one may find a further category of books which seek to influence managerial thinking by appealing to the readers' instincts and to their intuitive feelings. A good recent example is *The Fifth Discipline* by Peter Senge (1990), which portrays an ideal learning organisation as the organisation of the future. The author argues with messianic fervour the inherent value of 'five new component technologies' which he says are transforming organisations. These are 'systems thinking', 'personal mastery', 'mental models', 'building shared vision' and 'team learning'. We have, again, a list, this time of five magic nostrums, another cure-all for organisational ills. The main feature of books of this kind is the attempt to relate to the reader by means of deeper levels of agreement through the use of philosophical, spiritual messages so that the reader comes to buy into what could almost be described as a way of life.

Although books such as this may draw on the reader's belief in magic, they are persuasive. To begin with, as in the case of Peters and Waterman, we are all intrigued if someone claims to have found the secret to success. There is just enough proof at the level of personal experience to convince the reader to go on, even if only half-believing the message. These books are important also as opinion formers, as contributors to management thought. By influencing managers they have an impact on reorganisation, management style, organisational development and management development programmes. The messages are clear and, by stimulating managers to manage differently, they help to bring about change: a case of life imitating art.

The problems with prescriptive texts arise because the pat answers provided cannot be applied without adapting them, and what is missing is therefore an understanding of the particular organisational contexts where the golden rules apply. There is also, as indicated by Guest (1992), by Mitchell (1985) and by Berry (1983), a serious doubt about the validity of the messages themselves. What is required is a more convincing account from the prescriptive authors of how their ideas have transformed and improved organisational performance.

There are other ways we can sensibly use prescriptive texts. They represent data in their own right about managerial ideologies and the importance managers attach to their belief systems. The separation of ownership from control in organisations has resulted in the growth of managerialism. It has been argued that managers will become a new ruling class (Burnham 1962) and that the concentration of economic power in managers' hands will lead either to a more responsible business élite, a 'neutral technocracy' (Berle 1954), or to managers taking their stance as one powerful group among many within a pluralist democracy (Dahrendorf 1959). Nichols reminds us that 'business ideologies are about power', and that 'they consist of those patterned and selective self representations put forward by businessmen which pertain to its distribution' (Nichols 1969, p. 208).

Normative ideologies help to sustain the managerial prescriptions for success and fortune, and to legitimise managerial work. By finding good business reasons for treating employees well, normative ideologies give management a social purpose, provide managers with motivation and help managers to persuade employees of the significance of their work. Normative models of HRM become prescriptions for why as well as how to perform the HRM roles. These normative ideologies may well be strategic responses to the perceived need for a supportive belief system to underpin management actions. Unlike the other two model categories described in this chapter, normative models have an experiential reality because of their influence on the minds of managers.

Guest, whilst aware of the dangers in comparing normative models of HRM with other models of personnel management, clearly expresses a preference for human resource management to be regarded as something special, in particular as an attempt to set up policies, systems and approaches which produce employee commitment (Guest 1987). Briefly, the normative models of personnel management are mainly concerned with matching the needs of individuals with those of society, 'integrating' the interests of employees and organisations, if we are to believe the textbooks. As Legge (1989) points out, there is little difference between North American and UK normative models. Legge's analysis, however, reveals the inherent contradictions in the concept of integration, a phrase which is used to cover both the integration of HRM and business strategy, and the integration of individual and organisational interests.

ONE GENERAL THEORY?

The 'new industrial relations' and the changing economic climate have drawn attention to the personnel role just at a time when the term 'human resource management' has come into more general usage. Ironically, as the author's research with Alan Fell was revealing the many differences in personnel practice, and we were seeking to explain these by searching for 'models', so other academics have been seeking to find one general theory to cover all practice. The debate that results from these concerns tends to present two polarised models, one of which is called 'human resource management' and the other 'personnel management'. The explanations are then set out of how practice has moved from 'personnel management' to 'human resource management'.

It is not surprising that the structural changes to our society have focused attention on people management, and that this new emphasis has brought to the academic agenda a search for evidence of new directions in management thought. The search for one all-embracing theory of human resource management has thus become bound up with the search for a coherent, new approach at the organisational level which can be described by this new phrase 'human resource management'. The academic debate resulting from this happy coincidence of a need for a theory and far-reaching changes to management has been dogged by problems. Up until recently, one major problem hampering any advance has been the lack of empirical evidence to support the many bland statements about the personnel function (Guest 1989, Legge 1988, Storey 1989). A second major difficulty has been confusion over the types of model being used: sometimes they are normative or prescriptive, sometimes descriptive or analytical (Guest 1987, Legge 1989).

Each proposed model of HRM embodies a particular definition of the function and the values which underlie this type of work. The most thorough analysis so far is found in Storey's 1992 work which seeks 'recent configurations in the management of the employment relationship' (p. 23) by researching case studies of organisations. He sees the meanings of HRM along a continuum. These additive definitions are points on a line ranging from human resource management as a synonym for personnel management, through the notion that HRM is an integrated set of techniques, to the idea of a business-oriented approach, until we reach the position where HRM is all of these, plus a set of policies aimed at obtaining employee commitment to explicit organisational values.

The question addressed by this approach is whether HRM represents a distinctive managerial ideology, where certain truths about employee relationships are assumed always to be true. One obvious danger here is acknowledged by Storey:

'. . . the danger that one is contrasting an idealized version of HRM with a practical, lived-in account of the messy reality of personnel management'.

(Storey 1992, p. 33.)

However, the real danger is more fundamental. The problem is not just that these arguments compare reality with some form of ideal state, but rather the problem is where in reality are the concepts grounded? 'Human resource management' is a classification invented by a few practitioners and academics, as indeed originally was 'personnel management'. Both of these titles are also processes. Such processes do not have a simple physical existence. They can only be a set of ideas, recorded and sometimes spoken. Personnel management never existed as one entity, so comparisons with 'HRM' which make this assumption are flawed.

When academics set up a carefully constructed argument to demonstrate that human resource management is a new, normative approach, or an integrated strategic vision, the difficulty we face is that these approaches could always have been described since management first began, but never in a physical sense existed. Following Schopenhauer, we may say the difference is therefore between two different kinds of knowing: reflective, conceptualised knowing (from which categories such as 'human resource management' are drawn) and perceptual, living, empirical knowing by the experience of our senses. The search for 'HRM' as an existing, measurable phenomenon is therefore futile, since it is a search for empirical knowing by using the conceptualised categories invented by the researcher.

The difficulty is compounded because the specialist human resource or personnel occupation only itself exists to deal with management in the conceptual world. It is a kind of work from which there is no physical output. If we take the 27 points of difference between HRM and personnel management listed by Storey (1992, p. 36), we see these are based on assumptions and beliefs about what is strategic, and whatever is strategic is thought to be HRM. This method of seeking to define HRM suffers therefore from the weakness that it can only distinguish what is HRM by disaggregating management decisions and actions, and can only establish what is or is not HRM by reference to a prior definition taken out of context. Readers might therefore be forgiven if they feel this is a rather elaborate tautology.

What leads us into this sophistry is the tendency to attach precise, practical behaviours to ideas and to concepts. If we take a concept such as 'employee commitment', we can see how difficult it is to avoid making assumptions about what a policy on employee commitment could be, or indeed whether there are describable, or provable behavioural responses and thoughts which constitute 'employee commitment' to all observers. Does 'employee commitment' mean the same to managers, to employees and to their families as to academics writing about commitment? The word has connotations of agreement, accord between management goals and employee goals. But how do we know whether the behaviours which we see as signs of commitment are caused by motivation to help the company, or even if the employee believes in a mutuality of interests? Studies in organisational behaviour warn us to be wary of attributing motives to others. These studies reveal some of the complexities of individual differences. Given how difficult it is for anyone to divine another's motivation, or even his/her own, the assumption must be questioned that we know a particular set of managerial intentions, written as a policy document, will elicit a highly specific response from a diverse group of employees.

One of the reasons why we may find this academic debate on the nature of human resource management confusing is because the level of abstraction reached is usually unacknowledged, and it is not until the interpretation of results is attempted that we realise the significance of the shift from one sort of representation to another. Grundstein sums this up neatly:

> 'Schopenhauer made much of the differences between empirical knowing and mediate knowing. His differentiation, as will be seen, bears on the organizational process of thinking. Each of the two forms of knowing is a representation. A difference between the two is that the empirical is a direct representation. Another difference is that the empirical is not a reflective knowing but the mediate (which involves reason) is.'
>
> (Grundstein 1981, p. 131.)

The work performed by people who describe themselves as human resource specialists itself requires them to use a reflective, abstract approach. Human resource management deals in abstractions such as 'jobs', 'rewards', 'development' and, as we discussed earlier, 'commitment'. Jobs do not have a physical existence. Each job described is at best a collection of tasks which the person describing them imagines someone performing (Tyson and York 1982). Tasks themselves can be undertaken in a variety of ways, have uncertain outcomes, different durations and are, as we know, rarely as simple as they seem at the outset. Every day, industrial tribunals in the UK and various types of labour courts elsewhere try to grapple with this awkward fact of organisational life when attempting to discover or interpret contracts of employment.

Much of managerial time is spent dealing in organisational symbols. The same problems beset finance directors, who need to explain what the numbers they write down on pieces of paper actually mean for the business, and marketing directors who believe they are selling 'concepts' such as 'leisure' or 'dignity'. Indeed, all managers find it necessary to work with the symbolic order – that level of abstraction where decisions may be taken in a language where a rational assumption is made about behaviours, and the awkward, unspoken questions such as 'What is a job?' are not asked (Tyson 1987). The symbolic order is indeed a way of maintaining authority within organisations, and for managers such a legitimating property is essential. The rules which connect the various symbols are presented to organisational members as facts of existence. In most cases, to challenge them individually is unthinkable: such a challenge implies a critique of all organisational relationships. If, of course, one has a different view of the world, for example a Marxist perspective, this critique would seem valid. Most employees, however, who are socialised into the organisation's symbolic systems, will appreciate and come to interpret the signs, to endow the symbols with shared meanings (Bühler 1986).

Perhaps the most important aspect of Storey's 1992 account of human resource management is his evidence on how symbols are used in sustaining human resource strategies:

> 'The basic tenets of HRM would seem to be enjoying some wide appeal among managers – if only in furnishing an aspiration and a sense of direction. The crucial importance of symbolism in helping to conjure the nature of that goal was very evident.'
>
> (p. 116.)

He continues throughout the book to discuss HRM as a part of the symbolic order, since he perceives 'HRM' to be rich in symbolism, and the new directions taken within his case study companies frequently originated outside the specialist department, prompting a 'contest between symbolic realms' (p. 183).

What conclusions should we draw from this debate on human resource management? The many changes to the employment relationship represented by flexible working practices, the total quality movement, the pressure to measure value for money in both public and private sectors, and the overriding ideological changes discussed earlier in this chapter have resulted in a debate on the approaches available to manage the employment relationship (Brewster and Connock 1987).

Among the conclusions we may draw from our discussion are that: personnel management, whatever its variant or the classification used, operates at a high level of abstraction; those who work in the field, as with other senior managers, use the symbolic order to sustain the legitimacy of their actions; and personnel or human resource managers have a special role to play in creating the symbolic order. A useful entry point for creating a general theory of human resource management is therefore to examine the way symbols are used. In particular, the author believes that the special nature of the HR activity is to play the major part in reinterpreting symbols and changing meanings for employees (Tyson 1987). The HR function therefore has to work at both the mediate and the empirical level: to translate the organisation's symbolic order into actions by managing the meaning of the symbols.

A very simple example can be found in the management of rewards. If we interpret reward policy to be the effort–reward bargain, managing the constituent parts in that bargain to produce a coherent response from employees illustrates this point. The effort–reward bargain includes pay, benefits and management style on the reward side, and commitment, flexibility and responsiveness on the effort side. Management intentions are expressed symbolically by rewards and the key objective in HRM terms is to work on the meaning and use of these symbols in the minds of employees and managers to produce appropriate efforts. As far as rewards are concerned this is the only efficiency justification for the symbolic order, and the only way human resource specialists can use rewards to harness individual energy to corporate goals.

Bringing about change in a large organisation has been likened to steering a new course on a supertanker – the time-lag can be much longer than management anticipates. The HR role in managing strategic change is one way we might expect to see HR shift meanings through reinterpreting symbols. For example, top management may be subjected to various development and consultancy interventions aimed at shifting values and creating new shared meanings (Kakabadse 1983). In Grundstein's words a 'regulative architecture exists within mediate nature for the management of individual attitudes and sentiments . . .' (p. 164 *op cit*). The HR function's contribution to business strategy may be seen in the establishment of the 'architecture' and the use made of the 'architecture' to change the organisation.

From our discussion so far we may say that in order to create a general theory of human resource management, we require models of this activity which reveal the symbolic order within organisations, showing how this order is sustained and changed. The descriptive models so far discussed have alluded to the way human resource management is conducted. Analytical models should reveal the causes as well as the consequences of the actions performed by those who seek to influence the employment relationship. If we are to adopt an analytical approach to modelling this function, the theoretical base for the model becomes extremely important, because without a theory, analysis is impossible, for we would be unable to see whether or not the data explained causes and consequences. However, any general theory will have to be dynamic.

Normative models which have a prescriptive element can be experienced by managers, and represent one area for strategic choice for organisations. The threats to a coherent ideology come from a rapidly changing business, political and social environment where institutional changes are the norm. Finding a good fit between the business and the human resource activity therefore poses a further difficulty for a coherent human resource response when the dynamics of the business are in many different directions. Labour market changes, occupational changes, technological changes and changes in organisational structure favour the increasing use of the symbolic order as the mechanism by which the fit to business strategy will be achieved and managerial roles legitimised.

BIBLIOGRAPHY

Ackermann, K-F. (1986) 'A contingency model of HRM strategy. Empirical research findings reconsidered', *Management Forum* 6, pp. 65–83.

Armstrong M. (1992) *Human Resource Management. Strategy and Action*, London: Kogan Page.

Bassett, P. (1986) *Strike Free*, London: Macmillan.

Berle, A. A. (1954) *The Twentieth Century Capitalist Revolution*, New York: Harcourt Brace.

Berry, J. (1983) 'Review of In Search of Excellence', *Human Resource Management* 22(3), pp. 329–33.

Brewster, C. and Connock, S. (1987) *Industrial Relations: cost-effective strategies*, London: Hutchinson.

Brewster, C., Gill, C. G. and Richbell, S. (1983) 'Industrial Relations Policy: a Framework for Analysis', in Thurley, K. and Wood, S. (Eds) *Industrial Relations Management and Strategy*, pp. 62–72, Cambridge: Cambridge University Press.

Bühler, K. (1986) 'The Key Principle: the sign character of language' in Innis, R. (Ed) *Semiotics*, London: Hutchinson.

Burnham, J. (1960) *The Managerial Revolution*, Bloomington: Indiana University Press.

Child, J. (1974) 'Quaker Employers and Industrial Relations', *Sociological Review*, November.

Connock, S. (1991) 'H R Vision', *Managing a Quality Workforce*, London: IPM.

Crichton, A. (1968) *Personnel Management in Context*, London: Batsford.

Crozier, M. (1964) *The Bureaucratic Phenomenon*, Chicago: University of Chicago Press.

Dahrendorf, R. (1959) *Class and Class Conflict in Industrial Society*, London: Routledge & Kegan Paul.

Fox, A. (1974) *Beyond Contract: Work, Power and Trust Relations*, London: Faber.

Gowler, D. and Legge, K. (1982) 'Status, effort and reward' in Bowey, A. (Ed) *Managing Salary and Wage Systems*, Aldershot: Gower.

Grundstein, N. D. (1981) *The Managerial Kant*, Weatherhead School of Management: Case Western Reserve University.

Guest, D. (1987) 'Human Resource Management and Industrial Relations', *Journal of Management Studies*, Vol. 24, No. 5, September, pp. 503–21.

Guest, D. (1989) 'Personnel and HRM: Can you tell the diffence?', *Personnel Management*, January.

Guest, D. (1992) 'Right enough to be dangerously wrong: an analysis of the 'In Search of Excellence phenomenon' in Salaman, G. (Ed) *Human Resource Strategies*, London: Open University and Sage.

Herzberg, F., Mausner, B. and Snyderman, B. (1959) *The Motivation to Work*, New York: Wiley.

Hobsbawm, E. J. (1964) *Labouring Men*, London: Weidenfeld & Nicolson.

Homans, G. C. (1954) 'Industrial Harmony as a goal' in Kornhauser A., Dubin, R. and Ross, A. M. (Eds) *Industrial Conflict*, New York: McGraw-Hill.

Jackson, S. E., Schuler, R. S. and Rivero, J. C. (1989) 'Organizational characteristics as predictors of personnel practices', *Personnel Psychology* 42, pp. 727–86.

Kakabadse, A. (1983) *The Politics of Management*, Aldershot:Gower.

Legge, K. (1978) *Power, Innovation and Problem-solving in Personnel Management*, London: McGraw-Hill.

Legge, K. (1988) 'Personnel Management in Recession and Recovery: a comparative analysis of what the surveys say', *Personnel Review*, Vol. 17, November.

Legge, K. (1989) 'Human Resource Management: a critical analysis', in Storey, J. (Ed) *New Perspectives on Human Resource Management*, London: Routledge.

Mitchell, T. (1985) 'In Search of Excellence versus the 100 Best Companies to work for in America: a question of perspectives and value', *Academy of Management Review* 10(2), pp. 350–5.

Monks, K. (1993) 'Models of Personnel Management: A means of understanding the diversity of personnel practices', *Human Resource Management Journal*, Vol. 3, No. 2, pp. 29–41.

Nichols, T. (1969) *Ownership Control and Ideology*, London: George Allen & Unwin.

Niven, M. (1967) *Personnel Management 1913–1963*, London: IPM.

Peters, T. and Waterman, R. (1982) *In Search of Excellence*, New York: Harper & Row.

Pugh, D. S., Hickson, D. J. and Hinings, C. R. (1969) 'The context of organisation structures', *Administrative Science Quarterly*, Vol.14, March, pp. 91–114.

Radcliffe-Brown, A. R. (1952) *Structure and Function in Primitive Society*, London: Cohen and West.

Reader, W. J. (1975) *Imperial Chemical Industries*, Oxford: Oxford University Press.

Ritzer, G. and Trice, H. M. (1969) *An occupation in conflict. A study of the personnel manager*, Cornell University.

Schuler, R. S. and Jackson, S. E. (1987) 'Organizational strategy and organization' level as determinants of Human Resource Management practices', *Human Reso' Planning*, Vol. 10, No. 3, pp. 125–42.

Senge, P. (1990) *The Fifth Discipline*, London: Century Business.

Silverman, D. (1970) *The Theory of Organisations*, London: Heinemann.

Storey, J. (Ed) (1989) *New Perspectives on Human Resource Management*, London: Routledge.

Storey, J. (1992) *Developments in the Management of Human Resources*, Oxford: Blackwell.

Tyson, S. (1979) *Specialists in Ambiguity*, unpublished PhD thesis: University of London.

Tyson, S. (1980) 'Taking advantage of ambiguity', *Personnel Management*, February, p. 45.

Tyson, S. (1983) 'Personnel Management in its organisational context' in Thurley, K. and Wood, S. (Eds) *Industrial Relations and Management Strategy*, Cambridge: Cambridge University Press.

Tyson, S. (1987) 'The Management of the Personnel Function', *Journal of Management Studies*, Vol. 24, No. 5, September, pp. 523–32.

Tyson, S. and Fell, A. (1986) *Evaluating the Personnel Function*, London: Hutchinson.

Tyson, S. and Jackson, T. (1992) *The Essence of Organisational Behaviour*, Hemel Hempstead: Prentice Hall.

Tyson, S. and York, A. (1982) *Personnel Management*, Oxford: Heinemann.

Wächter, H. (1973) *Grundlagen der Langfristigen Personalplanning*, Berlin: Herne.

Watson, T. J. (1977) *The Personnel Managers*, London: Routledge & Kegan Paul.

Weber, M. (1947) *The Theory of Social and Economic Organisations*, New York: The Free Press.

Winter, G. (1966) *Elements for a Social Ethic*, New York: Macmillan.

Woodward, J. (1958) *Management and Technology*, London: HMSO.

CHAPTER 3

The changing business environment

We are moving from a turbulent present into an even more uncertain future. The pace of change, and the apparent contradictions with which managers are faced, produce a search for meaning, for interpretations and for interpreters. So-called 'primitive' peoples are said to appeal to oracles and magicians for signs in their attempts to reduce the uncertainty in their minds. In place of such a shaman we employ economists, political commentators, management gurus and corporate planners to put events, personalities, facts and figures into a coherent context.

The definitions of HRM which we explored in the previous chapter were attempts at constructing just such a set of coherent principles to explain changes in the employment relationship. The word 'change' has come to mean 'improve' in much of the management literature; that is, to be 'modern', relevant, and suitable to present needs. HRM as a concept has a particular virtue according to this perception since it is defined as being centred on organisational change. The paradigmatic shift towards HRM can represent all the new approaches to management we have experienced in the last two decades, and neatly place them into a vision which gives direction, and therefore comforts the reader with the thought that there exists a grand scheme where all the modes of managing can be made to fit together. This view is reinforced by studies which equate organisational effectiveness with the capacity to manage change (Kanter 1983).

The extent of political, economic, technological and institutional change over the past quarter century has been so great, any general theory of HRM must be dynamic. A list of words and phrases evoking the images of widescale change for organisations could include globalisation, political and economic turbulence, recession, raised expectations, new values, different life-styles, demographic shifts, new technologies and new occupation structures. The extensive academic debate on whether HRM does represent a shift from one steady state to another is all the more surprising, therefore. What is needed rather is an explanation of the forces which come to change the management of the employment relationship, and some analytical method for showing how these forces influence organisational life. In this chapter we will examine how economic and political ideologies have come to be embedded in organisational thinking during the shift to the right in British politics, and in particular how the two recessions have contributed to the way HRM has come to be defined. We will then go on to review the influences on HRM, external and internal to the organisation, by proposing a framework which establishes different levels of analysis in the study of HRM.

THE SHIFT TO THE RIGHT AND THE CONSEQUENCES

Human resource strategy can be described as the adjustment of what Schuler and Jackson (1987) called the HR policies, practices and philosophies, to the perceived opportunities and threats in the environment. Pervasive ideologies which are designed to reinforce managerial ideological positions, and which have come to be accepted as the received political wisdom at a particular time, are a part of the environment. They are a factor which needs to be accounted for, even if we are correct in assuming that the researcher has tried to exercise value-free judgements.

In 1979, the advent of the Conservative Government brought a new coherent ideology which came to be known as 'Thatcherism'. Based on a unity of beliefs: *laissez-faire* capitalism, the survival of the fittest and individualism, this new credo was sold to a receptive electorate by conviction politicians such as Keith Joseph and Margaret Thatcher who were scornful of the pragmatic decades which had gone before. To the celebration of capitalist economics were added the notion of 'sound money', interpreted as a reduced public sector borrowing requirement, and the goal of low inflation, and the 'privatisation' of any State-owned organisation which could be translated into a commercial business. The Labour Party, by the end of the Thatcher era in 1990, had dropped Clause 4, public ownership policies; had accepted many of the trade union law changes; and had moved in the opinion of some commentators from being a socialist towards a social democratic party. The dominance of the market-place was unchallenged.

These new political ideologies came at a time when the electorate felt a need for change to institutions. The failure of the Labour Party to solve Britain's economic problems was blamed in 1979 on the Party's original and continuing links with the trade unions. The attempts by the 1974–79

Labour Government to reduce inflation and to keep down public expenditure resulted in a series of damaging public sector strikes in the 'winter of discontent' just before the Conservatives came into office. The Thatcher ideology was therefore grasped as a new source of hope: Mrs Thatcher spoke of Britain regaining a sense of pride, and the 1982 Falklands war, and the strong links with the Reagan administration in Washington, gave the impression that the UK's world position was being restored. Even if this was political rhetoric, it was significant because the combination of a political ideology, an economic philosophy and a sense of pride became a source of inspiration and of motivation; indeed this helps to explain the persistence of the popular belief in Thatcherism, as evidenced by the subsequent General Election victories.

The Conservative Government was elected with a mandate to make changes to trade unions, and the Conservative Party manifesto made explicit the intention to reduce trade union power. The area of legitimate union action was reduced over a twelve-year period by the gradual removal of immunities from litigation for damages against trade unions. The final set-piece battles with the miners and with the printing trades in the newspaper industry resulted in victories for employers. A change in industrial relations' power gave credence to the new ideology. HRM moved from a concern for industrial harmony to being concerned with output goals (Bassett 1986). Public sector unions felt particularly under threat (Tyson 1988). The government also abandoned the hitherto accepted notion that the institutions which helped to govern industrial relations should be run by tripartite bodies, made up of employers, government and trade union representatives. Managerial prerogatives were accepted as most important (usually based on a unitary frame of reference), and interest in joint consultation declined. This was the era when corporate cultures were inculcated into employees, communication was often downwards and employers achieved control by manufacturing consent (Burawoy 1979, Legge 1989).

THE TWO RECESSIONS

The recession of the early 1980s turned the spotlight on people-management practices. The implications for HRM of the 1980/1981 recessions were that labour market strategies could be developed which emphasised flexibility, with 'flatter' organisations, simplified working practices and non-employment options such as outsourcing, to make companies more competitive (Atkinson 1985). These labour market policies, partly driven by skill shortages, were made possible by the new industrial relations' climate which had come to prevail. The changes to employment law, unemployment and the collapse of the old industries where trade unions had their strongest base had forced the unions on to the defensive. At the same time, the move to plant- or company-level bargaining had continued, and the readiness of employees to adopt new industrial relations practices had given management a new agenda, and the need for competitiveness had given them a strategic purpose.

This was the period in the mid-1980s when company culture was strongly emphasised, reinforced by reward systems and communication policies; corporate cultures could be 'built', the consultants claimed, by applying appropriate techniques drawn from social anthropology, such as the use of symbols, rituals, stories and myths (Deal and Kennedy 1982). We have already pointed to the contribution which management gurus such as Peters and Waterman can make to managerial thinking. The acceptance of their doctrines during the 1980s spread the idea that simplifying one's business and being close to the customer were key principles for success. The 'flexible firm' idea of Atkinson strengthened the notion that responsiveness to customer demands should be inherent within employment contracts. These ideas have been supplemented by the 'total quality' movement and by the Japanese exemplars already located within the UK. Expansion in the service sector as the UK came out of the first recession also helped to show how HRM can contribute to business performance in such organisations as British Airways, Marks & Spencer, Sainsbury and similar large retail operations, where the large scale of operation and proceduralised work routines made it possible for HR practices in recruitment, training and performance management to link into corporate customer-care programmes. The 1980s' recession gave HR interests a boost because new industrial relationships and new HR practices and policies helped organisations to recover and to become competitive again. In the eyes of some company chief executives, HRM was accorded a strategic status, therefore, rather than merely being asked to perform an administrative role.

The second major recession to hit the UK since 1980 has been the most serious since before the Second World War. This recession was different in scale and scope from the earlier economic downturns. The 1990s' recession has brought what are feared to be permanent levels of high unemployment, with an EC unemployment level of around 17 million people. Unlike previous recessions, this has reduced business levels drastically in the service industries, and big companies have been as badly affected as small companies. Unemployment levels in the South East of England have risen beyond those of the traditional unemployment blackspots in Wales, Scotland and North East England.

Organisations such as IBM and Marks & Spencer which had a 'no redundancy' policy have had to reverse this stance. For once there are no managerial solutions to the problems. World-wide trading conditions, the loss of business confidence and reduced investment are not matters which can be resolved by changing HR philosophies, policies or practices.

The recession has brought to the fore questions about employee commitment. In a recent survey, nearly 80 per cent of employers were shown to have a redundancy policy (Doherty and Viney 1993). Managerial labour markets are now expected to be as flexible as those for other workers, with the disappearance of career ladders (Inkson and Coe 1993).

The most notable impact of the 1990–93 recession can be found in the new attention given to issues of organisational structure. The restructuring and reorganisation of businesses have sometimes occurred because product groups have disappeared due to low demand, while industries such as construction and retailing have suffered severe cuts, and in many businesses operations have had to be scaled down in order to become viable.

Restructuring has taken a number of forms. There is a move away from bureaucratic structures towards flatter, horizontal reporting relationships where sub-units have greater autonomy. What have been described as 'federal structures' are now favoured (Handy 1989). This implies looser linkages with the centre, with clearer channels to market and a more responsive approach to change (Whitaker 1992). New forms of organisation have also been encouraged by the 'quality movement', through internal contracts specifying services and costs, with the increased use of external services for computing, security, public relations, marketing services and even personnel services. Product- or service-based organisational structures are typically found in organisations which have tried to create flexibility, often by using various matrix forms, sometimes organised across national boundaries with country-specific presidents on one part of the matrix.

The trend towards 'delayering' – removing levels from the bureaucracy – has continued over the last decade, and may have been accelerated by the recent recession. The large headquarters office has been reduced to a small corporate centre in many cases, with support staff pared down to a minimum. At the factory or shop level there has been a trend towards semi-autonomous work groups and larger spans of control. Supporting human resource policies, which have been adopted in organisations such as BP, include 'empowerment policies' which move responsibility down to the lowest level compatible with efficiency needs, and which give to all employees the power to make real decisions about their work. This results in many changes to policies: for example training, development, rewards and communication policies are more likely to be geared towards the team activity.

The two major recessions, coming at the beginning and the end of the dramatic move to the right in political ideology, illustrate how HRM is more than a management concern. These movements can be seen as one manifestation of how economic change and social development influence the employment relationship. The economic changes have shown how uncertain is the direction that HRM is taking. Normative purposes cannot be sustained over the varying stages in the economic cycle, and the values which management bring to their work are not constant, but are dependent upon the strategic choices which their companies face.

RELATING HRM TO FACTORS EXTERNAL TO THE ORGANISATION

During the 1980s it became unfashionable to ascribe organisational performance to the broad economic and social trends in British society. The then Prime Minister, Margaret Thatcher, remarked that 'society did not exist'. Success or failure was often attributed to the entrepreneurial zeal of the top managers and the owners, to the competitive nature of products or services (these being also a consequence of entrepreneurship), and to organisational cultures which espoused excellence. Companies such as IBM, Macdonalds and Coca-Cola, and Japanese companies, fell into the latter category, whilst entrepreneurs such as Maxwell, Walker, Nadir and the like were able to convince their business audiences that they had the special touch to spot opportunities and to exploit them.

From the HRM perspective, the organisational culture argument was attractive. The belief in organisational cultures was based on the assumption that the 'culture' was the most significant determinant of worker behaviour. Organisational culture, 'the way we do things around here' as it is so often defined, was refined as a concept. A 'cultural web' was said to exist which could be analysed according to the organisational structures, the routines and rituals, the power structures, control systems, symbols, myths and stories, to show what was the prevailing paradigm – the set of assumptions and beliefs which prevailed in the organisation (Johnson 1987). Since many of these elements within the cultural web could be influenced by HR policies, for example reward systems, this was good news for HR managers. The cultural argument also has the attraction that management can make a critical difference to organisational performance, and therefore results in a form of managerialism. Management ideologies become important to the success or failure of a business, if we accept this view.

The entrepreneurial thesis is another variant on the leadership debate. Here the argument is that the leader creates the team and organises the business around the principles in which he or she believes. Charisma and the power to implement new ideas are thus thought to be the *sine qua non* of good leadership. During the 1980s organisations had to be led through transformational change, whether it was Lord King of British Airways or Sir Graham Day at British Aerospace and at Rover. The role of HR under this interpretation is to provide the systems, policies, styles and techniques to support the new values which are to be espoused. This rather individualistic interpretation is not without historical precedents, if we think of Watson creating IBM, Rockerfeller with Standard Oil, Branson with Virgin Airlines, or Laura Ashley creating her retail chain.

These cultural or industrial explanations fail to show how the complex of variables influences an organisation and shapes its future. At the start-up phase it is easy and perhaps simplistic to look at the founding entrepreneurs as the source of all influences, or when a strong culture exists to see that as the template which moulds all behaviours. However, neither of these explanations helps us to understand how the economic, political, institutional and social aspects of the business environment influence business and human resource strategies. We have seen how political and economic changes during the 1980s created a climate which gave a direction and coherence to action, based on broadly accepted norms and a political philosophy. The question we should now explore is how do these broad societal values and philosophies come to be translated into organisational action?

In the development of a general theory of human resource management we need to discover what it is that links societal and economic change to management practice – that is, to link the two separate levels of analysis we have discussed so far. This might explain how social action in organisations changes as a consequence of societal variables. The trends and developments in HRM would then appear as distinct aspects to social and economic change, tying together the economic attributes of labour markets and product/service markets with organisational policy choices. One such attempt to express these relationships has been developed (Tyson 1979). This is shown in Table 3.

Table 3: Levels of analysis

SOCIETAL LEVEL VARIABLES				
Market size and product type	State of technology	Level of unemployment in specific labour markets	Climate of state activity on employment	Bargaining history and methods between employers and trade unions in specific industry
ORGANISATIONAL LEVEL: INTERVENING VARIABLES				
Market share	Investment policies	Personnel role – expressed in policies and actions	Management ideologies	Decision-making habits/rules
SENTIENT LEVEL: PERCEPTIONS OF WORK PEOPLE				
Deriving from group norms, concepts of justice, fairness and reciprocity				

This framework describes three levels of analysis: the societal level variables which impact on all organisations; that of the organisation itself, which intervenes between society and the perceptions of the employees; and the perceptions of the work people which are founded on their own social and economic positions. It is suggested that each of the societal level variables influences industries, and sometimes the particular organisations, by the size and type of product markets; the technology available; employment demand in specific labour markets; the climate of State activity on employment matters; and the industrial relations traditions in the industry in question.

We can define the headings more precisely in the following terms:

Market size and product type

The size of the market determines the potential scale of operations. The product type (which includes services) affects the speed of operations and the extent to which particular operating systems are used – for example, mass production, process production or craft production (Woodward 1958).

Market share

At the organisational level of analysis what matters is whether the organisation has a large share or a small share of the market. Big players can influence price, control entry for other companies, and take advantage of volume to achieve economies of scale. A small share of a large market produces a more responsive approach to the market-place, more rapid change and innovation as organisations look for new ways to make an impact. Highly segmented markets are clearly more difficult to control, and in many cases the company seeks dominance within a niche.

Evidence for the effects of the interplay between market size, product type and market share on human resource management can be found in Hendry and Pettigrew (1992). They argue from ten case study companies that 'life-cycle' patterns emerged from their sample (patterns they called 'rapid growth', 'severe retrenchment' and 'slow decline') which show differing emphases on human resource policies.

> 'In each of our cases what has generated change has been pressure on product life-cycles and, through this, pressure on the Company's overall product portfolio structure. Shifts occur when a product strategy is undermined and firms are forced either to strengthen or shift to an alternative basis of competitive advantage. This is likely to bring about changes in organisation structure.'
>
> (p. 140.)

They go on to conclude that while there are some obvious changes to HR policies when a company grows or declines, the more complex responses have to be evolved 'when monopolistic advantages decline', as then strategic management has to be 'practised'. According to the framework developed here, when market share declines, or the interplay between changing market size, product type and/or market share becomes complex, organisational structure and HR policy responses have to be developed to match these changes. A good example here would be the way organisations create European matrix structures in order to provide some coherence in functional strategies across national divides, as was found in the cases of 'Square D' and 'Chloride' (Tyson *et al* 1993), and the collaborative ventures such as Airbus Industrie (Tyson and Jackson 1992).

The state of technology

References to new technology, especially information technology, are now so common that any mention of the revolutionary changes which new technology has produced seem banal. The application of new technology in the workplace has resulted in a debate about the relative merits of technocentric or anthropocentric approaches towards manufacturing systems. It is argued that superiority of the latter, which allows for existing skills and for greater flexibility at lower costs, is becoming apparent with the need for market-responsive manufacturing systems which can design and manufacture products quickly to suit individual customer requirements (Brödner 1990). What is also becoming clear is the amount of strategic choice which organisations now have, and that different solutions are available according to particular needs. Competitive advantages are now possible through making choices which balance market pressures with human resource issues and the financial parameters of the business plan.

Investment policies

Advances in technology are sustained throughout a society and brought to bear on organisations as a consequence of competition. The investment policies adopted by organisations determine the take-up of new technology and its adaptation to the uses demanded by management and employees. It is the contention here that investment policies, which are themselves influenced by the market size/market share equilibrium, are intervening variables that condition how far new advances in technology are exploited, and the types of new technologies to be used. In turn, these decisions will impact on the number of jobs, and the type of work to be performed where job design factors also become involved. Significantly, it is the planning processes, through which investment policies are realised, which are now seen as critical to success.

> 'The increasing complexity of production systems, the interdisciplinary character of system solutions, the shortening of the planning phases, and the increased needs of the workforce all impose new demands on systems planning.'
>
> (Bullinger 1990, p. 29.)

Business and organisational process redesign is now one way to take a more holistic view of the organisation which brings together the various systems into alignment. The extensive literature on the effects of different technological systems includes evidence on relationships between technical complexity, organisational structure and decision-making (Woodward 1958, 1965), and the effects of rapidly changing technologies on organisational structures (Burns and Stalker 1961). There is a logic in the relationship between technical change and human resource management which leads researchers to use a systems approach when examining the issue, in the expectation that there will be a HRM systems involvement as a necessary consequence.

All the recent evidence shows that HR specialists are marginalised in technical change situations, which are dominated instead by systems engineers and line managers (Clark 1993, Legge 1993). However, this may be in the narrower, engineering, job-change aspects of new technology. Hendry's research at Hardy Spicer shows how the HR function there had a real involvement in technical change by creating a climate over a long period through managing the role relationships and industrial relations style (Hendry 1993). This required 'genuinely strategic behaviour which combines both planning and adaptation to an evolving situation' (p. 99). Such changes are usually accompanied by new organisational structures to reflect the new span of control, the new operational processes, and the range of computer-based information available: 'Technical change now appears to be framed within organisational change, rather than the other way round.' (p. 99.)

Level of unemployment in specific labour markets

Unemployment levels affect HR policies directly. The availability of labour influences recruitment policy, reward policy and training policy. Of equal significance, the unemployment levels create the general climate of economic activity, and affect trade union membership and militancy. However, unemployment lags behind economic recovery, as was demonstrated by the 1993 position, and general levels of unemployment are of less interest to employers than the operation of particular labour markets. Skills shortages or cheaply available labour, for example, influence strategic decisions on locations, acquisitions and expansion plans. Competitive advantages are gained and lost according to the capacity to acquire and develop specialised competencies.

Climate of State activity on employment

This describes the overall philosophy towards labour and the management of the employment relationship. It is created by laws, tax policies, social security policies, and by government propaganda. The 'climate' shift described earlier in this chapter illustrated how politicians with a strong ideological position helped to influence and to reflect the move towards the form of *laissez-faire* capitalism which has come to be called 'Thatcherism'. The economic policies and the degree of government intervention may be the crucial variables, but what is significant is the overall effect of government activity on managements, trade unions and the perceptions of working people. This effect is mediated by the prevailing ideological stance taken by managements at the organisational level.

Management ideologies

Whatever the general societal climate on employment matters, the ideologies that managers possess reinterpret these general trends. These ideologies are belief systems, and where the culture is strong the beliefs will be found in the everyday work of managers. Organisational cultures are sustained by the kinds of people who are recruited, promoted and rewarded. Their values can come to underpin management beliefs. These values about the employment relationship will have a major impact upon HR policies. For example, unitary or pluralistic frames of reference will influence trade union recognition policies (Fox 1974), or one might anticipate management styles of McGregor's Theory X and Theory Y persuasion influencing the level of trust in a company, with all the consequences for reward, development or 'empowerment' policies (McGregor 1966).

CHANGE IN THE LABOUR MARKET

The above-mentioned variables: unemployment, labour market factors, the climate of State activity and management ideologies, are associated in the way they reflect the available labour market strategies created at the societal level, and the organisational choices concerning which strategy to pursue. The labour markets and strategic choices are changing. Increasing labour productivity, additional pressures on the labour market from demographic changes, the weakening of the competitive position of the high-income economies and saturation in domestic markets have changed the labour markets in Western Europe (Offe 1985). The move to the right, and the major political changes over the last few years, mean the abandonment of Keynesian policies in favour of a free market mechanism. This has left firms with problems they cannot resolve, and which the State no longer wishes to solve. Some of the societal level choices are dependent upon governmental policies about welfare benefits: who should be included in the labour market and how unemployment benefits, health insurance and retirement benefits should be dealt with as between the State and the employer. To these uncertainties there must be added the changing nature of work, towards the knowledge worker. The proportion of professionals, managerial and technical occupations has been increasing, while in the period from 1950 to 1990 the numbers employed in manufacturing in the UK has fallen from 40 per cent to 22.4 per cent (Watkins, Drury and Preddy 1992). With the 1990 recession we have seen how companies have abandoned the career concept for managers, leaving the individual to negotiate her or himself through the labour market changes, as increasingly managers are treated like other workers – being subject to the same uncertainties and life chances.

In the framework, three levels have been suggested. The societal level is the aggregate level of concerns, expressed through legal, institutional and political action. The organisation level is the level of the firms, of company policies. Here there are choices about how the societal level issues may be resolved and, at the individual level of perception, the manager, professional and worker respond. The complexity of the HR function's position is due in part to its bureaucratic role. The problem is that strategic responses to societal-level opportunities and threats find the HR function trying to cope with the three different rationalities found in each of the levels of analysis. There is, as Offe reminds us, a political dimension to administrative action:

> 'The problem of administrative action is that it is at the same time suspended between these contradictory criteria and standards of rationality: it must simultaneously conform to its basic principles, its functions and the declared interests of its clients and reference groups.'
>
> (Offe 1985, p. 316.)

The juxtaposition of these different rationalities is exposed when the political/legal issues are brought into the organisational arena, and are especially evident when there are strong, clear employee interests. A good recent example is the case of British Coal seeking to use its pension fund money to contribute to the costs of making its workers redundant: an action which the courts ruled as illegal. Structural change within commerce, the public sector and industry is one side to the broad changes in political, institutional and legal structures.

When such monumental changes occur, the strain on the different rationalities increases. HR policies at this stage, when change has become discontinuous and severe, frequently play on inappropriate symbols and fail to change meanings quickly to correspond with societal-level rationality. For example, 'individualism' as part of the management ideologies of the 1980s often expressed through reward policies, seems to deliver an outdated message in the 1990s when people increasingly work in teams, and cooperation and the facility to adapt quickly are competencies more in tune with current needs.

Bargaining history and methods between employers and trade unions

During the last twenty years there has been a steady move away from bargaining at the industry level towards company or plant bargaining. Changes to the bargaining methods impact across all organisational boundaries. Where there is local-level negotiation there is still an effect on settlements in related industries. Trade unions (with a membership still of around one-third of the working population) have an influence even beyond the industries where they are well represented. The 'going rate' for pay increases resonates from agreements in such companies as the Ford Motor Company to other industries employing workers in engineering and similar occupations, just as public sector pay rises are watched by all employers. The changes to traditional industrial relations activity has brought change to the models of HRM at the company level (Tyson and Fell 1992). It could be argued that recent changes have come about because management decision-making has changed: managers now wish to talk more directly with their employees and increasingly to take the initiative with new HR policies.

Decision-making habits and rules

Collective bargaining traditions are reinterpreted and amended at the organisational level, according to the decision-making habits and the rules of the enterprise. Here we are defining decision-making as a formal process, which will involve the dominant coalition of the organisation, but may also be affected by the many interest groups and delegated authorities concerned. For example it may be affected by divisional boards, strategic business units, empowered supervisors and the particular posts found in specific sectors (shop managers, police authorities, hospital trusts and so on). Decisions about managing the employment relationship will frequently be taken from the very local perspective of these managers, i.e. according to their 'bounded rationality'.

The phrase 'decision-making habits' is intended to convey the semi-formal nature of much top team decision-making, where personalities and 'political' behaviour have considerable strategic significance (Kakabadse 1991). The importance of 'rules' in decision-making is attested by sociologists such as Crozier (1964), Cyert and March (1963) and Jaques (1976).

Organisational rules which are relevant here may include different approaches to employee involvement, problem solving, and joint consultation. The chief effects are on organisational structure and on management ideology. These variable relationships are not simple causal chains, therefore, and societal-level changes do occur as a consequence of the aggregate of organisational changes.

THE 'SENTIENT' LEVEL

One of the main gaps in HRM research is the absence of data on what people who actually experience HRM policies think or feel about them. Even with all the attention paid to HRM, the consumers of these policies seem only to be consulted by the HR functions within a few organisations. This 'market research' is rarely published. From what the author has learned in the many HR policy audits conducted by Cranfield's Human Resource Research Centre, and the published accounts of surveys, it appears that there are always some surprises for management (Tyson *et al* 1988).

In one organisation of 40 000 people working in textiles, the communication policy stipulated by the main board was only partially put into operation. Although the personnel director thought the policy to be very effective, in one plant there had been redundancies, for named individuals, announced on the noticeboard, and in another not only was the policy not practised, but the factory manager had not even heard of it.

Issues of justice, fairness and reciprocity are of significance to employees because they are on the receiving end of policies which regulate their working lives. The instrumental attachment to work identified by Goldthorpe *et al* (1968) is surely more evident now. Societal norms are expressed through individuals, and one medium for transmitting these norms is the organisation. The framework proposed suggests that the organisation mediates the societal-level factors listed and reinterprets them into HR policies and organisational behaviours – which are then the source of each person's vivid experience of working life.

SUMMARY OF THE ARGUMENT

In this chapter the effects of the business environment on HR policies have been placed in a framework which shows three levels of analysis. These levels equate to the subjective, 'objective' and social worlds, each of which carries its own concepts of rationality. It is argued that the perceptions of members of an organisation are affected by the reinterpretations of societal trends and therefore that symbolic meanings extend beyond the workplace. That is, HR policies and practices define the societal norms and values in certain important, specific areas.

Reward policies offer a good example of this process. The value society places upon an employee's work is experienced by the employee through the organisation's compensation and benefit policies, in most instances. Because of the consumer orientations in our modern society, the economic reward also confers a social status. You are what you can buy. Now there are, of course, certain professional groups whose earnings are believed by themselves and others familiar with their work not to represent the 'correct' social value. Medical doctors, nurses, ambulance staff, schoolteachers among others would fall into this category. But this apparent anomaly serves to prove the point. It is the 'unfairness' of the reward which is at issue – the professionals in question *should* receive more salary, it is argued, in order to overcome the disparity between their economic and social status.

The notion that societal-level variables have a big impact on HRM is not new. However, too often writers on HRM are content to deal with this topic by reference to 'the environment' – a black box from which various influences are acknowledged to flow – without distinguishing the different elements. In the framework described here, we have attempted to show how one element affects another, and to describe how the dynamic in HR policies derives from the interaction between the societal, the organisational and the sentient levels. The intention is not to convey the idea that all changes to HR policies are predetermined by society; on the contrary, the mediation of societal-level changes within the organisation necessarily requires some accommodation between the subjective perceptions of the employees, and the interactions between organisation-level variables and the influences from society upon them. Policies may also exist which encourage employee involvement in the creation of policies, for example through joint consultation or employee involvement schemes. In any case, the creation of policies has been described as an outcome from the interaction between varying stakeholder interests: top management, line management, trade union representatives and strategically powerful employee groups, as well as HR specialists.

While the description here is very Anglo-Saxon, there is a strong likelihood of the framework being relevant in other continents. The idea of the three levels, and at least some of the variables (such as market size and shape, State policies and technology) are likely to be the same. No doubt further research would show what other variables are important. One remarkable aspect of the current business environment is that it is possible to generalise about the speed of change. Global branding, new technology, outsourcing, the new trading blocs (EC, ASEAN, the Gulf States) and the institutional arrangements for world trade have encouraged the 'global village' idea. Travel between countries and between continents is commonplace. This degree of interaction itself encourages change. Internationalism combined with ever-growing human wants provides the need, and the restless search for competitive advantage, sometimes even for survival at a time of widescale political changes, is the engine which drives organisations to change working methods, size, structure, products and services and to seek alliances, mergers, acquisitions, divestments and joint ventures. For most people working in organisations these broad, sweeping changes, often even to the ownership of the company they work for, must be bewildering and one would anticipate might lead to apathy. The rationalities used by the key decision-makers at each level are unlikely to be compatible at the current rate of change.

At the sentient level, the reasons for investment policies which change rapidly or for new management ideologies are not easily appreciated, even if as an employee some of the societal level changes are visible. This is because there are strategic choices to be made, and with a high degree of uncertainty, senior managers can only make decisions on the balance of probabilities, that is assuming their decision-making has a rational basis.

For academics engaged in the sisyphean labour of theory building, constant change also brings doubt. But from the doubt comes the possibility to see new relationships between phenomena. The study of industrial relations has a long history, and has always up until now been based on theories about the relationship between capital and labour which were formed at the end of the nineteenth century, and developed in the first half of the twentieth century. The changes experienced over the last twenty years have challenged many assumptions. The search for new theoretical certainties is a common cause amongst sociologists and philosophers who have recognised the implications of economic, social and technical change as well as the changes to ideologies.

> 'The destruction of the historico-philosophical certainty that the industrial working class and the European labour movement were targets for possible, theoretically induced processes of enlightenment and bearers of a politically pursued, revolutionary transformation is not, in my view, entirely a disadvantage.'
>
> (Jürgen Habermas 1982, p. 222.)

Human resource management has inevitably become caught up in the changes which are taking place in the institutions; economies and societies in Western Europe. Any theory of HRM has to account, in outline at least, for societal change. Habermas is concerned with the dynamics of modern society, and seeks to explain through his theories of labour and interaction how, in the process of forming the 'self', society is achieved. It is in the clash between the rational, or official, world and the human, where the desire for choice and for spiritual, emotional states of mind is represented, that the individual comes face to face with the 'objective realities' of power and money. Any new theory of industrial relations will need to take into account the mediation process which occurs at the organisational level of analysis. HRM seeks to make the 'objective' rational world a subjective world, at this level. The symbolic order is the process by which the translation from one level of rationality to the other is achieved.

BIBLIOGRAPHY

Atkinson, J. (1985) 'Flexibility: Planning for an uncertain future', *Manpower Policy and Practice* 1, Summer, pp. 25–30.

Bassett, P. (1986) *Strike Free*, London: Macmillan.

Brödner, P. (1990) 'Technocentric–anthropocentric approaches towards skill-based manufacturing', in Warner, M., Wobbe, W. and Brödner, P. (Eds) *New Technology and Manufacturing Management*, Chichester: John Wiley.

Bullinger, H.J. (1990) 'Integrated Technical Concepts. Towards the Fully Automated Factory' in Warner, M., Wobbe, W. and Brödner, P. *op. cit.*

Burawoy, M. (1979) *Manufacturing Consent*, Chicago: University of Chicago Press.

Burns, T. and Stalker, G. M. (1961) *The Management of Innovation*, London: Tavistock.

Clark, J. (1993) (Ed) *Human Resource Management and Technical Change*, London: Sage.

Crozier, M. (1964) *The Bureaucratic Phenomenon*, Chicago: Chicago University Press.

Cyert, R. M. and March, J. G. (1963) *A Behavioural Theory of the Firm*, New York: Wiley.

Deal, T. E. and Kennedy, A. A. (1982) *Corporate Cultures*, Reading, Mass.: Addison-Wesley.

Doherty, N. and Viney, C. (1993) *Organisational Perspectives on Outplacement*, Human Resource Research Centre, Cranfield University.

Fox, A. (1974) *Beyond Contract: Work, Power and Trust Relations*, London: Faber.

Goldthorpe, J. H., Lockwood, D., Bechhofer, F. and Platt, J. (1968) *The Affluent Worker: Industrial Attitudes and Behaviour*, Cambridge: Cambridge University Press.

Habermas, J. (1982) 'A reply to my critics' in Thompson, J. B. and Held, D. (Eds) *Habermas. Critical Debates*, London: Macmillan.

Handy, C. (1989) *The Age of Unreason*, Boston: Harvard Business School Press.

Hendry, C. (1993) 'Personnel Leadership in Technical and Human Resource Change' in Clark, J. (Ed) *Human Resource Management and Technical Change*, London: Sage.

Hendry, C. and Pettigrew, A. (1992) 'Patterns of Strategic Change in the Development of Human Resource Management', *British Journal of Management*, Vol. 3, No. 3, September, pp. 137–56.

Inkson, K. and Coe, T. (1993) *Are career ladders disappearing?*, London: Institute of Management.

Jaques, E. (1976) *A General Theory of Bureaucracy*, London: Heinemann.

Johnson, G. (1987) *Strategic Change and the Management Process*, Oxford: Basil Blackwell.

Kakabadse, A. (1991) *The Wealth Creators*, London: Kogan Page.

Kanter, R. M. (1983) *The Change Masters*, New York: Simon & Schuster.

Legge, K. (1989) 'Human Resource Management: a critical analysis' in Storey, J. (Ed) *New Perspectives on Human Resource Management*, London: Routledge.

Legge, K. (1993) 'The Role of Personnel Specialists: centrality or marginalization' in Clark, J. (Ed) *Human Resource Management and Technical Change*, London: Sage.

McGregor, D. (1966) *Leadership and Motivation*, Cambridge, Mass.: MIT Press.

Offe, C. (1985) *Disorganized Capitalism*, Cambridge: Polity Press in association with Basil Blackwell.

Schuler, R. S. and Jackson, S. E. (1987) 'Linking competitive strategies with human resource management practices', Academy of Management Executive 1.3.

Tyson, S. (1988) 'The dilemmas of Civil Service Personnel Management', *Personnel Management*, September, pp. 49–53.

Tyson, S., Ackermann, K-F., Domsch, M. and Joynt, P. (1988) *Appraising and exploring organisations*, Beckenham: Croom Helm.

Tyson, S. (1979) *Specialists in Ambiguity*, unpublished PhD thesis, University of London.

Tyson, S. and Fell, A. (1992) *Evaluating the Personnel Function* (2nd Edition), Cheltenham: Stanley Thornes.

Tyson, S. and Jackson, T. (1992) *The Essence of Organisational Behaviour*, Hemel Hempstead: Prentice Hall.

Tyson, S., Lawrence, P., Poirson, P., Manzoline, L. and Vicente, C. S. (Eds) (1993) *Human Resource Management in Europe*, London: Kogan Page.

Watkins, J., Drury, L. and Preddy, D. (1992) 'From Evolution to Revolution. The pressures in professional life in the 1990s', Bristol: University of Bristol.

Whitaker, A. (1992) 'The Transformation in Work: Post-Fordism revisited' in Reed, M. and Hughes, M. (Eds) *Rethinking Organizations*, London: Sage.

Woodward, J. (1958) *Management and Technology*, London: HMSO.

Woodward, J. (1965) *Industrial Organization Theory and Practice*, Oxford: Oxford University Press.

CHAPTER 4

The contribution of HRM to business strategy: the planning process

Change is experienced as a natural feature of organisational life, but it has now assumed a different dimension. The societal level variables are changing in ways which make any understanding of what would be an appropriate organisation-level response difficult to imagine. The pace of change, its fundamental nature, and the uncertain political and institutional structures in the UK and Europe raise the odds for any bet on the future.

Uncertainty about the UK's European future, large swings in the economic cycle and the outbreak of international peace alongside national wars have brought into the open questions about economic and political stability, and the appropriateness of institutions. The *fin de siècle* atmosphere which prevails mixes 1980s' solutions with the next millennium's problems. How do we fund the social benefit needs of our ageing populations? To what extent is *laissez-faire* capitalism the solution to economic ills? How do we find a medium for expressing nationalist aspirations which maintains the peace and encourages economic cooperation? The 'reforms' of the 1980s, which included privatisation and unleashing market forces, European-based economic policy and an individualistic ideology, no longer seem appropriate. The difficulties which are experienced in carrying through changes throw doubt upon their purpose.

During the early 1980s attention was switched from the societal level of analysis, where the issues were often taken for granted, to the possibilities for improving and evolving corporate strategy through corporate controls, of which human resource management was one element. This is not to deny senior management's fascination with change, and the seriousness with which predictions were taken about the coming of a 'post-industrial' society, where 'knowledge workers' would be at a premium, collaborating in networks from electronic cottages (Tofler 1980, Handy 1989). We have already noted how the 'demographic time bomb' was also prophesied to explode in the early

1990s. One suspects that the intense interest caused by all of these predictions was for two reasons: the impact on people management was expected to be considerable, and as we know from children's behaviour, there is some kind of primitive need within the human psyche to be frightened with stories of catastrophe, so we can enjoy the comfort of our everyday reality. The truth in many of these predictions has been seen, but has had different effects in different organisational contexts, and has been ameliorated or distorted by other, unpredicted changes, such as the rise in unemployment and the effects of the recession.

Much of the HRM literature quoted so far in this book derives from research conducted in the mid 1980s, when to leading commentators and to some companies, there seemed to be a new managerial approach to the management of the employment relationship. The change focus for such studies provided insights into strategic positioning and into the change processes themselves, in which HRM played a major part. However, what we do not yet know is how changes to management practices and the normative ideologies espoused by some managements at that time have withstood the depredations of the deepest and longest recession to hit the UK since the 1930s.

One might anticipate important differences would be found in HRM according to the levels of unemployment in the economy and whether market share/size ratios are changing. Expansionist policies are easy to envisage in fields such as recruitment, training and development. By contrast, recession reverses policy objectives, and redundancy and reduced career expectations become the norm (Doherty and Tyson 1993). The excellence literature of the early 1980s has moved on through a concern with change management (Kanter 1983) to the study of turbulence and chaos (Peters 1987).

Much of the literature on business strategy focuses on how to reduce uncertainty and therefore to clarify options for business plans. We defined business or corporate strategy in Chapter 1 as a process for positioning the organisation to take best advantage of the prevailing business environment. The purpose of this present chapter is to look at the planning process. We have established so far that there is a relationship between business and human resource strategy, and that we would therefore expect some impact on business performance from HR policies and practices. We have also shown that it is necessary to understand the organisational context, because of the complexities of the intervening variables between the sentient, organisational and societal levels. The high degree of turbulence and institutional, political and economic uncertainty currently experienced in the UK lead us to expect the contribution of HRM to business strategy to be affected.

In this chapter and the chapter that follows we will examine a research project which has sought to discover what is the contribution of HRM to business performance and how the planning processes are undertaken, and describes HRM in the UK in recession and recovery.

DIFFERENT ROUTES TO EXCELLENCE – A RESEARCH PROJECT

The starting point for the project was a desire to discover the reality of the relationship between HR and business strategy, partly to counter the rhetoric of the mid 1980s, when so many prescriptive statements were made. These had seemed to regard in a simplistic way 'good' HRM as synonymous with business success and tended to be based on assumptions about what all businesses should do, without regard to the need for different models of HRM according to the context – which can be described at the three levels of analysis. The fact that the simplistic nostrums of Peters' and Waterman's text (1982) had been questioned was also influential. Seventeen of their 'excellent' companies were in some kind of difficulty within two years of the book's publication. There are strong arguments for regarding 'excellence' as a broad categorisation which can be partially in evidence rather than an absolute state (Sharma *et al* 1990).

There are varying approaches to HRM (*see* Chapter 2), and the notion of 'fit' between business and HR strategy is well developed by Schuler and Jackson (1987). This would suggest that the 'fit' would itself be dependent upon how the organisation level variables were reinterpreted to be in tune with the business strategy: the strategy being a response to the interpretation of the societal-level factors by the organisation's dominant coalition.

The process by which the reinterpretation of business strategies turn these into functional strategies has also been the subject of debate. We have seen from Ackermann's work that some HR policy areas are more sensitive to changing business strategies than others. Purcell (1989) argues that HR strategies are 'second' order strategies, which follow on from 'first order' strategies. Personnel policy choices are typically 'downstream' from the main strategic decisions, especially in diversified organisations, where the main strategic issues are which businesses to invest in, or divest from, how to capitalise the business and so on. The possibilities for strong linkages remain in single product businesses, or those with one main area of operations. To some extent this debate centres on the distinction between corporate and business strategy: the former being the phrase used to describe a portfolio of businesses, and the latter the strategy used to develop a particular business. By contrast, Lengnick-Hall and Lengnick-Hall (1988) theorise that there is a 'reciprocal interdependence' between a firm's business strategy and its human resources strategy.

They put forward a model of interdependence where the 'demand' for skills and employees is a function of the competitive strategy, and the organisation's availability and readiness is a product of the human resource strategy, but where the HR strategy necessarily conditions the competitive strategy. This is because only certain competitive strategies can be considered, in view of the constraints and opportunities provided by the HR strategy – they thus stress the multi-dimensional nature of the relationship. (*See* Fig. 2.)

As we discussed in Chapter 2, the way managers are conditioned only to consider certain strategic options has become of interest to researchers, and the reminder that we are considering a multiplicity of influences on both business and human resource strategy does at least shift attention away from single towards multi-causal explanations. Searches for 'final causes' in human affairs are invariably frustrating, and instead of looking at 'why' we should concentrate instead on discovering 'what' happens and 'how' at the organisational level of analysis.

RESEARCH OBJECTIVES

The research study described here therefore sought to examine the broad issue: to what extent and how do organisations which are well known, and/or which have consistently achieved good business results, integrate their business and human resource strategies? Underlying this broad research topic are the questions in our terms of how personnel functions at organisation levels are adapted to fit the business strategies, how the symbolic order is used to obtain linkages between the three levels of analysis and if, as we assert, there are different models, what are the different routes to excellence adopted by high-performing businesses?

Even as these questions were formulated, the methodological and conceptual pitfalls were seen to be of a considerable magnitude. The difficulties experienced by all those who have researched into this area seemed to be vested in this one project. These potential problems can be summarised as deriving from the need for in-depth but representative data, the effects of many variables and the problems of defining organisational performance.

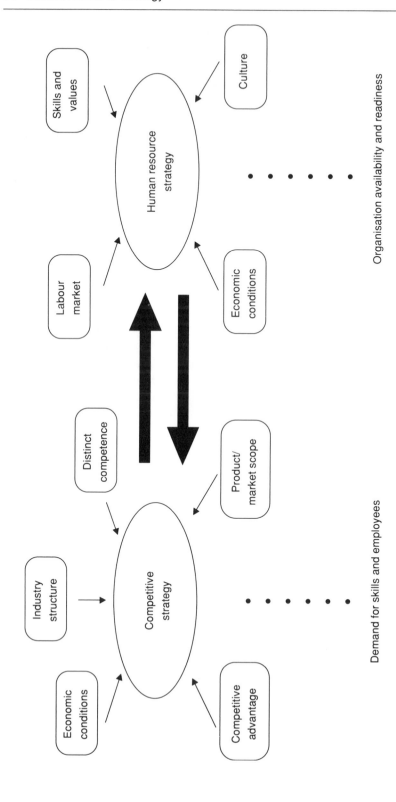

Fig. 2 'A perspective on business strategy and human resource strategy interdependence'

C. A. Lengnick-Hall and M. L. Lengnick-Hall (*Academy of Management Review*, 1988, Vol. 13, No. 3, pp. 454–70).

The most crucial problem is how to research at the organisational level but also to obtain data which is broadly representative. The need to take into account contextual variables and the specific conditions which give rise to strategies was reviewed in our discussion of contingency theory. All that we know about the way strategies are developed leads us to the conclusion that general surveys, whilst providing representative data, can be interpreted in many ways, and can fail to place the data in a context which gives the results meaning (Legge 1989, Tyson and Fell 1986). The approach therefore was to use case studies, with a sufficiently standard interview format to permit comparisons between the companies studied.

The second difficulty is also a consequence of the need for representativeness. We know from the study of organisations how significant industry type, technology and size can be in the variations in human resource management. The number of variables for which we would have to control, if we were to attempt to make direct comparisons without these variables affecting the results, is far too many for even a large-scale survey, let alone a series of case studies. However, it is not the intention here to seek the precise effect of a particular business strategy upon a human resource policy, or then to trace an irrefutable cause all the way to the business results. There are too many intervening variables between the strategic option being chosen and the end business result, some years later. *Rather, the intention here is to see how the intervening variables interrelate at the organisational level of analysis, and what effect the human resource management policies in general have on business performance, both qualitatively and quantitatively.* Some broad controls on size and industry type can be applied in order to make the influence explicit.

METHODOLOGY

We therefore decided to select from a comparatively small range of industries, but to include two groups or organisations which were typically British – conglomerate industries and recently privatised industries. Also, while making no size restriction on the number of employees, we sought organisations with at least a £500 million turnover per year.

The industry groupings we decided upon were:

- Pharmaceuticals

- Chemical/industrial
- Textiles
- Engineering
- Conglomerates
- Publishing
- Retail
- Leisure/hotels
- Power/electrical/communications

The third major problem was how to define good performance, and the concomitant difficulty of how to generate an acceptable sampling frame to include a representative group of organisations. The debate on this topic is well summarised by Saunders, Brown and Lavernick (1992). As they point out, the highest-performing companies, if we use financial criteria, are likely to have the greatest fluctuations in performance, assuming we measure return on investment and risk. Industries vary in their performance according to the trade cycle, and some may be particularly susceptible to the recession (for example, the construction industry). Profitability and growth are likely to be different at different stages of product life cycles, and the financial indicators shown in the company's annual report and accounts may represent creative accounting, for example to impress the shareholders and financial pundits when a rights issue is to be launched, rather than to demonstrate the actual long-term performance of the company.

The solution to this problem is to use a combination of measures. This leads us to the question of what combination of measures is most suited and how should they be combined? Purely non-financial measures unfortunately suffer from the same problems as the financial ratios which could be used. For example, Norburn and Birley (1988) used employment growth and sales per employee. These are unlikely to be accurate measures of success in a recession, especially when profitability has been maintained by cutting employment numbers, and comparisons of sales data are difficult across industries due to pricing (e.g. retail), regulatory differences (e.g. airlines), and volume differences (e.g. Rolls-Royce cars versus Ford).

The solution proposed by Saunders, Brown and Lavernick (1992) to this problem of how to measure success was a peer-group evaluation. They constructed a sampling frame from the largest British companies quoted on the Stock Exchange, based on their capitalisation value in July 1990, divided into 21 industry groupings. A peer-group evaluation on defined criteria was then attempted by asking seven senior managers, including the chairmen, managing directors and personnel directors, to rank their named competitors on an 11-point scale. The eight criteria used were: quality of management; financial soundness; quality of product and services; ability to attract, retain and develop top talent; value as a long-term asset; capacity to innovate; quality of marketing; and community and environmental responsibility. A response of 64 per cent was achieved, but mostly from only one person (usually the chairman or a director) out of the seven mailed in each company.

While peer evaluation is an intriguing dimension, there are a number of problems with this approach. Collecting a large number of subjective opinions together does not make them objective. Although one could argue that top managers in the same industry have a good knowledge of their rivals, their opinions are most likely to be based on past performance and on corporate image rather than on facts or future trends. The second problem is the reliability of the data over time, and the reliability of ratings between sectors. Do the ratings change with the economic cycle? For example, under the leisure industry grouping Thames TV was first, Carlton Communications second and the Rank Organisation third. Also, would people inside the financial services sector rate banks the same as those outside, who probably only knew their own banks? New contracts, or changes to franchise arrangements would clearly make a difference. Nevertheless, Saunders *et al* acknowledge the limitations of the methodology used, but point to the high response rate and to the expertise they have been able to tap because of the peer group's qualifications and experience.

The methodology adopted in the 'different routes to excellence' study relied on a mixture of financial criteria, the broad reputation and size of the businesses, and comparitors within the industries chosen, which meant an element of 'convenience' sampling was adopted. The companies chosen because of the case study method had to be those who were prepared to cooperate in the discussion of relatively sensitive data. The sampling frame was also affected by the recession, during which the study was completed (1990–92). During this period some companies who said they would cooperate found themselves unable to do so, and other companies entered the sampling frame as the closest acceptable substitutes.

Our original intention was to research 30 British companies whose business performance was successful over a period of time which included recessions and economic growth. The criteria we established were:

● Quoted on London Stock Exchange and British based (even if international in scope).

- Turnover in excess of £500 million per annum.
- Within the defined industry sectors.
- Rated according to three main financial criteria as good performers.
- With a good reputation within their industries (the reputation criterion could not apply to privatised companies who were too new to have gained a rating).

The companies selected are shown in Table 4 on page 70.

The basic sampling frame was constructed from an index published by our research collaborators, PE International. This index was based on the following parameters.

Companies were ranked on three criteria to produce an overall ranking:

- **Profit margin**. This was defined as the ratio of profit before tax : sales. This is a fundamental business ratio, since without profits there will be no long-term business.
- **Return on total assets**. This ratio was selected because it showed how a company was using its total physical and financial assets. This ratio was used rather than return on capital employed, which is affected by liabilities and can be changed by how well a company is using its creditors' capital in place of its own.
- **Added value:pay**. This measures the value of the wealth created and the cost of the human resources in producing it. It is one of the best measures of productivity.

The three ratios therefore cover the full width of a company's performance, by taking into account profit and the use of human and financial assets to produce the profit. ROTA and added value:pay ratios were included so that both labour and capital intensive companies could be compared. More details on the ratios and the performance of the companies chosen are given in Appendix 2.

The PE database consisted of *The Times* top 1000 companies, together with a range of other companies whose performance on the key financial indicators had in the past shown high levels of performance. The UK database is updated from the interim and preliminary statements. The ratio for margins is updated from the interim accounts to give the margins for the latest 12 months. If the latest information is for the interim period, the latest six months' figures plus the second half-year's figures for the previous year were taken. Ratios which required the balance sheet could not be updated in the same way, as only a few companies issue balance sheets at the interim stage. The definitions for all the terms are in Appendix 1.

The 'finance', 'property' and 'energy' sectors were not included as their ratios were incompatible. One of the uses to which the data was applied was to produce profiles which compared a company's performance to that of others in the same industry. A company's performance on each of the ratios was compared to the median, and the spread of all the database companies. One profile shows how the latest accounts compare with the database. This is the static profile. The dynamic profile shows how the company moved in the previous year compared to how all the others moved. The companies selected for our sampling frame were high performers on the static profile within each of the chosen industry sectors. Comparisons were then made against the dynamic profile, to see if they were rising or falling.

It is interesting to note that, using these criteria, the listing for our database included 12 out of the 39 companies ranked one to three in the similar industry sectors in the Saunders *et al* (1992) study. Bearing in mind our study was two years earlier, and that we were unable to gain entry to all of our first-choice companies, there is considerable overlap between the peer-group ranking and our original list using mostly financial criteria.

Having established the database of companies, and reached a position where we could agree with some confidence which British companies were suitable for investigation, the broad 'case study' method required further refinement so that we could find a way to discover the 'fit' between human resource and business strategy. The HRRC questionnaire and its development are described more fully in Appendix 1. We should be quite clear here about the difficult methodological problems encountered in any attempt to find the fit between business and human resource strategies.

From our discussion in Chapter 2 we can see the significance of discovering the nature of the 'fit' between business and human resource strategies. Human resource management as a separate new development in the management of the employment relationship has at its heart the notion that human resource policies are integrated in two directions: there is integration with business goals, and sufficient integration between the policies themselves for policies to be coherent (Fombrun *et al* 1984, Legge 1989).

In order to discover this integration we decided to conduct interviews with senior management in our case study companies, to explore three areas:

1 The business and corporate strategy and its development. Here we were searching for the way HR concerns came into the planning

process, and by asking HR directors we were seeking confirmation of their knowledge of the strategy.

2 The explanations by the senior management teams of whether they sought to integrate the 'functional' strategy of the HR function, who was involved, and how and why the integration occurred.

3 We were also looking for practical examples of how the HR policies had supported the business strategy in the recent past. We were aware that some of our sample were large, diversified businesses. We knew that holding companies which controlled by the imposition of financial criteria and little else, and where autonomy was highly decentralised, would require a different approach. In these cases it was decided that, in addition to the corporate-level interviews, research would take place within the most successful operating divisions, which the corporation should nominate as being most representative of the corporation as a whole. Prior and careful researches into company performance and other external factors were undertaken.

The interviews were conducted by a group of researchers, with a semi-structured format and a common questionnaire on which all responses were recorded.

Table 4: Different routes to excellence – research companies

Industry sector	Companies
Pharmaceuticals	Wellcome, Amersham International, Glaxo
Chemicals/Industrials	ICI, BOC, Laporte, Blue Circle
Retail	Marks & Spencer, Kingfisher
Textiles	Coats Viyella
Leisure/Hotels	British Airways, Ladbroke, Forte, Scottish and Newcastle, Rank Organisation
Electrical/Communications	BT, Racal Security
Food/Tobacco	Reckitt & Colman, Cadbury-Schweppes
Engineering	Vickers, British Aerospace
Conglomerates	RTZ, BAT
Publishing	Reed International, Fine Art Development
Power/Utilities	BNFL, London Electric, National Grid, Scottish Power, SW Water

DISCOVERING HUMAN RESOURCE STRATEGIES

The difficulties and issues raised in the description of the methods used in our study are intended as an acknowledgement of the research problems contained in this area. There is one further hurdle to be discussed. In defining 'strategy' in Chapter 1 the notion that strategies are also 'stratagems' was mentioned. The purpose of a strategy may well be to outwit the competition, to develop some new product or service, to move more quickly than others, to merge, acquire or direct businesses as a part of the strategy. By their very nature, strategies may be 'hidden'. We also are aware that strategies may only be considered rational in the particular context of the organisation. How then can a researcher expect to discover these potent secrets? The solution to this problem seemed to be to work on management actions. The benefits from the study of strategy as an approach for the analysis and explanation of managerial actions is summarised by Thurley and Wood:

> 'Its use lies in the possibility of comparing the likely results of different strategies in different situations and in the awareness that only selected aspects of industrial relations may be judged as an important condition for the success of a given business strategy.'
>
> (Thurley and Wood 1983, p. 221.)

The approach we took to solving this problem was therefore to work at the organisational level of analysis, to discover through interviews the 'direction' of the changes, asking how these changes came about, and what the strategy was on each business issue. There was a danger that the answers received might have been far from the truth. This is not just because in some cases the respondent may have wanted to deceive the questioner. There were also likely to be answers from respondents who were not entirely sure of the truth, and from those who thought they knew, but who were not fully aware of what had been happening. This is a weakness of the interview method in general. The interviewers attempted to resolve this difficulty first by looking at the sequence of events, and then sought to explore the rationale for the decisions taken in relation to that sequence. Wherever possible, several managers were interviewed within each organisation, and the interviewer asked for practical examples of the contribution of HRM to business strategies.

Even with these safeguards, the practical processes of organisational life are most likely to result in various kinds of distortion. Individuals see the importance of strategic issues from their own perspective. Human resource specialists were therefore likely to exaggerate the significance of human resource issues, and to believe in their own propaganda. Nevertheless, the multiple realities represented by these responses are themselves data. The rhetoric, the propaganda, the 'official line', whether partially or entirely believed, influence the senior managers' definitions of the situation. As we know, if people define situations as real, then they will act upon that belief.

STRATEGIC PLANNING

A primary area for investigation in this research must be the extent to which human resource issues are taken up or in fact play a leading role within the strategic plans of high-performing organisations. This question has two aspects: how do organisations undertake their strategic planning and what is the HRM content of these plans?

To begin with we should delineate what would constitute the approach to corporate planning which is advocated in texts and which is 'officially' supported by business school academics as a preferred system. This is illustrated by the formal planning processes of a US multinational with $5 billion sales in the fashion/consumer products business. The European part of the business which operates in most of the main economies in Europe recommends the following planning process to its various European companies.

The strategic planning process

Agree company mission and values	What kind of business are we; where are we placing ourselves in relation to the competition?
Set company objectives	Financial and non-financial.
Undertake situation analysis	External and internal strengths, weaknesses and opportunities analysis, and assumptions explicitly stated.
Create strategies	In the fields of efficiency improvement, cost reduction, growth and diversification.
Establish resources needed	People skills, financial and physical assets.
Undertake a financial analysis of the risks and contingencies	Agree rates of return, financial targets, probability, costs of failures, etc.
Implementation plan	Showing the roles of each functional area, with timetables for achievement.

The Mission Statements were broadly similar for each European country (UK, France, Germany, Spain, Portugal, Ireland, Italy and Benelux), but with slightly different emphases according to the national competition, the different organisation of selling in each country, the different laws, etc. For example, the UK's variant stated that it wished to serve more customers by:

- Leading and dominating in their market.
- Motivating and supporting the sales representatives.
- Satisfying customers' needs with quality, value for money products.
- Serving customers through convenient, contemporary sales and distribution networks.
- Building on the company's established heritage.
- Living the principles of the company's founder.

The financial objectives were recorded in sales volume, operating profit, return on investment and cash flow. Non-financial objectives were expressed in terms of customer growth, channel to market, image development and management effectiveness. Each functional area, including HR, produced its own functional plan to integrate within the strategic plan. The HR strategies which emerged were in the policy areas of organisation development, resourcing, reward, working climate or culture, and employee development.

In practice, the strategic issues which HR addressed within these plans were the development of their representatives, who were seen as an under-utilised resource; the reassertion of the company image (which had become blurred) through strong relationships and marketing; and the support, therefore, for better ways of managing and raising volume through training, better regional management and a new rewards scheme. There was support also for new product launches, with improved internal communications and changes in organisational structure.

In some parts of the European operation, the HR function saw itself serving internal customers and sought, through appropriately-expressed objectives, to broaden access to HR 'customers' and to enhance HR customer service. There were then HR programmes or 'products' which were designed to meet these objectives.

Although one could see in this planning process many of the textbook-recommended features, the reality of HR planning revealed by examining this HR function's response showed:

1 There were different objectives in each European HR function.
2 There was no agreement across Europe on the priorities.

3 There were different perceptions of the HR role (ranging from HR as an administrative service to the notion that HR was itself marketing services).
4 The formal expression of plans was more sophisticated than the mechanism for implementation.

Even with these reservations, the formal planning process in this American multinational was sufficiently well developed to show that business and human resource strategies were interlinked, consciously by senior HR practitioners, who did believe that they were able to give effect to the corporate plan through their HR programmes. The extent to which HR issues were considered within the corporate planning process itself is more difficult to answer from this example. The HR contribution was stated by each HR director to have been sought from the 'situation analysis' stage onwards. This implies that non-financial objectives (although influenced by the HR strengths and weaknesses) were not seen as an HR concern, but as more of a matter for marketing and corporate affairs functions. The process described here is 'top–down' and there are clearly weaknesses with such an approach, where objectives are handed down. The 'formality' of the description may disguise a more iterative, informal process by which managers and staff are able to contribute their ideas before strategic objectives are formulated. Companies do not begin the planning process with a *'tabula rasa'*. The choices faced and the possible actions are very often limited to a well-known range, and therefore the analysis and fine tuning of the response is what counts.

HR PLANNING

During the 1970s long-range corporate planning was thought to be the solution to business problems. Lack of success was attributed to planning failures, in particular failure to define objectives and prepare the organisation to work towards the objectives. This was at a time when 'management by objectives' came into vogue, and informal organisational processes were thought to lack thoroughness and precision in analysis, and to be based on incomplete information.

Not surprisingly, manpower planning, as it was then described, was also thought able to deliver precisely the correct number of people, with the appropriate abilities to do the work needed, by forecasting demand and supply over periods of five years or more (Bowey 1973, Department of Employment 1968). The case for manpower planning was strong. It was argued that, by planning, companies would be able to avoid the undesirable social consequences of a 'hire and fire' policy where people moved and perhaps even changed career, only to become surplus to requirements shortly afterwards. Similarly, by planning for labour requirements well in advance, companies would not be hindered in the exploitation of their business plans by any shortage of labour. Planning encouraged employee development and skill acquisition over long periods, it engendered confidence in trade union relationships, and resulted in a more rational weighing of costs, and hence was an aid to decision-making.

Much attention was therefore given to the development of planning techniques, especially on the supply side. The Civil Service pioneered an elaborate series of computer models, such as MANPLAN which was designed to help planners to understand what was happening in a given hierarchy of jobs (Smith 1976). Age at which promoted, recruitment and promotion rates were thus considered important variables which could be manipulated to suit different policy objectives. Models were either 'push' models or 'pull' models. 'Push' models showed what would happen to 'stocks' (numbers in a particular grade) if a given set of 'flows', such as recruitment, promotion and wastage, were maintained. 'Pull' models took the numbers required in each 'stock' level as a constant, and then showed what changes would occur in the 'flows' or change rates as a consequence of the number being maintained in each grade (stock). On the demand side, the variables have always been more unpredictable: the marketing mix, consumer demand, extraneous factors such as interest rate changes and factors at the societal level of analysis, are subject to rapid and unplanned change. However, attempts at improving on work study techniques and simple extrapolations based on a sales forecast were tried, for example by using principal components' analysis and the factor analysis of workloads. The attempts to bring rationality into the planning process at a corporate level therefore had their counterparts in the attempts to create long-range manpower planning techniques.

The ideological changes and the rapid pace of change in the 1980s have made detailed planning over very long periods seem unrealistic. Indeed, the uncertainties of the 1990s have also fuelled the notion that detailed planning in the long-range period is an unproductive exercise. The successors to the manpower models of the Civil Service are now more used in scenario planning. The Institute of Manpower Studies developed 'microprospect' and its later version 'Sussex' to give managers the opportunity to set out on their microcomputers the likely consequences for changes to HR policy. Using the same principles of 'push' and 'pull' models the HR function can now give the Board the costs and HR consequences of any major policy change, such as a recruitment or a promotion freeze, early retirement or the expansion of any particular 'stock' or strategic group of personnel.

A good example of the use of this model is given by Bell (1993) in his account of manpower planning at the TSB. He shows how a 'branch establishment' model of the demand for labour was created, based on a work study of transactions at the Bank's branches, which allowed for rest times, training and any systems changes. This was then used as a basis for deciding the target number of employees. The microprospect model was then used to plot what was happening to the internal labour supply. The differences and imbalances in labour then showed the recruitment, training and utilisation policies required.

The problem with all of these models is best summed up by Bell, himself a strong proponent of manpower planning:

> 'I ought to add that we have had some problems in carrying out proper manpower planning over the last few years as a result of the very considerable reorganisations that have been going on in TSB Bank. The branch establishment model has been invalidated by significant changes in the organisation of work.'
>
> (Bell 1993, p.121.)

He goes on to explain how he expects to adapt the model to the new organisation, having lost the staff who could use microprospect in the reorganisation. The problem of discontinuous change, reorganisation and the movement of key people in HR makes planning much more difficult.

In practice, however, one wonders when there has been a period of sustained stability, and whether the rational approach to planning is not just an ideal. Perhaps the forces of individual ambition, chaos and the political processes in organisations are too powerful for decision-making ever to be more than a haphazard, short-term affair, contingent upon personalities, perceived opportunities and the struggles for power. Mintzberg has suggested that strategies emerge as a pattern in a stream of decisions (1987), and even apparently clear-cut financial decisions are not easy to link to corporate strategy according to Grundy (1992), let alone the unquantifiable and sometimes debatable human resource strategies. Grundy shows how there are conceptual, organisational, process and systems problems in linking financial appraisal into corporate strategy. In addition, strategic decisions are often made in an incremental way, not as large-scale wholes, and there are pressures to make decisions, as a 'bandwaggon' effect occurs. Given the political pressures, Grundy's solution for financial analysis of concentrating on value chains, and computing the net present value of different strategic options, seems to be only applicable in the human resource area when or if human asset accounting develops to this pitch of precision.

STRATEGIC PLANNING PROCESSES IN THE RESEARCHED COMPANIES

Our questions began in each case study by enquiring about the processes normally adopted by the Board, and those with specific responsibility for strategic and for human resource planning. The responses varied according to industry type, organisational structure, the degree of change taking place and the approach to involving staff in the process.

One might have anticipated different planning processes in different industries, since the technologies involved and the markets in which companies operate are likely to have an effect, as we discussed in Chapter 3. The time horizons for planning, with a few notable exceptions, were remarkably similar. Most plans fell in the range of three to five years, with annual updates and reviews. The exceptions were at both ends of the time span. In certain of the retail businesses, where the detailed planning is very short term, the plans become increasingly general targets to aim for over the three-year period foreseen. In those businesses where large-scale capital projects are involved, for example BNFL, or where mining and extraction require planning consents and negotiations with governments, as in RTZ, the time frame will stretch out to 10 or 15 years.

Although the majority of the 30 companies fell into the three- to five-year period, what was significant here was the view expressed by senior managers in those companies where they were forced by circumstances to plan for up to five years, when planning was perceived often as a constraint on business. Academics writing on this topic have not given sufficient weight to managers' desire for quick action, and their wish not to be caught up in a rigid framework when seeking to exploit a volatile environment.

Divisionalised and highly devolved structures also have an influence on the planning process. A typical organisational structure is as shown in Fig. 3.

Various types of matrix structure are then imposed on the organisational structure, for example, with country general managers, if the business operates internationally; or with divisional or even

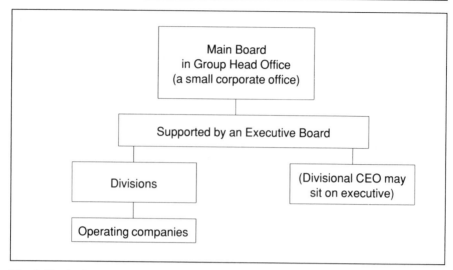

Fig. 3 Typical structure of an organisation

corporate functional specialists, such as marketing, finance or human resource directors who work across the divisions or companies.

Planning processes are also made more complex because of previous decisions to diversify. For example, Scottish and Newcastle operates a traditional brewing division, a rapidly-changing retail division for its public houses and a leisure parks division. These all fit together in an entirely coherent business strategy. However, they are all competing in different markets, with very different customers, traditions, capital requirements, legislative frameworks and different types of employees.

The most obvious effect of diversification on the planning process is on the consequential need to plan at divisional or diversified company level. Chandler's famous maxim 'structure follows strategy' may be challenged, therefore, since divisionalised structures are expected from our evidence to put forward strategic plans to meet the needs of their particular market-places. Whilst the companies in our study gave to their divisions varying degrees of autonomy, and divisional managers had different perceptions of how much autonomy had been granted, those with divisional structures (about 25 of the 30) all expected input of a detailed kind from their divisions into the corporate plan.

It was impossible to judge precisely from our study the relationships between divisions and their parent groups, since this would have required longitudinal research, but from our research there is evidence of both a 'top–down' and 'bottom–up' approach to corporate planning in these companies. The role of the Main Board is critical to the process. In most cases, the Main Board established the 'vision' and published the company's 'mission'. Although these mission statements were not necessarily brilliant guiding lights in the corporate jungle, the involvement of managers and sometimes other staff with their creation had produced debates which fruitfully explored questions such as 'What business are we in?' and 'What business should we be in?' Similarly, vision statements also tended to incorporate 'values'. The reference points thus created were used as criteria on which to base judgements about future direction.

Only around a third of this sample of companies employed specialist corporate planners at corporate level, although all senior managers partially played this role. The CEO's office and/or chairman's office often coordinated plans, and in some instances there were specialist sub-committees formed from the Executive Committee or the Main Board, whose role was to vet corporate planning proposals before the final version was put before the Board. In one organisation, a 'business development department' existed, which worked with marketing and human resource management specialists to review the corporate objectives and plans. There were also 'executive strategy committees', 'directors sub-committees', 'regional directors' and many other idiosyncratic formats. In virtually every case, the plans were reviewed annually and updated through these mechanisms. The planning process thus revealed shows how some degree of integration is attempted to counter the divisional pull and to look for coherence. As Lawrence and Lorsch (1967) observed, the drive for diversification also brings a need for integration at the corporate level. The main aspects of these plans were financial objectives, so the issues which were adjusted (sometimes in a very informal, iterative process) were the likely financial consequences of plans. The overall corporate plan in most instances therefore represented the financial and other detailed business objectives which the Board could endorse as being the best current way to achieve the stated mission.

A sub-set of our data were a group of newly-privatised businesses. Our evidence shows how these organisations have now embraced with enthusiasm the corporate planning concept. Mission statements, reorganisation into strategic business units, financial ratios and profit projections, scenario planning and all the trappings of market-driven strategic planning have been taken as necessary in order to participate as private sector players. One consequence of this new-found interest is the continuous succession of changes which have beset their managements. Paradoxically, therefore, the felt need for corporate planning has occurred in these newly-privatised businesses just at the moment when detailed planning is made more difficult.

Whatever the industry, the size, the structure or the history, one common feature for these organisations was the desire to adopt the most flexible stance possible in relation to their markets. The different approaches to human resource planning had in common the desire by senior managers to be responsive to the fast-changing world where they traded.

Three distinct approaches to corporate planning were discerned:

1 **Formal, long-range planning**. These companies followed the route to realising their corporate goals described earlier in this chapter when we outlined the planning processes used by the US fashion/consumer products company. Corporate development departments seem attached to this approach, but even where the top–down method was adopted, there was always some consultation, discussion and often informal meetings and conversations with the various interest groups in the organisation. The formal plans could be seen as a framework for planning, and were most usually recorded in financial terms, with appropriate commentaries.

2 **Flexible strategies**. The majority of the 30 companies fell into this category. Plans in the medium timeframe were reviewed and changed frequently, and were expected to be highly responsive to changes and to new initiatives from competitors. What differentiates these companies from those who adopted a long-range planning approach is that, whereas the latter created long-term plans and then put in place mechanisms to assist deviation, to revise and reforecast, those designated under the 'flexible' label intentionally planned short term, and tried to set up processes which would assist their organisations to change rapidly: such as smaller, flatter structures, strong emphasis on values but not on detailed plans, good communications systems, flexible HR policies, and placing the management focus on change as a process, rather than on any long-term goal. Divisions whose strategies fit an overall mission and values, and which deliver against financial targets, can be flexible and adaptive because of the autonomy they enjoy, but so too are those companies without Divisions, which have no written strategy, but whose senior executives closely monitor changes in the competitive environment and adapt accordingly.

3 **Attributional strategies**. In these companies, perhaps a third of our sample, the approach was 'one step at a time'. Only after some years could a strategy be attributed to the actions taken. The rationalisation of previous actions does give a sense of purpose and direction to the

strategies to be adopted in the future, but in reality, whatever gloss is placed on the steps, the company is not committed to any one strategic direction. This approach is similar to the notion of 'emergent' strategies. It is another variant on the flexible theme, because in these businesses caution is prevailing over strategic thinking, which does permit changes to direction.

The findings outlined above find echoes in the previous research conducted into the strategic planning process. The research into 'different routes to excellence' was carried out during a deep recession, at a time of economic turbulence and political change. When faced with discontinuous change, and sudden surprising developments, the old strategic planning approaches are ineffective. The logical predictions from historical trends are not an option. Structural changes nullify the economic assumptions on which corporate growth is predicted. The problem is then that the information is inadequate and changing quickly.

The flexible approach to planning described here is a strategic response to this problem:

> 'A solution to this paradox is to change the approach to the use of strategic information. Instead of letting the strategic planning technology determine the information needs, a firm should determine what planning and action are feasible as strategic information becomes available in the course of the threat/opportunity. Early in the life of a threat, when the information is vague and its future course unclear, the responses will be correspondingly unfocussed, aimed at increasing the strategic flexibility of the firm. As the information becomes more precise, so will the firm's response, eventually terminating in a direct attack on the threat or opportunity. But the prior build up of flexibility will make this attack or opportunity occur earlier, and the attack will be better planned and executed.'
>
> (Ansoff 1975, p. 23.)

What Igor Ansoff described as a 'graduated response' to weak signals in the market place is consistent with the results. He goes on to propose that, in addition to seeking to amplify the information, so that the signals from competitors or from the environment become stronger, other response strategies could also be followed, including changes to organisational structure, heightened contingency planning and greater internal flexibility.

The results here also suggest that organisations in recession, and just entering recovery, are in a state of flux. ICI, one of the great pillars of stability, was on the verge of dividing into two; British Aerospace was reeling following the ending of long defence contracts with the cessation of the Cold War; BT was in the midst of a major culture change; and so on.

The dynamic nature of the organisations we researched in the midst of the recession meant they were always 'about to change'; whatever strategic direction was planned, revisions were likely. This is the emergent aspect of strategy: strategies are not constant, nor is there necessarily agreement amongst all managers on what is the strategy. By the time the strategy comes to be implemented the different people involved will no doubt also make whatever adaptation they believe necessary (Bailey and Johnson 1992).

The human resource management role in strategy development was explored through our research, but we were conscious of the indeterminate, vague and shifting character of business strategies themselves. Thirteen out of the 30 companies we studied employed a human resource director on the main board. HR issues were often represented on the board by a director, even if from another functional background, such as the 'Group Services Director', 'the Information Director' and the 'Finance Director'. Significantly, nearly all companies in our sample had HR or 'Personnel' representation at the lower level management meetings, especially at 'divisional' level. HR directors would mostly therefore provide their input to the divisional HR strategy. From our research there is strong evidence that divisional management creates detailed strategies and in many cases the role of main boards is to coordinate and shape these strategies in support of the mission and the published vision/values. HR divisional directors play an important role therefore. It is perhaps less significant that HR is so infrequently represented at main board level since HR may be seen as a 'second' or 'third' order strategy (Purcell 1989). However, it is at this level of detail that HR policies need to be established if they are to have an effect. There is evidence of how, by using scenario forecasting techniques, HR functions can feed back to first order strategies the likely consequences of undertaking any new company direction.

This raises another question on the role of HR in establishing the corporate mission, values and vision. There are two possible responses to the question, from our evidence. Following the argument above, we could assert that it is unreasonable to expect HR specialists to predominate when company values and mission are decided. There is no reason why marketing, finance, operations and other functional areas including corporate affairs departments or sales departments should not have an equal input. Non-executive directors might also bring wide experience and the kind of broad understanding needed in order to help a Board phrase corporate statements of this kind, or even to help executive directors to think through the mission and its implications. The second argument concerns the persuasiveness of HR policies and their long-term influence. Recruitment, promotion and development policies have both a practical impact and a symbolic impact. From the alignment of these two pressures HRM generates leverage to establish the organisation culture and, as Hendry (1993) has pointed out, can help to shape change over a number of years. Through recruitment, development and reward policies HRM can also help to bring about the mind set which decides what strategic issues are considered.

In practice, HR directors are fulfilling a spectrum of roles. For example, in BT the strategic objectives reside in the need for a new culture and the change agent role is most to the fore. In BNFL strategy is centred around the achievement of divisional targets, to which HR is fully committed. In Coats Viyella the HR mission is incorporated into the group vision, based on common values, and the same could be said of Marks & Spencer although less formally.

There are different routes to excellence. The chapters that follow will explore in more depth the HR role, but here we can state that whatever the generality of HRM as a new paradigm for managing the employment relationship, there is ample evidence that there are significant differences in the way HRM is performed in different businesses. There are also different emphases given to the various aspects of the planning process. This process is shown in Fig. 4.

The process may be broken down into three levels (Walker 1977). What Purcell described as 'first order strategies', and those which are addressed by the mission and the vision statements. These become guides to future action, but more importantly the process of discussing the issues clarifies where the business is going. Many of these issues will be HR-oriented, but are only of relevance in regard to their impact on the business in the future. Thus, although HR might be influential in shaping management thinking, the overt issues which are debated are most likely to be about future markets, products and services, competitors, costs and operational modes.

The second level of planning focuses down the issues into particular plans and policies. Here, HRM will be involved in scenario planning, and perhaps with forecasting the requirements for strategically important groups of people. At this level we would find detailed Divisional strategies, but not, according to our evidence, for long periods ahead, three years being the most often stated time frame. At Divisional level HRM helps to create the business plans, which are, after adjustment, the basis for most corporate plans.

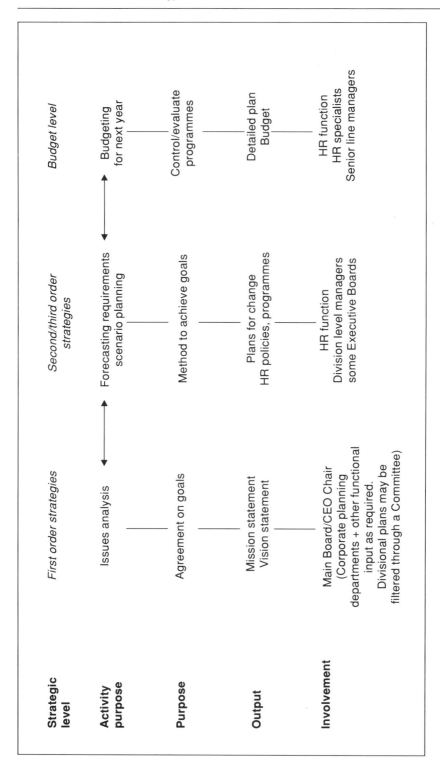

Strategic level	*First order strategies*	*Second/third order strategies*	*Budget level*
Activity purpose	Issues analysis	Forecasting requirements scenario planning	Budgeting for next year
Purpose	Agreement on goals	Method to achieve goals	Control/evaluate programmes
Output	Mission statement Vision statement	Plans for change HR policies, programmes	Detailed plan Budget
Involvement	Main Board/CEO Chair (Corporate planning departments + other functional input as required. Divisional plans may be filtered through a Committee)	HR function Division level managers some Executive Boards	HR function HR specialists Senior line managers

Fig. 4 The planning process

HRM here would be most concerned with policies relating to recruitment, development, promotion, redundancy and change programmes. The two areas since the 1990 recession which predominate are those related to new organisational structures and forms, and the management of the change process itself. The outcome of this planning process is a series of policies and programmes. In a sense, these are the HR products.

The third level is the 'next year' or budget level, where precise numbers are attached to the preferred option and the tactics, the mechanisms for making things happen, are pulled out into a plan. Again, there is a relation to the second level of planning, because detailed costings may produce a rethink, with alternative courses of action being considered. Such a plan will contain actions affecting various people, deadlines and a budget for each activity.

One inhibitor to detailed planning is the rapidity of organisational change. The flexible approach to planning discussed throughout this chapter is not just one option. Most organisations, including the significant number of high performers in our sample, set a general course, but did not engage in long-range, detailed planning at corporate level. As one HR director said, 'We're preparing the organisation to implement the plan'. This is closer to tracking through a jungle than to a rational debate weighing ends, means and costs. There is little detailed HR planning, except for management succession planning and planning for strategically important groups such as research scientists, high potentials and senior managers. Plans for people in a broad sense do exist, and there are plans for the business. The most important and difficult task for HR is to make both the people and the business flexible enough to fit them together.

Flexibility in managing human resources is the most obvious strategic response to the high levels of uncertainty in the business environment. The organisation needs to be flexible to meet market-place demands, to avoid predatory competitors and to cope with unforeseen challenges. The rapidity of change was evidenced in our research, for example when the decision to split ICI into two corporations was announced during our series of interview meetings with their HR staff.

The current approach to change can be summarised in the identity: flexible goals = flexible structure = flexible people. For HRM, the involvement in creating flexible strategies is at two levels. There is practical work to be done in devising contractual, task and time flexibility, and at the second level of symbolic actions there is a role for the HR function to create the meaning structure, where agreement with and understanding of the goals makes it possible for people to be adaptive and to be flexible in response to the unforeseen challenges of the modern market-place.

BIBLIOGRAPHY

Ackermann, K.-F. (1986) 'A contingency model of HRM strategy. Empirical research findings reconsidered', *Management Forum*, Band 6, pp. 65–83.

Ansoff, H. I. (1975) 'Managing Strategic Surprise by response weak signals', *California Management Review*, Vol. XVIII, No. 2, Winter, pp. 21–33.

Bailey, A. and Johnson, G. (1992) 'How strategies develop in organisations' in Faulkner, D. and Johnson, G. (Eds) *The Challenge of Strategic Management*, pp. 147–78, London: Kogan Page.

Bell, M. (1993) 'Manpower Planning in the TSB Group' in *Human Resource Planning in the Banking Sector, Conference Book*, Commission of the European Communities, pp. 109–26.

Bowey, A. (1973) *A Guide to Manpower Planning*, London: Macmillan.

Department of Employment (1968) 'Company Manpower Planning', *Manpower Papers*, No.1, HMSO.

Doherty, N. and Tyson, S. (1993) *Executive Redundancy and Outplacement*, London: Kogan Page.

Fombrun, C. J., Tichy, N. M. and Devanna, M. A. (1984) *Strategic Human Resource Management*, New York: Wiley.

Grundy, T. (1992) *Corporate Strategy and Financial Decisions*, London: Kogan Page.

Handy, C. (1989) *The Age of Unreason*, Boston: Harvard Business School Press.

Hendry, C. (1993) 'Personnel Leadership in Technical and Human Resource Change' in Clark, J., *Human Resource Management and Technical Change*, London: Sage.

Kanter, R. M. (1983) *The Change Masters*, New York: Simon & Schuster.

Lawrence, P.R. and Lorsch, J. W. (1967) *Organisation and Environment: Managing Differentiation and Integration*, Boston: Harvard University Press.

Legge, K. (1989) 'Human Resource Management: a critical analysis' in Storey, J. (Ed.) *New Perspectives on Human Resource Management*, London: Routledge.

Lengnick-Hall, C. A. and Lengnick-Hall, M. L. (1988) 'A perspective on business strategy and human resource strategy interdependence', *Academy of Management Review*, Vol. 13, No. 3, pp. 454–70.

Mintzberg, H. (1987) 'Patterns in Strategy Foundation', *Management Science*, May, pp. 934–48.

Norburn, D. and Birley, S. (1988) 'Top Management Teams and Corporate Performance', *Strategic Management Journal* 9, pp. 225–37.

Peters, T. (1987) *Thriving in Chaos: Handbook for a Management Revolution*, New York: Knopf.

Peters, T. and Waterman, R. (1982) *In Search of Excellence*, New York: Harper & Row.

Purcell, J. (1989) 'The impact of corporate strategy on human resource management' in Storey, J. (Ed.) *New Perspectives on Human Resource Management*, London: Routledge.

Saunders, J., Brown, M. and Lavernick, S. (1992) 'Research notes on the Best British Companies: A Peer Evaluation of Britain's Leading Firms', *British Journal of Management*, Vol. 3, Issue 4, pp. 181–95.

Schuler, R. S. and Jackson, S. E. (1987) 'Linking competitive strategies with human resource management practices', Academy of Management Executive 1.3.

Sharma, S., Netermeyer, R. and Majajan, V. (1990) 'In Search of Excellence Revisited: An Empirical Evaluation of Peters' and Waterman's Attributes of Excellence', *Proceedings of the American Marketing Association Education Conference*, Chicago, Vol. 1, pp. 322–7.

Smith, A. R. (Ed.) (1976) 'Manpower Planning in the Civil Service', *Civil Service Studies 3*, London: HMSO.

Thurley, K. and Wood, S. (Eds) (1983) *Industrial Relations and Management Strategy*, Cambridge: Cambridge University Press.

Tofler, A. (1980) *The Third Wave*, London: Pan Books.

Tyson, S. and Fell, A. (1986) *Evaluating the Personnel Function*, London: Hutchinson.

Walker, J. W. (1977) 'Linking Human Resources Planning and Strategic Planning', a paper presented at XIII International Meeting of the Institute of Management Sciences, Athens, August.

CHAPTER 5

The contribution of HRM to business strategy: philosophies and policies

The fascination for most managers of looking at high-performing companies probably derives from the hope that there are some secrets or special lessons which can be learned and applied to make their own businesses more successful. What are the practical ways in which a company uses its people resources to achieve corporate objectives? Are there special lessons to be learned? A central question in the search for the HR contribution to business strategy is whether we should be looking at particular policies and individual practices or should be examining overall management philosophies. The question, as with so many in this field, requires clarification because the terms used have many meanings, and yet words such as 'policy' or 'philosophy of management' are usually taken for granted, the meanings assumed and treated as unproblematic.

THE RELATIONSHIP BETWEEN HR PHILOSOPHIES, POLICIES AND PRACTICES

Human resource policies are sometimes taken to be the same as HR strategies (Brewster and Bournois 1991) and as 'practices' (Jackson, Schuler and Rivero 1989). There is also a narrower definition of HR policies as the formal official guidelines applicable to specific areas in the management of people. Schuler and Jackson (1987)[1] seem to be taking this as the way to describe what they call 'HRM practice menus', that is a menu of choices which management may make for the company to follow in order to achieve the corporation's strategic goal. (For example, behavioural criteria versus results criteria in appraisal policies; a standard, fixed package versus a flexible package in reward policies; and so on.) A further complication comes from the distinction which may be drawn between espoused and operational policies (Brewster, Gill and Richbell 1983). They define espoused policy as the 'summation of the proposals, objectives, and standards that top management hold' (p. 63), which are formalised when managements write them down as policies. The operational industrial relations policy is the way management actually order priorities ('often unconsciously'), and is influenced by both the espoused policy and by custom and practice. From these definitions we may say that the key distinction is between the formal and the informal in management's actions towards employment relationships. Espoused policy is identical to formal policy, and operational policy is the informal action, custom and practice, which have come to be accepted irrespective of the formal policy.

To summarise then, we will use the term 'HR policy' to describe the formal policies which are adopted towards the management of employees, which may be written and which are the organisation's official guides to action. 'HR practices' is a phrase best used to describe any informal process or norm in management which has the sanction of custom, but which is not codified or written. Human resource strategy was defined in Chapter 1 by reference to choice, when we stated that human resource strategy is 'a set of ideas, policies and practices which management adopt in order to achieve a people management objective'. Policies and practices are used as part of the strategy, but equally other ways to motivate and direct behaviour might be adopted. For example, a strong corporate culture may be created, or anti-union action may be sanctioned to frustrate any attempt by employees to achieve solidarity, or the company may use sub-contract, franchise or outsourcing approaches as a part of its human resource strategy.

This still leaves the idea of a distinctive 'HR philosophy' to explain. This expression takes us into a broader field. The implication is that there are different philosophies of management which result in different types of employment relationship: that there are different psychological contracts between employers and employees, which are the reasons why people work for the organisation and what it is that determines their performance. Management style at the individual level may illustrate the general philosophy of management. Managers holding similar values may be attracted to work for corporations where these values are welcomed and rewarded. In the selection process there is a two-way exploration by applicant and company to discover any congruence in values. The socialisation process is also designed to inculcate particular values and attitudes. The cognitive dissonance experienced by those whose attitudes are antipathetic to their colleagues might be expected to result in a preferred organisational style emerging.

Taking management style as a matter for choice, McGregor's (1960) description of the Theory X and Theory Y approaches suggested that managers could best achieve results by adopting a style which gave employees an opportunity for self-fulfilment, which helped staff to derive satisfaction from their work and gave them responsibility, and assumed they had the best motives, rather than the worst. McGregor contrasts this 'Theory Y' perspective with the 'Theory X' attitude which seems to have antecedents in Taylor's scientific management school, the central tenet being that managers should control behaviour through the carrot and the stick, expecting their employees always to act only in their own interests, in a low-trust environment. Likert (1959), in the McGregor Theory Y approach vein, similarly argued that managers should trade on work group solidarity and use the group, through appropriate supervision, to encourage interest in the work, and to give responsibility and job satisfaction. This overall stance, which has been labelled the 'human relations' approach, is based upon a number of assumptions about people at work (Silverman 1970). In particular, there is the assumption that workers *want* to be involved, to take responsibility, and that they identify sufficiently with the task to work enthusiastically in factories, shops and offices for someone else's profit, with all the subordination of their inherent creativity and humanity which the act of compliance on entering the labour market implies. What seems equally plausible is the opposite assumption: that people enter the labour market reluctantly, to obtain money, so that they can spend at least a part of their lives with their families and friends, enjoying their personal interests. This 'instrumental' attachment to work (Goldthorpe *et al* 1968) would imply a very different kind of contractual relationship. This is alienation in the Marxist sense of being alienated from one's true self by the capitalist system.

The technical production or service processes have also been described as key variables leading to an alienated condition, deriving from the way people are used as adjuncts to machines (Walker and Guest 1952, Blauner 1964). This technological alienation is what job design experts are able to address. 'Fordism', is the corporate expression of this management of the labour process through large bureaucratic organisations using the principles of the division of labour and the mass production/service systems and was the characteristic feature of the 1950s, 1960s and 1970s. This interpretation gave rise to the view by socio-technical systems theorists that by altering the technical system to better match the social, informal system found in the work groups, the worst aspects of alienation could be removed (Trist *et al* 1963, Miller and Rice 1967).

However, 'Fordism' was not just organisationally specific; it was vested in society and in the institutions of industrial relations. The philosophies of management which emerge from the patterns of societal relationships are more deep-seated than is implied by the human relations school. Using the phrase 'industrial relations trajectories' Grahl and Teague (1991) seek to explain how changing economic conditions and new political ideologies produce new approaches to industrial relations:

> 'The notion of trajectories is predicated on the belief that economic development passes through specific phases within each of which a clearly defined pattern of production becomes the organising principle for most economies. A feature of such a production system is that it gives rise to specific forms of social, industrial and work organisation which in turn influences the character and content of industrial relations.'
>
> (p. 70.)

Grahl and Teague go on to argue that, following the demise of the 'Fordist' industrial relations trajectory, two alternative approaches are available as broad human resource strategies, each of which carries a particular management philosophy within it. The flexible industrial relations trajectory is based upon using labour and machines in as flexible a way as possible to respond to market demands. There are two aspects to this: flexible production seeks economies of scope rather than of scale, which results in smaller business units, decentralisation and less division of labour, with quality management built into the work; whereas 'competitive flexibility' is used to gain competitive advantage through minimising costs, reduced trade union influence and freedom from controls in the labour market. The alternative trajectory is termed 'constructive flexibility'. This is said to consist in an attempt to achieve economic flexibility within a protective social framework, and to concentrate on output expansion rather than on competition through cost reduction, which is seen as limited in its long-term utility as a strategy.

The Ford Motor Company in its drive for competitiveness has sought to achieve both of these outcomes, in a variant on the ideas described here which seeks to improve its learning through employee involvement (Starkey and McKinlay 1993). This was not without difficulty as the management process was at odds with the change process.

Whilst these two 'trajectories' undoubtedly exist as a set of ideas about how enterprises in a modern industrial state should compete, the analysis by Grahl and Teague is not intended to explain reality at the organisational level. Managers will certainly recognise the first trajectory, but the second assumes a societal perspective which UK companies normally do not take. In part, this is Grahl's and Teague's point – that Continental Europeans who believe in the European Union and its emerging institutions have a vision for their future society.

SOFT AND HARD CONTRACTS

The trajectory concept sits easily with the notion that organisations as a whole adopt their own management philosophies. From the philosophy flows the range of policies. These are not static but change in response to shifts in the economy, especially when supported by a convincing political ideology. Thus new trajectories are born out of what appears to managers to be the best strategic approaches available which could exploit the political, economic, social and technological environment. What is rational therefore changes according to circumstances. For example, it would seem madness to create elaborate management development schemes when facing a collapse in demand for the main product or service, whereas a merger or acquisition may be just the trigger needed to prompt new policies in this area.

The policy range available is enormous. Different contractual positions are likely under different philosophies, with the consequential supporting policies. Tonnies (1955) described these as different kinds of association, ranging from *Gemeinschaft* to *Gesellschaft*, from community (with its emphasis on belonging to a group brought together by common experience and shared values) to association (where people are drawn together for purely economic interests). Different types of associations between employer and employee are reflections of different managerial philosophies, which work according to their own rationality. We can expect to see the associative differences within the employment contract. The nature of contractual relations, if we follow the preceding argument, sets down the reciprocal duties and obligations, and so the expectations of each party. Managerial philosophies will provide the values on which these expectations about behaviour and reciprocity are based.

Relationships between the contractual form, the competitive strategy adopted and the organisational structure are explored within the markets and hierarchies paradigm developed by Williamson (1973), the management philosophy implications of which are described by Williamson and Ouchi (1983). We will discuss the implications of Williamson's thesis for the study of organisational structure in the next chapter, but here we can see that the old ideas of 'community' and 'association' have found a new lease of life in the notions of hard and soft contracting.

'As with market modes of contracting, there are two general options, which we designate as 'hard' and 'soft' contracting respectively. Under hard contracting, the parties remain relatively autonomous, each is expected to press his or her interests rigorously, and contracting is relatively complete. Soft contracting, by contrast presumes much closer identity of interests between the parties, and formal contracts are much less complete. This is the clan-type management style.'

(Williamson and Ouchi 1983, p. 26.)

Soft contracting implies an elaborate internal labour market, managed by a sophisticated HR function, with strong HR policies to govern relationships, pay, promotions, appraisal and development. Hard contracting implies a link back into the wider labour markets with a more legalistic and instrumental attachment to work as the norm for the effort-reward bargain. Soft contracting relies on social controls and socialisation, whereas hard contracting is the 'associative', formal type of relationship, bound by official rules. As Williamson and Ouchi go on to point out, the task specificity of hard contracting may produce problems when organisations face great uncertainty in their markets, and soft contracting can only work in a culture (or with a management philosophy) which is conducive to maintaining this form of social relationships.

In terms of alternative approaches to HR policies, the two alternative forms of contracting can be further explained as shown in Table 5.

Table 5: Key features of the 'hard' and 'soft' contracts

Hard contract	Soft contract
Emphasis on transaction costs.	Emphasis on vision and values of the organisation.
Service agreements between departments inside organisations.	'Clan' culture is supported.
Non-employment options are openly canvassed.	Long-term socialisation is normal.
'Taylorism' in reward policies is accepted.	Experience and length of service are rewarded.
People are employed in 'jobs' not careers.	Employee and management development policies are sophisticated, with emphasis on careers, appraisal.

In these two representations of HR policy alternatives, we can see 'community' or 'association' are the values which underlie each version of the employment contract. The hard contract version represents a position close to the market, where negotiation over the effort–reward bargain is never far away. The soft contract responds to market changes through the internal 'governance structure' of the enterprise – that is through the management of the internal labour market. Hard contracts offer choices to employees and the freedom to negotiate; soft contracts are more invidious in expecting employees to respond cooperatively to whatever changes or new demands are required. It is difficult to opt out of the clan. The power to negotiate under the hard contract is dependent upon conditions in the external labour markets, whereas under the soft contract it is dependent upon status and influence inside the organisation. In this sense, management philosophies and values are more apparent under the soft contract.

One benefit in analysing human resource policies in this way is the connection which is made clear between philosophies of management and the policies adopted. Some of the characteristics associated with Japanese management philosophies can be seen in the soft contract; long-term socialisation, the 'slow burn' approach to development, promotion from within, and the guarantee of lifetime employment in larger Japanese enterprises were the subject of comment during the 1970s and 1980s (Abegglen and Stalk 1985, Thurley 1983). Changes towards a 'hard contract' by Japanese companies as they face the recession will require a new management philosophy. In the UK, some organisations which have typically adopted a soft contract may also have to move towards 'hard' contracting – for example British Rail on privatisation, the Civil Service 'agencies' and the National Health Service are amongst those which are changing. Many of the changes by companies during the recession have required a rethink of HR philosophy, policies and practices. The upheaval in the way the HR functions operated was continuing while the research described here was being undertaken.

HR POLICIES AND PHILOSOPHIES IN HIGH-PERFORMING BUSINESSES

The argument for adopting a distinctive management philosophy or for pursuing a coherent policy range is, one assumes, to contribute to business success. This is where we encounter the hub of our search for a human resource theory – in the claim that certain ways of treating employees will, at the least, assist the business in achieving its goals. HRM prescriptions carry with them the implicit principle that behaving towards employees in an 'adult' way (by which is meant a participative, trusting way), if supported by appropriate development and reward policies, will produce a committed, highly motivated team. The next step in the logic is that such a team is more likely to perform well and to generate good customer relationships than an uncommitted, demotivated group of individuals.

Nowhere is this assertion better expressed than in James O'Toole's description of US 'vanguard' companies (O'Toole 1985). He takes the argument a stage further through his belief that it is possible to identify the policies and practices which a company should adopt in managing its employees in order to be effective as an enterprise. The HR management attributes that he associated with effective organisations were:

- A stakeholder status for the unions.
- Employee stock ownership.
- A fair measure of job security.
- Life-long training.
- Benefits tailored to individual needs.
- Participation in decision-making.
- Freedom of expression.
- Incentive pay.

(O'Toole 1985, p. 35.)

His vanguard list was formed by asking appropriate business people which big American corporations they would want to work for and it included Atlantic Richfield, Control Data, Dayton-Hudson, Deere, Honeywell, Levi-Strauss, Motorola, and Wayerhauser. He saw a strongly normative philosophy within these businesses, which he argued was the reason for their effectiveness. Giving unions which already had bargaining rights a stakeholder status, stock ownership, participation and freedom of expression were all part of forming an 'adult-to-adult' relationship, as opposed to a paternalistic style. The policies offering stable employment, life-long training, flexible benefits and performance pay were seen as a means to produce the right climate, to operationalise the values. Chief Executives were quoted to support his contention that the reasons for these policies were based in the companies' ethical stance. His economic justification rested on an unproven assertion that: 'Treating employees as shareholders works to the benefit of customers, dealers, suppliers, local communities and shareholders. Hence there is no trade-off necessary between people and profit.' (p. 65.)

The unitary frame of reference offers a convenient way out. O'Toole's analysis is very much a product of the full employment of the 1980s. Retaining staff was a priority for many companies at that time and, when profits were not being squeezed and there were still long-term corporate careers, the HRM priorities were rather different to those today. Some statements appear particularly dated. For example: 'Abbott, Data-General, DEC, Delta, Eli Lilly, Hallmark, Hewlett-Packard, IBM, Up-John and Wrigley are ten large US corporations that have found it possible to completely avoid lay-offs.' (p. 45.)

Even within the narrow sample of companies he researched, the disparity in policy provision was considerable, and he interpreted such broad values as 'freedom of expansion' and 'participation' in a number of different ways in order to accommodate his sample.

Two conclusions from this kind of study are important. As with the 'in search of excellence' approach to the HR contribution, there is a danger in making assumptions about the persistence of the apparent relationship between management practice and business success. If the relationship does not hold good over time, clearly we cannot claim that adopting the policies presented leads on to business success. Rather than engaging in the futile search for the special HR policy ingredient, the Golden Fleece of HR policies, we should avoid starting this particular voyage. The thesis argued by O'Toole is the mirror opposite to reality: corporate survival and success over long periods results from a refusal to be locked into particular policies. The recent decision by IBM to declare 40 000 redundancies world-wide signals a desire and need to adapt, and to change. This conclusion therefore throws doubt upon normative approaches to HRM.

The second conclusion is that we must look to all three levels of analysis: societal, organisational and the sentient level, to explain HR policies and how they contribute. The position taken throughout this book is that what matters is the fit of HR policies and strategies to the business strategies, and that we should direct our attention to the way strategies are formulated and the fit is achieved.

It is sometimes argued that the HR philosophy produces an organisational culture, and that it is this set of underlying values which creates the possibility for matching policies to strategic needs. We have already discussed in this chapter the linkages between policies and philosophies of management. The 1980s' emphasis on organisational culture (Deal and Kennedy 1982) was mostly approving of this phenomenon, as in the Nissan case (Wickens 1987). Here the culture was seen as a sort of liquid solution, a 'culture' in a different sense of the word, in which policies which are appropriate are inclined to grow.

The implication here is that socialisation is so strong that the soft contract is enveloping all practical policies, giving a high degree of adaptability within the contract's boundaries. This is an intriguing idea which deserves investigation. One question which must be raised is whether such a culture would naturally produce more rather than less successful organisations, since the culture is stronger than the market-place where it exists, and one might anticipate problems with adaptivity. There is also the question of how organisational structure and complex organisational objectives can all be served by basic values and culture in an organisation, without any attendant mechanisms for adjustment. If there are ways to adapt cultures, what are they?

POLICY AREAS WHICH CONTRIBUTE TO BUSINESS PERFORMANCE

In our research into the different routes to excellence, we found all companies in our sample regarded three main HR policy areas as major contributors to business strategies. Employee and especially management development, employee relations and organisation development were the strongest levers which were pulled to make the organisations change. Organisational change is not a special case in modern business life; it is the norm. When organisations are making significant changes, the strategies are more prominent. Discovering strategic HR influences within the change processes at the organisational level of analysis does therefore seem a legitimate technique for discovering the HR contribution.

Management development

Management quality was seen by all our sample as a potential source of competitive advantage. Management development as a total policy area includes many sub-systems, for example: systems to identify potential, to appraise staff, to determine training needs, to manage succession and careers. The mechanisms for delivering development, whether through line managers delegating and coaching, or through formal programmes of various kinds, were also important to most of our sample. This was because the method selected carried implications for the way the company as a whole was managed: delegation, for example, required the manager to possess a management style and sufficient confidence in his or her accountability to be able to give a part of the job to a subordinate, and to have both sufficient trust and a learning environment enabling development to take place. Thus, policies on development depend upon the sentient level, and the strategic significance of development stems from the translation of broader societal influences into the organisational arena.

For most of our sample, management development and business development went hand in hand. Young high-potentials were seen as the seedcorn of these companies, to be preserved, developed and encouraged. The connection to the strategic level is illustrated by the significance many organisations gave to learning and adapting. Competency and skill development have moved centre stage. As Reckitt & Colman put it:

> 'Developing the whole range of skills and abilities at all levels in the company is part of the value proposition of the organisation.'

For some businesses, staff training is expected to have an almost immediate effect on company performance. Where the staff interface with customers there is a felt need to train new employees in skills techniques and attitudes. At the point of sale and service delivery critical judgements are made about what the company is providing for the customer. How the service is delivered is as important as what is delivered; indeed, for those businesses which rely on relationship-marketing techniques, the exhibition of company values and the philosophy of management at the point of sale or service are essential to developing their businesses. Similarly, even where the sale is more a mechanical process, as in retail stores, the strategy is built upon repeat business, and on the overall company image.

Management development has strategic significance as a lever to change or to reinforce the management philosophy. There are other strategic benefits in management development policies. Development policies make the corporate values visible. Development has a future orientation: it is concerned with the kind of company which will exist and the competencies which will be required. This connects development to the business which the company wants to be in, and to the mission and values espoused.

Employee relations

The management of employment relationships was perceived to be a strategic matter, whether or not the companies concerned recognised and negotiated with trade unions. All high-performing companies need to have a policy agenda to create relationships with their working people which supports their business objectives. That being said, there were many variations in policy content amongst the sample. For many companies, there were explicit employee relations policies, which stipulated the company's values and the management approach. For others, there were covert policies, for example to reduce trade union influence through changing the bargaining arrangements, especially by negotiating only at local factory or unit level, rather than at the corporate level, and by limiting the range of issues over which bargaining could take place.

What was common amongst the companies was the felt need to have an employee relations stance, to be clear about the kind of relationship the business strategy required, and to push the execution of employee relations policies down to the lowest level possible, compatible with the corporation's overall values. There is no doubt that within the broad field of 'employee relations' policies, corporate values are most clearly read. For example, in the reward policies, which in some cases were used to inculcate specific values. Through profit share schemes or performance-based pay, for instance, the values are made real. Similarly, policies in the communication field also indicate the corporate position on relationships (for example attitude surveys, with the data fed back to the employees, briefing groups and focus groups). In both the case of rewards and of communications there are strong symbolic overtones. Monetary rewards may not motivate in the long term, but they certainly symbolise the value corporations attach to specific behaviours – for example rewarding long service, interpreted as loyalty, or rewarding performance above other attributes. Communications is also a policy area steeped in symbolism: what is communicated is less important than how and to whom the communication is addressed.

As one might anticipate, our survey showed that there was considerable variation in HR policies, and the industrial relations policies within our sample showed the effects of different traditions. This is exemplified by companies such as ICI with its history of joint consultation, or Marks & Spencer with its strong culture and paternalistic philosophy. Within some groups of companies there are a variety of traditions. For example, Scottish and Newcastle has a very traditional approach to industrial relations in its brewery, whereas its leisure division and retail outlets are completely different in approach. The 'confectionery' business stream in Cadbury-Schweppes is totally different in culture from the 'drinks' business stream, being more production-oriented, in contrast to the drinks stream's marketing orientation and global outlook. Rolls-Royce, the motor car manufacturer, is different from the other businesses within the Vickers Group.

One way to distinguish these differences is to contrast the strong, central cultures of some businesses with the more diffuse cultures in divisional operations. Industrial relations management was most frequently left to the divisional or company managements in the 'M' form structures. We can therefore see that diversification strategies are significant influences on industrial relations strategies, depending upon whether the share of the product/service market is large or not. Where a company has the stability deriving from a large share of the product market, issues such as joint consultation and other harmony-preserving measures come to the fore. Where the whole market is fragmented, competition on price and on product/service quality becomes more important. Unless the trade unions are a party to management's concern to compete on quality and/or cost, the unions would become marginalised, as they would be seen to be no longer in touch with a generally accepted strategic need. An example of unions cooperating in order to facilitate change can be found in the Rolls-Royce car plant, where multi-skilling, team working and quality initiatives have gone hand in hand, as Rolls-Royce faces increased overseas competition and problems of surviving in the US export market whilst needing to develop new products for the future.

Employee relations practices were, in every case in our sample, being updated either to carry through a major change programme or to express in a more modern way the same traditional values and approaches to management which had always formed part of the culture. The common feature here is the way companies were changing employee relations practices in order to adapt their organisational cultures. The pressures for change from the competitive, social and economic environment are constant, causing companies to review and to shift attitudes, and to tie new employee relations policies into quality and customer service initiatives.

There were many examples of employee relations strategies to support the business strategies:

- Some companies used vision and 'values' to gain employee commitment. The strategy was only regarded as effective if the corporate communication policies were adequate. The reality of the values had to be seen to be acted out by management on a day-to-day basis.
- In some cases reward systems were used to encourage particular employee behaviours. Profit-share schemes and various bonus schemes were commonly adopted. Although respondents acknowledged that

profit-share schemes may not directly motivate people, they believed employees would improve their understanding of the business. Initiatives in this area were therefore aimed at a general improvement to the climate of relationships and to attitudes, and sought to achieve a broadening of employee commitment.

● The movement of negotiations down to SBU, company or sometimes divisional level was also for some organisations a useful strategy to control bargaining and to avoid costly leap-frog claims across the whole corporation. In some instances, by leaving employee relations to the lowest line-management level possible, two objectives were achieved: trade union recognition was avoided, and line managers were empowered to solve local problems, 'to manage their own patch'.

For most of the well-known businesses identified here, the flexibility battles with trade unions had been largely won during the 1980s. The challenge from the late 1980s onwards was to move the industrial relations agenda on to major on quality issues. The changes to organisational structure and to management philosophy have had an impact here: by devolving quality and customer service responsibilities down to the lowest possible levels, this strategy sought to engage the problem solving and creative abilities of employees in the company's interests.

Organisation development

The phrase 'organisation development' is used here to categorise the multiplicity of change programmes we encountered when discussing the contribution of HRM to business strategy. There were direct strategic interventions which often combined employee relations strategies with new organisational forms in order to produce organisations which were more responsive to markets, more efficient in product or service delivery, and with organisational cultures which were inherently adaptive.

Change programmes of one kind or another were essential to these strategies. The variety of change programmes or initiatives was a function of the different situations in which companies found themselves. The constant need to carry out change, however, was a prompt to the use of the tactics deployed. In the words of Sir Graham Day, Chairman of Cadbury-Schweppes, 'If you're not changing, you're not managing'. Reorganisations in the face of competitive pressure and to exploit market opportunities had driven most organisations to review structures. Divisionalisation and the divestment and acquisition decisions over the past decade had encouraged this trend. Most of the organisations in our survey had been involved in some form of restructuring, and the delayering, downsizing or 'rightsizing' manoeuvres which resulted were one reason for organisational development policies. Sometimes, as with recently privatised companies, organisation development was a response to the changing nature of the business, and often management development was the means for supporting and directing the changes. Few companies were concerned to engage the trade unions in a dialogue to lead these changes, although managing the change process did very often involve employee relations activity at the SBU level.

The attempts to change values in organisations were quoted as examples of HRM strategic contributions, which were intended to shift fundamentally the way the company worked. One example here included BT, which used development activities and an element of employee participation in its 'change management forum'. This was designed to change the culture from an originally traditional public sector culture to a more dynamic, entrepreneurial approach, whilst allowing divisions to create their own versions for their own markets. In another case, British Airways sought to harness the pride in the company felt by all employees, in order to motivate change. At the time of privatisation, and subsequently, BA had undertaken a series of change programmes, which attempted to manage the hearts and minds of their employees. These programmes, such as 'winning for customers', picked on key values and sought, through special events, changed role descriptions and objectives, top management commitment and communication techniques, to keep employees on the 'edge of performance'. Glaxo Pharmaceuticals UK was engaged in a major culture change programme designed to help it launch new products and to become more adaptive to market conditions. Focusing on values and beliefs, they were attempting to bring about 'organic' change from the lowest levels upwards, using change workshops and team-building activities to aid cross-functional team effort, to reduce competitive conflict within, and to enhance the flexibility and productivity of their newly empowered teams. This is another example of a company seeking to imbue employees with their core values: role clarity, acceptance of change, team working, innovation and output orientation, in order to govern the way they should behave in order to be competitive in the 1990s.

DIFFERENCES IN HUMAN RESOURCE PHILOSOPHIES AND POLICIES

The differences between the companies studied were more significant than the similarities. When one compares human resource policies in companies within the same industry sector, even the variation is considerable. Most striking are the different management philosophies. These might be seen as distinctive 'cultures', but we were not seeking here to encapsulate the total culture of the organisation, rather it was the approach to corporate strategy and the organisation structure consequences, the intentions of management towards employees and the model of HRM adopted which gave rise to the many differences. The intervening variables at the organisational level of analysis were seen to cause change in the features listed above.

It was interesting, for example, to see how HRM was strategically placed within recently privatised businesses (including those which, although still technically owned by the Government, had moved to a private sector stance). All the companies which are part of this subset of data had moved into the private sector during the 1980s and early 1990s. Ranging from BT to SW Electricity (Retail) and London Electric, they had all embraced private sector strategic planning processes with enthusiasm.

Unlike most old-established private sector companies, in many of these cases the companies enjoyed a near monopoly position. This was evident from their strategic concerns, which for example focussed on high-quality service, devolving parts of the business into stand-alone operations in their desire to satisfy shareholders for the first time and their wish to be seen to be as profitable as other privatised companies. A feature of all the companies in this group was the use of OD strategies. Change brought about by privatisation had gone far beyond just the rhetoric of competition, and the marketing concepts found in the private sector. All of these businesses had been engaged in pushing through changes to organisational structures, combined with changes to their management styles and their industrial relations systems. The changes they sought provided their HR functions with high-profile strategy work, and were initiated by their changing market-share position and by their wish to adopt private sector management ideology.

Another distinct set of companies comprised those businesses where staff interface with consumers. Employee relations strategies, based on communications, service quality standards and employee development within a distinct and sometimes evolving culture were priorities for these companies, in retail, travel, leisure and similar activities. Good customer relationships were perceived to be central to the strategic concerns of these businesses. The need for an 'enabling culture' to support the relationship at the interface between customer and staff derived from the requirement quickly to socialise people from a fragmented labour market, including part-time, casual and temporary staff, into delivering a specific kind of service. Within these businesses the way customers are served is a part of the organisation's value proposition. HR policies in training, development, reward and the employee relations field therefore reflected the labour market, the management strategy and the traditional relationships within the industry sector.

Traditional industrial relations concerns still predominated within the engineering companies in our sample. Here the organisation-development activity centred upon changing attitudes, values and bargaining structures, as a part of the totality of improving competitiveness. For example, Rolls-Royce cars, part of the Vickers Group, had introduced team working, semi-autonomous work groups and the more flexible use of labour along with quality and training initiatives designed to maintain the quality of the products while also controlling costs and meeting the demanding standards they had set for themselves. Traditional patterns of bargaining were breaking down in engineering and in the ex-public sector companies. Traditions within industrial relations were therefore still exercising some influence over decision-making habits and rules. So too were the attempts to harness the sentiments and perceptions of the work people from the sentient level, in socio-technical systems fashion, to the organisation's goals through semi-autonomous work groups, team briefing, new supervisory roles and quality circles.

International businesses typically espoused very different management philosophies and policies from those companies which were very largely operating only in the UK. Organisational culture issues became enmeshed with national cultures in the international businesses. Policies on expatriate management and policies to sustain corporate (perhaps also national) presence, together with the representation of interests and the political sensitivities of the host countries were all influences on international businesses which were not relevant to national companies. Similarly, the changes occurring internationally affected those businesses, and influenced marketing and human resource strategies – illustrating the effects of market size/share and state policies on the human resource function.

A salient feature distinguishing company philosophies is the managerial value set. In some corporate cultures, strong humanistic values were espoused. In other businesses managers were more manipulative with values, seeking to shift and to change values in line with shifts in business strategy. This latter form of social engineering was most noticeable in companies stressing OD strategies, rather than the changes to the institutions of collective bargaining which we found in companies with a strong industrial relations tradition. For example, the history of companies such as ICI, Reckitt & Colman, Cadbury-Schweppes, and Marks & Spencer explains how the company in question has come to believe in certain values and to adopt particular industrial relations policies. We need to remember that managements view their changing situation from inside their own corporate cultures. Other companies, such as Coats Viyella, Vickers and BAT had a mixture of cultures, acquired along the way as the business was developed through the purchase and divestment of companies with cultures different from the original parent business.

In this analysis companies have been taken as 'wholes'. It would be quite possible, however, to locate many of the companies in our sample in more than one grouping, since often parts of their operations were more similar to other businesses than to the parent corporation. For example, SE Electricity could be considered as a recently-privatised business, or along with other retail companies; Scottish and Newcastle are in the leisure business, but the traditional brewery part of the company would probably have more in common with, say, the confectionery business stream in Cadbury-Schweppes than the drinks stream in that company; and ICI has, since this research was completed, subdivided into a pharmaceutical business and a plastics/chemicals business.

What conclusions should we draw from all of these differences therefore? Generalisations on human resource management philosophies and policies are likely to conceal important differences which exist not only between companies in different industries, but also between companies within the same industry. Corporations are sometimes amalgamations of different businesses, or even parts of businesses and, if we expect HRM to exist solely for the purpose of making those businesses successful, we must anticipate differences in HRM within businesses. This question was addressed in the discussion on different models of HRM. Different models may indeed coexist within the same business, although often not without some strain on relationships (Tyson and Fell 1986).

The search for the HR contribution has to be at the organisational level of analysis. However, if it is the mechanism by which HRM contributions are being made, there is merit in a broader debate to establish the frameworks or models which will explain how contributions can be measured. Such frameworks should also seek to explain, as has been done here, how HRM changes over time, and what the influences are from the societal level of analysis to the organisational level of analysis. The contribution of HRM to business strategy may therefore be explained as the content of HR philosophies and policies which relate to business objectives and as a mechanism for adjusting philosophies and policies to business needs over time.

One reason for the differences between organisations is the way the increasingly fragmented labour markets are exploited by the varying sourcing strategies adopted by companies. The creation of more federal structures is also a feature of the changing and more complex organisations encountered in this study. Divisional structures, collaborative working arrangements, joint ventures, holding companies and different kinds of SBUs were all found amongst the respondents. The change to federal structures and the increasing use of short-term or sub-contract work has supported the move towards the 'hard contract'.

That different models of HRM were co-existing within the same organisation was a source of tension over HR policies. For example, to avoid talent hoarding and conflict over high-potential development, companies usually differentiated between the cadre of high-potential managers and the rest of management. For the high-potential managers special programmes were run, and they were regarded as 'corporate property' whereas the development of the rest of the management population, was left to the SBU or divisional level. In this way 'strategic' development is a role for the centre, with wide implications for other human resource policies, including recruitment, promotion and appraisal policies. Another area for conflict arose where contractors were employed alongside employees. This could be expressed as a conflict between the two different forms of contracting. In organisation development there were the tensions between local interests and head office change management concerns.

BUSINESS STRATEGIES AND HUMAN RESOURCE POLICIES

The data gathering for the research quoted here took place in the midst of a recession. All the companies in our sample were suffering from highly competitive market-places, which pushed human resource policies into a second place after marketing strategies. Yet, the strategic levers were being pulled to adapt and to change organisations. The strength of global competition and difficult trading conditions at home have, on this evidence, forced companies to be highly pragmatic. A more openly strategic approach may be evident from the human resource management point of view, but the corporate strategies have if anything become more short-term, 'attributional' and reactive to the recession. HR policies reflect this, with the emphasis on policies which will take out costs from the organisation, encourage flexibility and exploit any potential savings from the labour market.

Schuler and Jackson (1987)[2] argued that different competitive objectives resulted in appropriate HR practice in order to use policies to the company's advantage. Broadly, Schuler *et al* are suggesting that 'effective' HR strategies, which could be called 'HR philosophies', can be adopted to exploit the business strategy opportunities. What is argued is that there are typical business strategies, for which appropriate HR 'strategies' can be formed. They identified three strategy clusters, 'utilisation' 'accumulation' and 'facilitation' policies, which they claimed were related to the typical business strategies. The 'utilisation' cluster is closer to the 'hard' contract and the 'accumulation' to the soft contract, whereas the 'facilitation' strategy implies a readiness to move between the two. If we were to interpret the facilitation HR strategy as a hard contract approach for the peripheral workers (working on a short-term, sub-contract basis) and as a soft contract for the core workers, the model proposed could be adapted as shown in Fig. 5.

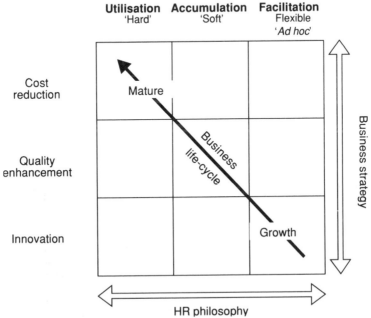

Fig. 5 Effective HR strategies

While this may seem convincing, our research did not reveal such a simple, linear relationship. What confuses the problem is that business strategies at corporate level do not frequently fall into the three simple categories described. Additionally, although one might anticipate quality to be a key concern for companies with long-term employment and development strategies (the 'soft' contract), the accent on utilisation does often go hand in hand with a concern for quality, expressed by the tight performance standards and internal contracts found in hard contracting.

The move towards hard contracting may indicate the cost pressures from the highly competitive business environment. For those companies with a 'soft' contract approach, further evidence of companies trying to manage their way out of the recession came from the way 'vision' and 'values' were often stressed. Leadership abilities for senior management became ever more important when the messages were not always good. Managing through vision and values encourages compliance, and along with appropriate communication policies helps management to put over difficult messages.

Although all the companies in our sample subscribed to the idea that HR policies should be coherent and be totally integrated with business strategy, there were few who could claim to have achieved such a state of perfection. The process of strategy formation gave considerable power to divisional-level HR functions, where the classic 'M' form existed. The time-lags and the problems in gaining agreement to the various strategies militated against the production of one simple, agreed and accepted set of HR policies to give effect to the corporate plan. Instead, HR policies more accurately could be described as being constantly in 'play', negotiated, reviewed, revised and adapted.

There is little doubt that there are different routes to excellence. Whatever the basis for comparison, companies do not have one approach to HRM in common. Where there does seem to be some basis for comparison is in the three main strategic levers identified. Here again, however, the actual policies show considerable variation. The variables at the societal level, reinterpreted at the organisation level, conditioned the HR role adopted and the policies supported. The evidence of differences does not mean there are no patterns. Taking these variables and the perceptions of the work people into account, the evidence is present from the 30 case study companies for the move to hard contracting, the way companies use the three main policy areas as strategic levers, and that there are different models of HRM. Different routes to excellence derive not only from different policies but also from different industry norms, different structures and from the different philosophies of management adopted.

BIBLIOGRAPHY

Abegglen, J. C. and Stalk, G. (1985) *Kaissha, The Japanese Corporation*, New York: Basic Books.

Blauner, R. (1964) *Alienation and Freedom: The factory worker and his industry,* Chicago: University of Chicago Press.

Brewster, C. and Bournois, F. (1991) 'Human Resource Management: A European Perspective', *Personnel Review*, Vol. 20, No. 6, pp. 4–13.

Brewster, C., Gill, C. G. and Richbell, S. (1983) 'Industrial Relations Policy. A Framework for Analysis' in Thurley, K. and Wood, S. (Eds) *Industrial Relations and Management Strategy*, pp. 62–72, Cambridge: Cambridge University Press.

Deal, T. E. and Kennedy, A. A. (1982) *Corporate Cultures*, Reading, Mass.: Addison-Wesley.

Goldthorpe, J. H., Lockwood, D., Bechhofer F. and Platt, J. (1968) *The Affluent Worker: Industrial Attitudes and Behaviour,* Cambridge: Cambridge University Press.

Grahl, J. and Teague, P. (1991) 'Industrial Relations Trajectories and European Human Resource Management', in Brewster, C. and Tyson, S. (Eds) *International Comparisons in Human Resource Management*, London: Pitman Publishing.

Jackson, S. E., Schuler, R. S. and Rivero, J. C. (1989) 'Organizational characteristics as predictors of personnel practices', *Personnel Psychology*, 42, pp. 727–86.

Likert, R. (1959) 'A motivational approach to a modified theory of organization and management' in Haire, M. (Ed.) *Modern Organization Theory*, New York: Wiley.

McGregor, D. (1960) *The Human Side of Enterprise*, New York: McGraw-Hill.

Miller, E. J. and Rice, A. K. (1967) *Systems of Organisation: The Control of Task and Sentient Boundaries*, London: Tavistock.

O'Toole, J. (1985) 'Employee practices at the best managed companies', *California Management Review*, Vol. XXVIII, No. 1, pp. 35–66.

[2]Schuler, R. S. and Jackson, S. E. (1987) 'Linking competitive strategies with human resource management practices', *Academy of Management Executive*, Vol. 1, No. 3, pp. 207–19.

[1]Schuler, R. S. and Jackson, S. E. (1987) 'Organizational strategy and organizational level as determinants of HRM practice', *Human Resource Planning,* Vol. 10, No. 3, pp. 125–41.

Silverman, D. (1970) *The Theory of Organisations*, London: Heinemann.

Starkey, K. and McKinlay, A. (1993) *Strategy and the Human Resource*, Oxford: Blackwell.

Thurley, K. (1983) 'How transferable is the Japanese industrial relations system? Some implications of a study of industrial relations and personnel policies of Japanese firms in Western Europe', *Paper at the 6th World Congress of International Industrial Relations Association*, Kyoto, 28–31 March.

Tonnies, F. (1955) *Community and Association*, London: Routledge & Kegan Paul.

Trist, E. L. *et al.* (1963) *Organisational Choice*, London: Tavistock.

Tyson, S. and Fell, A. (1986) *Evaluating the Personnel Function*, London: Hutchinson.

Walker, C. J. and Guest, R. H. (1952) *The Man on the Assembly Line*, Cambridge: Harvard.

Wickens, P. (1987) *The Road to Nissan. Flexibility, Quality, Teamwork*, London: Macmillan.

Williamson, O. E. (1973) 'Markets and hierarchies: some elementary considerations', *American Economic Review* LXIII, pp. 316–25.

Williamson, O. E. and Ouchi, W. G. (1983) 'The markets and hierarchies programme of research: origins, implications, prospects', in Francis, A., Turk, J. and Willman, P. (Eds) *Power, Efficiency and Institutions*, London: Heinemann.

CHAPTER 6

Organisational structure and the human resource function

Whenever accounts are written of management activities, recourse is inevitably made to organisational structure explanations as the causes of actions, role demands and influence. It is only a short step then to question the theories of organisations in which organisational structure solutions are framed. Since human resource management is itself organisational work, designed to sustain, develop or in some way to influence management intentions, any general theory of human resource management will be dependent upon organisational theories. The question can be pushed further – to what extent is a general theory of HRM possible without an equally convincing and all-embracing theory of organisations?

While accepting the need to take organisational structures and the theoretical explanations of them into account when theorising about HRM, the starting point in this chapter is that no one organisational theory would ever be adequate to explain the variety of activities within organisations and the many possible perspectives on organisations (Morgan 1986). In this chapter, however, the case is argued that in the post-recessionary period HRM is determined by organisational structure variables.

THE CHANGING NATURE OF ORGANISATIONS

One characteristic response by senior management to the second, deeper recession in a decade, from 1989 to 1993, has been to re-examine their organisation's structure. 'Delayering', 'downsizing' and 'rightsizing', the well-worn euphemisms of the period, are the words used to describe the sometimes brutal process of removing costs from organisations. In simple terms this has meant dispensing with large numbers of employees, especially middle managers, and holding down all controllable costs, such as wages and salaries for lower level employees. In the paradoxical way that social life happens, top management teams and chief executives have often awarded themselves large pay rises for achieving these cost savings.

Commentators witnessing these major organisational changes have seen within the apparent reaction to short-term problems a sign that a more serious, long-term reappraisal is taking place, in which work flexibility, new technology and new governance structures are all playing a part. Handy (1989) forecast the move towards 'federal' organisations, where the various units collaborate with each other, undertaking joint ventures, combining over research, marketing or production, or in some linkage of all of these (as was the case between Honda and the Rover Group, prior to the BMW takeover in 1994). Similarly, the emphasis on smaller, leaner organisations and on responsive structures, as in the case of Scandinavian Airlines (SAS), was forecast by Schumacher (1973) in his notion that 'small is beautiful'. There seems every reason to believe the claims of the post-modernist theorists that we are witnessing the end of the large bureaucratic production era, when enormous factories produced vast quantities of standardised goods, and were organised on the classic basis of the division of labour, with a central unity of control, operating a large pyramid of managers and supervisors, working in remote command chains.

Some researchers have roughly equated 'modernist' organisations with Weberian bureaucracies, which are sometimes (as in the work of Grahl and Teague 1991, already cited) described as 'Fordist', following Gramsci's notions (1971). By contrast, post-modernist organisations are described as 'organic' and flexible, using technology to service niche markets, with multi-skilled workers employed through a variety of contractual and working time arrangements (Lash 1988). Sometimes, 'post-modernism' is a shorthand label for the popular conception of Japanese management in large organisations (Clegg 1990). Such contrasts are made usually to the disfavour of older 'modernist' approaches, at least on the tacit basis that self-evidently Japanese organisations are more successful than most British companies. An equally convincing account of the changes defines the transition as being not towards 'freer', more flexible or participative structures, but instead interprets the changes as new ways for management to gain control over labour, through 'attitudinal restructuring' (Wood 1989), a reworking of Fordist production methods (Hudson 1989) and the use of technology to achieve flexible specialisation, productivity gains and deskilling (Whitaker 1992).

These different interpretations may reflect different images of organisations, which as Morgan (1986) has shown can range from

metaphors of organisations as machines or systems, to organisat
psychic prisons. In much of the 1980s' literature, organisational structure
issues were subsumed into cultural categories. For example Harrison
(1972) and later Handy (1978) represented organisational form as
organisational culture, going beyond a description of the formal
reporting relationships into matters concerned with style and informal
relationships. Whether or not structure is a part of culture, or is a
framework within which certain cultures develop is not clear. The
linkage between culture, structure and strategy may be represented as a
circular relationship (*see* Fig. 6).

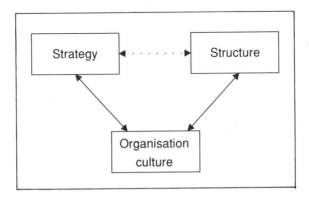

Fig. 6 The relationship between structure, culture and strategy

If structure follows strategy, it also helps to create culture, which in
turn is influential on the strategic decisions made. Structure limits
strategic choice, but also prompts exploitation of opportunities. For
example, a large TV rental business was facing the collapse of its market
when consumers turned to purchasing televisions rather than renting
them. Although technological innovations had allowed the company to
survive previous recessions (BBC2, colour TV, etc), the change to the
market-place was long term. By seeing its regional and branch network
as potential assets to be exploited, with sophisticated distribution
channels, skilled TV repair technicians and loyal management, the
company was able to move into new fields, such as home computers,
video games, etc, within a broad 'home entertainment' product portfolio
(Tyson and Kakabadse 1987, Chapter 17). The structure helped to
determine the strategy.

Culture is usually defined as pervasive and multifaceted. It is
supported by values and beliefs, and includes not only management's
ideologies but also the belief systems of various sub-groupings who

create their own sub-cultures, for example 'professionals' such as medical doctors in the health service. The relationship between structure and culture is more complex than is implied by contrasting the 'machine bureaucracy' with the 'task-oriented' organic structure. Managerial approaches to decision-making are filtered by different levels and sub-groupings within organisations. When implementing HRM policies, therefore, managers need to work at both the 'organisation' and the 'sentient' levels of analysis. To change organisations strategically requires work on employee attitudes and beliefs. This aspect of the HRM strategic contribution was evident from our research, which showed how OD policies were designed to influence values and relationships.

Morgan (1993) proposes that new technology and what he describes as the holographic nature of culture (the way that attitudes, values and social practices are characteristic of the whole, but also are latent within the parts) can be harnessed by appropriate structures and HR policies in areas like empowerment and leadership styles to change the way people behave, and to inculcate a sense of shared vision and values.

> 'Bring these ideas together and we have a novel way of thinking about how we can create and manage decentralized organisations that are completely unified, because people are on the same 'wavelength', and have the capacity to reproduce the character and style of their organisations naturally and spontaneously. Organisations designed and managed in this way have much more in common with dandelion seeds and spider plants than with bureaucracies of old.'
>
> (Morgan 1993, p. 10.)

This certainly strikes a chord in our research with the methods for achieving strategic goals. Companies in our sample were using various techniques to manage values towards a particular direction, as a process to implement strategy. However, values and style are not enough. Company management also needs a linkage back into the societal level of analysis, with its attendant economic threats and opportunities, from which the HRM policy responses show how HRM can contribute towards successful business outcomes. For private sector organisations, financial performance is inevitably the *raison d'être* for change, albeit sometimes as a long-run strategy and sometimes as a result of the need for basic survival. The organisations we were studying were 'economic organisations'. This is what makes the non-rational actions of an organisation's members so important: it is the departure from the assumptions usually made about economic activity which generates interest in culture, values, beliefs and the influences managers bring to their work. This should not, however, blind us to the processes of capital accumulation and economic exchange on which the whole organisational edifice is built. What seems to be needed, therefore, is a theoretical understanding of how the three levels of analysis connect.

CONTINGENCY THEORY

The most appropriate work on how to fit organisational-level variables with societal level variables is found amongst those organisation theorists whose work became known in the 1960s and 1970s, sometimes called 'contingency theory'. This is not one theory, but rather a collection of different theoretical perspectives which share the notion that what happens in organisations is contingent upon a range of variables, and that explanations of the actions within organisations must take account of the variables within society which impinge upon the organisation as well as on the intra-organisational variables including relative power, and the dependency between organisational units or departments. Legge was the first to see the significance of contingency theory for the study of personnel management (Legge 1978). The theoretical issues raised by the original thinkers in this field remain unresolved and significant for our analysis of HRM today. The early attempts by Burns and Stalker (1961) to find a relationship between the level of uncertainty in the product market and the utilisation of the mechanistic, bureaucratic form in organisations is still relevant. Although they were arguing from the case of the electronics industry, which was changing rapidly after the end of the Second World War, to the general point that technological innovation gives rise to 'organic' rather than mechanistic organisational structures, this dichotomy between rigid, stable, large organisations and smaller, responsive, more fluid structures is a construct with relevance in post-recessionary Britain.

Joan Woodward (1958, 1965) was originally interested in which structures were most likely to bring commercial success, and went on to discover technology and organisational structure linkages. Thompson (1967) looked at how firms try to obtain control over their environment, and began to develop the argument about different diversification strategies and different forms of production, which require coordination. Among the first self-avowed contingency theorists, perhaps of most relevance, are Lawrence and Lorsch (1967) who suggested that different amounts of uncertainty are found in different industries, and in the varying environments where the different departments within an organisation do business. They found that departments facing the highest degrees of uncertainty were the most influential in the firm.

Managers needed to adopt different strategies according to their trading environments. This differentiation of activity produced a counter need for greater integration within the firm. The integration mechanisms suggested included individual integrating roles for managers across functions, temporary integrating project teams, specialist integrating departments, paper systems and rules, formal planning schemes and personal contact between departments. Lawrence and Lorsch sought to demonstrate that the high-performing firms in their study had successfully organised their integrating mechanisms, having recognised appropriate levels of diversification in their activities.

There are a number of HRM lessons from the notions of differentiation to meet market needs and integration to achieve organisational efficiency. It is worth noting the prescience of Lawrence and Lorsch, who argued the case for flexible and informal, as well as formal, integration mechanisms. Matrix structures and project groups have now become well-established integration devices. The human resource function could be seen as an integrating department itself, since its remit usually extends across departmental boundaries, as does the finance function and the corporate communications activity, where this exists. From our research, the internalisation of corporate values was also an integrating device, often through major communication programmes. Corporate culture and the 'managed heart' are corporate control devices, managed by the HR function, as much as being normative human resource management philosophy.

MARKETS AND HIERARCHIES

The discussion on strategic choice and organisation structure has built upon Lawrence and Lorsch's earlier work, in order to connect structure to the way the organisation reacts to the economic environment. As we mentioned in the last chapter, the markets and hierarchies paradigm seeks to connect structure to strategy and then to attach policies to the strategy. Williamson's thesis is particularly appropriate to our discussion since he uses the transaction and transaction costs as the basic units of analysis. In addition, his work on the relationship of the firm with its economic environment brings the various internal modes of contracting into the study of how markets affect organisational structures. Using two assumptions about behaviour: that some organisational actors will be 'opportunistic' (exercise 'calculating behaviour' in their own self-interest), and will be subject to 'bounded rationality' (actors simplify and try to understand the world through their own perceptions of what is reasonable); organisation design is explained:

> 'Faced with bounded rationality on one hand, and the proclivity for some human agents to behave opportunistically on the other, the basic organisational design issue is essentially reduced to this: organise transactions in such a way as to economise on bounded rationality while simultaneously safeguarding those transactions against the hazards of opportunism.'
>
> (Williamson and Ouchi 1983, p. 17.)

The contribution of Williamson's ideas to the discussion on organisational structure and HRM can be summarised by saying that the markets and hierarchies paradigm takes the differentiation/integration discussions a stage further. It shows how divisionalisation, which arises from the need to differentiate products and services in order to compete and to respond to the special conditions of each market-place, produces different types of relationship within the firm, which have been termed 'hard' and 'soft' contracts. From the perspective taken in this book, the benefit of this approach is that it attempts to explain how what happens at one level of analysis (the firm operating in the economy) results in different contractual relationships with employees at the organisational level, and how it therefore influences perceptions of work, career, rewards and attachment to the employer at the sentient level.

If we accept that HRM is a control mechanism for the firm, the question arises of how the ways companies are organised and managed condition their performance. The argument stated here about different routes to excellence can best be pursued by examining how corporate governance arrangements influence corporate performance. The evidence on this may be adduced from the different types of devolved structures, and the relationship between divisions and head office. One function for head office is to be the mechanism by which the various influences on the firm are interpreted into strategies and policies. This is consistent with our definition of corporate strategy as the way corporations exploit opportunities and resist threats from their business environment through exercising choices.

ORGANISATION STRUCTURE AND HRM IN THE RESEARCHED COMPANIES

From our research the significance of devolved structures soon became clear, since the delegation of strategic planning to divisions and therefore the delegation of the supporting HR policies were consequences of divisionalisation, itself often a result of diversification strategies. This had a major impact on the consistency of policies, and their integration at the corporate level, and on the role of HRM in the firm itself. In order to respond to the markets for which the division had been established, particular business strategies had to be pursued. If the HR strategies were to support the business strategies, different HR policies were often needed within divisions. The integration of HR strategies with the business therefore inhibited the integration of HR strategies at corporate or group level.

Some of the companies in our sample were 'single product' businesses. Although in one sense all the companies were multi-product, i.e. they offered a range of services or products, there were differences between, for example, Marks & Spencer, British Airways, Scottish Power and BT on the one hand and, say, RTZ, BAT, Forte and Coats Viyella on the other. Corporate strategies within diversified or conglomerate businesses rarely accorded any role at the centre to HR strategies, except as a minimal service to headquarters staff. Sometimes a senior executive provided general advice and 'firefighting' on HR issues at the behest of the CEO or other board members. This contrasted with the more centralised businesses where strong organisational cultures were sustained through HR policies.

There was also a distinction between companies heavily engaged in overseas operations and companies which were very largely operational only in the UK. In the former cases questions of organisational culture became enmeshed with the impact of national cultures. Influences on international businesses, which were not relevant to national companies, included policies on expatriate management, on sustaining a corporate (and sometimes a national) presence, the representation of interests and the political sensitivities of the host countries. In addition, for companies whose interests were very much overseas, international changes influenced marketing strategies. Hendry (1994) argues that different approaches to control and staffing result in different approaches to all HR policies within multinational or international firms. Illustrating his argument with the case of BP, he shows how the company moved through different structural approaches with consequences for staffing philosophies and HR objectives: from an integrated structure in 1960s, with an enthnocentric philosophy, to a 'horizontal' structure (that is, one which is closer to a federal structure) in the 1990s, with regiocentric and geocentric staffing philosophies.

The structure of international companies has to resolve the dilemma of whether regions, countries or products should be the basis for divisionalisation. In the case of Philips, the Dutch-based electronics company, the highly diversified product portfolio was supported by a matrix structure (van Houten 1989). The main board of management set the policy for the company, and product divisions were grouped around the components and products, headed by MDs with world-wide responsibility for their products. National organisations within 60 countries carried out the full range of responsibilities, including manufacturing and marketing, and in some cases research. The corporate departments at head office provided a coordinating function world-wide, with staff development as the main HR contribution. More 'regional management' was said to be emerging, as were interlinked product divisions to assist with a need for integration. The balance and 'timing' of centralised *versus* decentralised management were described as a part of the management process.

Amongst the researched companies in our study, many were involved with international operations, but there was no single pattern of organisation. At the time of our research, ICI was splitting up and a new company, Zeneca, was formed for the pharmaceutical part of their business. Marks & Spencer were emerging as a more international player, with stores in an increasing number of overseas countries. RTZ was a well-established global player, with a highly decentralised group of mining companies and many joint ventures. Of all the companies in our survey, the majority of RTZ's 70 000 employees were employed overseas, and for the most part regarded the local company as their employer rather than the group as a whole. One point of comparison between BP and Philips (which were not in our study) and the whole 30 companies we researched was the extent to which organisational structures were constantly under pressure to change. The international dimension adds another pressure source. The need to be responsive to local conditions, markets and socio-political influences has to be balanced against the need for control in distant areas where local managements are accountable to a remote office and mistakes are costly. One general consequence is the prevailing view in most companies that their structures are not entirely satisfactory: the need to change and adjust is therefore a continuing trend. In this sense managements can never be said to have the 'right' structure. The 'right' structure is one that needs to be changed. The wrong structure is one that is not being changed or is too rigid to change easily. Organisation structures are designed to control organisation members. The hierarchy, along with the price mechanism and cultural or socialisation strategies are alternative ways to arrange this control (Hennart 1993).

From our research, the position of the head office in relation to the subsidiaries or divisions revealed how the governance structure in each company was organised. The central HR function, whether or not represented on the main board, represented the position of HR in the decision-making apparatus and was extremely influential on the coherence and integration of HR policies. The integration of HR strategies within business strategies was not always a matter for the main board. As reported in the previous chapters, integration frequently occurred at divisional level. This is not surprising in organisations which have made considerable efforts to diversify and thus to create organisational structures which are close to their respective markets.

The role of head office was researched by the Cresap consultancy in 1987. From its research into 45 leading British companies, it concluded that four head office types could be discerned:

- 'Targeting' types, which defined fundamental objectives, set and monitored financial targets and delegated all operating decisions to the operating divisions.
- 'Guiding' types, which coordinated business strategies, set and monitored objectives, and contributed to major operating decisions.
- Directing types, which participated in the development of business strategies, in their implementation and in major operating decisions.
- 'Running' head office types, which developed and monitored plans, guidelines and policies.

From the HR perspective, the main issue is what sort of HR services are supplied from these head offices. This sample showed 95 per cent of company head offices had personnel functions. These ranged from a minimalist role of adviser under the targeting type, to selling and 'telling' personnel staff in 'the running head office' type, with various coordination roles in the other types. One suspects that these results from the 1980s would not be replicated in any modern study, and we will discuss the changing role of the HR specialist in the next chapter. The conclusion from our study was that divisional level management for HRM was now more significant than board level HR and that the structural changes which have occurred, forcing decision-making out towards the market place, have resulted in a realignment in power.

Decisions coming up from divisional boards to the main board would usually carry the whole weight of divisional senior management with them. In Cresap's terms there has been a shift towards the 'targeting' type head office functions (RTZ, BAT, Reed, Forte, Scottish and New-castle, for example), although there were also 'guiding' types (Vickers, Cadbury-Schweppes, Glaxo, for example), 'directing' types (Marks & Spencer, Coats Viyella, BOC, for example) and 'running' types (British Airways, BT, Scottish Power, for example). Making precise judgements on this scale is impossible, but the notion of different types of head office is useful as an analytical device for capturing the very different functions served by a headquarters within an organisational structure.

The categories created by Cresap were echoes of the work of Goold and Campbell (1986). They distinguished three different approaches to planning and control by corporate offices:

Strategic planning companies build portfolios of activity around a small number of 'core' businesses. There is long-term planning and organic, if slow, growth. Business units may not feel strongly involved with corporate strategy and rely instead on consistently good financial performance. Cadbury-Schweppes is an example from our study.

Strategic control companies are more interested in short-term results with more emphasis on financial performance. Long-term strategies are encouraged, but there is a more ruthless approach by business unit managers to divestment and the motivation to perform. Typically, growth is less steady than in strategic planning companies. Vickers plc is a good example of this type of company.

Financial control companies have a strong focus on financial performance. Growth is often achieved through acquisitions, with less interest in long-term planning and an emphasis on profits. The business is often brought together with a portfolio of good performers. BAT may be quoted as an example in this context.

Classifying companies according to these broad approaches to strategy formation and control was a less clear action than is implied by these definitions. Companies might easily be moving from one approach to another, and in the recessionary period our research revealed companies moving from the 'strategic planning' type towards 'strategic control' type. This reflection of the more ruthless attitude to SBU performance by group senior managements seemed from our research to be a permanent rethink of control criteria. With these provisos, Table 6 represents the position of the companies in our sample, in the period 1992/1993.

Most of the recently-privatised utilities have been shown under the strategic planning heading in view of their approach at this time which no doubt derived from the more sedate strategic control attitudes of their past. However, all were rapidly embracing the opportunities for new management approaches, and were moving into long-range planning with the passion of the recently converted. There was also a movement between strategic and financial control approaches – perhaps a cyclical swing according to the economic circumstances and according

Table 6: Companies listed according to strategic approach of head office or group

Strategic planning	Strategic control	Financial control
Blue Circle Industries	Kingfisher	Coats Viyella
BNFL	Reckitt & Colman	BAT
Scottish Power	BT	Laporte
SWEB (Retail)	Forte	BOC
National Grid	Vickers	ICI
London Electricity	British Aerospace	Ladbroke
Cadbury-Schweppes		Rank Organisation
Glaxo		Racal
RTZ		Fine Art Development
Marks & Spencer		Scottish and Newcastle
British Airways		Amersham International
Wellcome		Reed

to the way companies sought to react to the changes internally prompted by recession, competition and new opportunities.

What conclusions can we draw from this for the strategic management of the people part of the businesses? The shifts towards different approaches, from a strategic planning or a strategic control towards a financial control approach, mean more emphasis on cost control and on the measurement of transaction costs. A shift towards 'hard contracting' is likely therefore. Growth through acquisition in the 1980s and the strengthening of SBU HR functions in some cases were at the expense of central HR planning and policy-making. The recession seems to have had two different effects: pressure for more control; and the opposite trend towards pushing accountability down to the lowest level possible. Perhaps these apparently opposing trends are compatible, since the overriding requirement is for clarity, with responsibility to be shouldered by managers at all levels.

The removal of organisational layers has also encouraged these trends. Pushing power down to divisions is a two-edged sword. Although slimmed-down headquarters staff may devolve more responsibility, the senior team will be able to identify readily where the results are coming from. Hard contracting also implies more non-employment solutions – more subcontracting, more outsourcing and fewer services provided by the core or group headquarters. If divisions want the benefits of particular policies (for example training centres, industrial relations services, pension schemes, use of office space), they will have to pay for them.

ORGANISATIONAL STRUCTURE AND HR POLICIES

Organisational structure is such an all-pervasive term that the HR policy implications can be traced in all the ways people are managed. Industrial relations policies, for example, are dependent on the organisational level at which bargaining takes place. The drive to local-level bargaining in the 1970s and early 1980s facilitated the strengthening of divisional, or SBU-level HRM. Policy initiatives at SBU level have the closest relationship to the business strategies created at that level. The removal of whole layers of management has often been accompanied by empowerment initiatives and culture change programmes aimed at increasing flexibility, reducing costs and improving services to internal and external customers, and improving product quality. The way all these policy initiatives intermingle should not blind us to the saliency of organisational structure. Management style, organisational culture and employee attitudes may be the flesh of organisations, but it is the structure which is the skeleton on which these softer, more indeterminate factors cling.

Two examples may serve to illustrate the point. Glaxo Pharmaceuticals UK is a part of the Glaxo Group and stands as an independent entity. The existing senior management described the business in 1989 as hierarchical and rigid, with a strong functional structure and culture, and with almost all its communications through vertical channels. There was little inter-divisional exchange of ideas. The success of the drug Zantac had resulted in complacency and management had stopped trying to improve the organisation. However, the culture change programme as described in the previous chapter sought to inculcate the core values of role clarity, acceptance of change, team working, innovation and output orientation as a means to develop the organisation for the 1990s by creating a responsive, flexible group of people. The programme was instituted through a series of workshops and policies in communication and above all was designed to help people to understand change and to be able to adopt new behaviours to increase cooperation and communication. These were the means by which a multi-disciplinary approach to sales, marketing and distribution was achieved. The team effort improved coordination of sales and marketing and the structure of the distribution chain. The sales teams of two trading subsidiaries were merged. The new culture assisted in the launch of three new products and the multi-disciplinary project teams have now become a normal feature of the organisational structure. Glaxo Pharmaceuticals UK described this as an organic rather than just a 'flattening' of structures, and saw the benefits from changing attitudes and motivation alongside new roles and relationships.

In the case of Cadbury UK, a part of Cadbury-Schweppes, the HR function was conducting an organisational audit, reviewing structures and management resources in relation to future needs. The company has broken down layers of management and increasingly involves the shop-floor workers in the immediate decisions which affect their work. The 1991 management audit included an organisational structure and function review which was a function-by-function analysis of organisational structure issues, training, development and succession issues and plans. The backdrop was a scenario of organisational change and of three years of effort on total quality management, a main vehicle for changing culture, which has had strong support from the TGW Union. The combination of structural change, high-profile TQM programmes and development programmes based on an analysis of future needs, was the version of organisational development favoured by Cadbury UK. This coherent approach to strategy, structure and supporting policies reveals how policies are influenced by structure changes and are used to help institute structural change.

From these two examples we can see how in both cases subsidiaries of the holding company were setting the pace with strong divisional or SBU strategies, which brought HR policy changes in their train. The structural changes, which were partly forced on Cadbury UK and which were foreseen as necessary by Glaxo Pharmaceuticals UK, led to new HR policies in support. In Glaxo Pharmaceuticals UK, the main emphasis was on values, attitudes and increasing collaborative behaviour, whereas in Cadbury UK the change programme was more formal and structural. Both cases show that structural change strategies can only be carried through with the aid of change programmes aimed at both helping people to be more adaptive and developing the required new attitudes and behaviours. This is a major contribution from HRM to achieving strategic objectives.

THE DETERMINING VARIABLES

In our search for a 'general theory' to explain HRM, the three different levels of analysis have been shown to impact on the HR function and role. The discussion on organisational structure within this chapter has revealed some of the ways in which the different levels of analysis interrelate. The social, political and economic context (sometimes described as the 'institutional' context or the business environment) creates pressures for change and offers opportunities for organisations to exploit. Our level of analysis is the organisational field (Di Maggio and Powell 1983) and this type of explanation, which draws on institutionalisation theory (Zucker 1987), stresses the way organisations have to be structured in order to meet societal needs as expressed by institutions and by economic forces.

The Williamson thesis can be modified to the extent that, although the provision of goods and services is organised either by markets or hierarchies, or some mixture of these forms of relationship, the organisational structures and processes which are created for this purpose are themselves subject to wider pressures, including political and social institutional pressures. This is well represented by the recently privatised or neo-privatised organisations in our sample. Including British Airways and BT, seven of the 30 companies fell into this category. The fact that they were privatised in the first place was partly because of a change to a Conservative Government in 1979 and the consequences of a particular political ideology. The restructuring and total repositioning to which each of these organisations has been subjecting itself has been explained by the senior managers in every case by the need 'to be competitive', 'to cope with change and customer demand' and 'to be efficient'. The responses, for example the creation of divisional structures, could be described as a consequence of environmental pressures towards isomorphism, that is the adoption of an organisational form which is common in the organisational field. ScottishPower, for example, was highly integrated as a power-generation, distribution and retail organisation, and at the time of our research was trying to formulate a divisional structure. It was experiencing all the difficulties of subdividing units, deciding on levels of authority and looking at the question of what HR policies should be common and what should be divisional. Benchmarking with other organisations is common in this stage and organisations which are newly formed have a strong pressure to emulate what is regarded as 'best practice'.

Some departments within companies are more subject to environmental pressure than others (Westney 1993). The human resource function, because of its role as interpreter of environmental pressure (e.g. laws, social conventions, norms and values) is just such a vulnerable unit. The role of interpreting requires the department to be in touch with what is required, but also places strains on the credibility of the function when challenged by managers who have a strong desire to maintain the *status quo*. One could say that it is via these kinds of departments that societal and institutional norms enter organisational life, and become internalised by organisation members. The 'business environment' in this sense is not 'out there' but is within people: the idea that man is in society, and society is in man (Berger 1966).

The differentiation argument of Lawrence and Lorsch always contained within it the need for integrating mechanisms. From this research the inculcation of company values and the legitimation of these values through the interpretive role of HRM is one process for integrating the company and for binding together the different levels of analysis. We will explore this issue further in the next chapter. The divisional structures observed here in our research have provided HRM with the opportunity to contribute to business strategy. This is because senior managers in organisations believe they must meet the demand from their customers to tailor their products and services to the customers' needs, in order to compete effectively. Organisational structure changes have therefore brought HRM into the fore as a means of delivering business strategy. The particular policy contributions were outlined in the previous chapter. This change in decision-making challenges Purcell's (1989) notion that HR strategies are necessarily third order strategies.

Because of the way the environment enters the organisation, HR strategies such as empowerment shape the structure and relationships, and adapt the attitudes and values of employees, forming a link back into what has been called the sentient level. The characteristic features of empowerment are that decisions are pushed down to the lowest levels possible, work groups are given the power to do a good job and an environment is created of high trust, in which learning and creativity are encouraged. Many of the organisations in our study were using semi-autonomous work groups, which made a considerable impact on working relationships. Decisions in these groups were left to group members, including the allocation of work, minor disciplinary matters, on-the-job training and quality-improvement activity. Changes in structure, when such changes are accompanied by new approaches to decision-making, therefore produce changes in management style and in the way employees perceive work. These are not normative strategies. The flattening of organisational structures results in larger spans of control. An effective response is therefore to grant greater autonomy to the groups of people who work together, and to encourage flexible working within those groups. One output from such a reorganisation was often said to be improved quality together with some reductions in costs.

The changes to which all the organisations in our study were subject were not carried out in an ordered way, from one steady state to another. The continuous processes of change, the misunderstandings and the renegotiations were in many cases part of an environment of continuous and competing pressures for change. The fact that chaos was not found is perhaps surprising. The integrating roles which managers play in these circumstances, and the strength of the organisation's culture are counter-balances to the forces of chaos. The shift towards the short-term in strategic planning and the more flexible, responsible organisation have nevertheless made working life far less comfortable. One major contribution that the HR function plays in the modern corporation, which should be recorded is to be both the catalyst for change and the regulator of working life: a role forced upon the function by the need for continuous organisational change.

BIBLIOGRAPHY

Berger, P. (1966) *Invitation to Sociology*, London: Penguin.

Burns, T. and Stalker, G. M. (1961) *The Management of Innovation*, London: Tavistock.

Clegg, S. (1990) *Modern organisations: organisation studies in the post-modern world*, London: Sage.

Cresap/BIM (1987) *The Effective Head Office*, report published jointly.

Di Maggio, P. J. and Powell, W. W. (1983) 'The iron cage revisited: Institutional isomorphisms and collective rationality in organizational fields', *American Sociological Review* 48, pp. 147–60.

Goold, M. and Campbell, A. (1986) *Strategies and Styles. The Role of the Centre in Managing Diversified Corporations*, Oxford: Blackwell.

Grahl, J. and Teague, P. (1991) 'Industrial Relations Trajectories and European Human Resource Management' in Brewster, C. and Tyson, S. (Eds) *International Comparisons in Human Resource Management*, London: Pitman Publishing.

Gramsci, A. (1971) *Selections from the Prison Notebooks*, London: Lawrence & Wishart.

Handy, C. (1978) *The Gods of Management*, London: Penguin.

Handy, C. (1989) *The Age of Unreason*, Boston: Harvard Business School Press.

Harrison, R. (1972) 'How to describe your organization', *Harvard Business Review*.

Hendry, C. (1994) *Human Resource Strategies for International Growth*, London: Routledge.

Hennart, J. F. (1993) 'Control in Multinational Firms: The role of price and hierarchy in organization theory and multinational corporations' in Ghoshal, S. and Westney, D. E. (Eds) *Organizational Theory and the Multinational Corporation*, London: Macmillan.

Hudson, R. (1989) 'Labour market changes and new forms of work in old industrial regions', *Environment and Planning Society and Space* 7, pp. 5–30.

Lash, S. (1988) 'Post-modernism as a regime of signification', *Theory, Culture and Society* 5 (2–3), pp. 311–36.

Lawrence, P. R. and Lorsch, J. W. (1967) *Organization and Environment: Managing Differentiation and Integration*, Boston: Harvard University Press.

Legge, K. (1978) *Power, Innovation and Problem-solving in Personnel Management*, London: McGraw-Hill.

Morgan, G. (1986) *Images of organization*, London: Sage.

Morgan, G. (1993) *Imaginization*, London: Sage.

Purcell, J. (1989) 'The impact of corporate strategy on human resource management' in Storey, J. (Ed) *New Perspectives on Human Resource Management*, London: Routledge.

Schumacher, E. F. (1973) *Small is Beautiful*, London: Blond and Briggs.

Thompson, J. D. (1967) *Organizations in Action*, New York: McGraw-Hill.

Tyson, S. and Kakabadse, A. (Eds) (1987) *Cases in Human Resource Management*, London: Heinemann.

van Houten, G. (1989) 'The implications of globalism: New management realities in Philips' in Evans, P., Doz, Y. and Laurent, A. (Eds) *Human Resource Management in International Firms*, London: Macmillan.

Westney, D. E. (1993) 'Institutionalization Theory and the Multinational Corporation' in Ghosal, S. and Westney, D. E. (Eds) *Organization Theory and the Multinational Corporation*, London: Macmillan.

Whitaker, A. (1992) 'The Transformation in Work. Post-Fordism revisited' in Reed, M. and Hughes, M. (Eds) *Rethinking Organizations*, London: Sage.

Williamson, O. E. and Ouchi, W. G. (1983) 'The markets and hierarchies programme of research: origins, implications and prospects' in Francis, A., Turk, J. and Willman, P. (Eds) *Power, Efficiency and Institutions*, London: Heinemann.

Wood, S. (1989) (Ed) *The Transformation of Work*, London: Unwin.

Woodward, J. (1958) *Management and Technology*, London: HMSO.

Woodward, J. (1965) *Industrial Organization Theory and Practice*, Oxford: Oxford University Press.

Zucker, L. G. (1987) 'Institutional Theories of Organization', *Annual Review of Sociology* 13, pp. 443–64.

CHAPTER 7

Human resource management models and roles

The research described in this book occurred in the midst of one of the worst recessions to hit the UK economy this century. The question arises therefore of how the human resource management role has changed as a consequence and whether the changes observed are likely to be permanent? The new agenda for Human Resource Management will, no doubt, soon be regarded as conventional wisdom: *'Tempora mutantur, et nos mutamur in illis'* times change, and we change with them. Many of those who are currently active in the field of HRM can recall the highs and lows of unemployment, the effects of strong trade union power and periods of high inflation. The particular combination of economic and social circumstances at the societal level of analysis gives rise to the conditions prevailing at the organisational level of analysis. The recession of the early 1990s has proved to be a watershed since it coincided with a time when all UK political and social institutions were under review. At such a period one would expect the new human resource management agenda to be debated and its formulation is thus emerging (Tyson and Witcher 1994).

The second edition of *Evaluating the Personnel Function* (Tyson and Fell 1992) set out what constituted the 1990s' new realism. The Atkinson type of 'flexible firm' with its new contractual relationships, the impact of the social charter and European legislation, high levels of long-term unemployment, the break-up of the old organisational structures, and the changes initiated outside the personnel function (for example, the total quality movement, business process redesign and reorganisation into flatter structures) have shifted the function on to new ground (Tyson and Fell 1992). Our original notion that there were three main models of the personnel function prevailing in the UK, the 'clerk of works', 'contracts manager' and the 'architect', has stood the test of time. However, new models may be emerging and we are clear that more than one model may exist within an organisation, a point that becomes all the more relevant when the models of the personnel function are changing.

The issues which dominate discussion on Human Resource Management as an occupation centre around: the delegation to line management of work areas previously claimed by Human Resources specialists; the question of what activities should be devolved to SBUs and what should be kept in the centre; the nature of the employment contract; the role of Human Resource Management in change, managing acquisitions, mergers and collaborative ventures; the subcontracting of the function; performance standards and competencies; and the strategic role to be performed in the face of such changes.

At first, it seemed that in the late 1980s, the 'contracts manager' model with its strong emphasis on industrial relations systems and processes was disappearing. However, the 1990s is seeing a new need for industrial relations management, partly through the collectivist legislation emanating from Brussels and partly because British trade union membership has held up well during the recession, especially in the public sector, and the unions are merging to become bigger and stronger, and are seeking to be better managed. The complexities of the many different types of employment contract (including European contracts) which the Human Resources function has to handle are literally re-emphasising the 'contract manager' role for the function. The functional devolution to line managers has also encouraged the 'clerk of works' model where a minimal range of services is required.

Although it may have seemed that time was on the side of the 'architect' model, the 1990s has seen the managed culture become a part of general management. Where strong cultures remain, the core of workers sustain the culture and the problem becomes how to inculcate the culture in a rapidly changing group of temporary, sub-contracted, and part-time employees. The 'architect' model was also conceived as a proponent of the utilisation of the people assets, or the management of the costs to the best advantage for the firm. Outsourcing and joint ventures therefore naturally fit the ethos of the 'architect' model.

HUMAN RESOURCE MANAGEMENT MODELS AND CHANGING ORGANISATIONS

The changes at the societal level have produced new organisational forms and this has put pressure on the adopted approach to corporate governance. If we take the Goold and Campbell typology, the majority of companies in our sample were either financial control or strategic planning types. The personnel function as described from the corporate, head office perspective was analysed in our study to show that, as one might expect, the majority fell into the 'architect' category. From the evidence, the cases can be analysed as shown in Table 7.

Table 7: Personnel function according to strategic type of corporation

| Corporate office approach | Personnel function model | | |
	Clerk of works	Contracts manager	Architect
Financial control	3	7	2
Strategic planning		5	7
Strategic control			6

The results can be explained in terms of the definition of the six coinciding models so far described. There is a diversity of approaches possible for financial control companies. This is reflected in the different levels at which the human resource function operates. This can be strategic at the SBU level. However, concerns with financial results and short-term solutions favour the 'clerk of works' or the 'contracts manager' models because corporate head office acts as a buffer between the SBU and the market-place. Thus, market disciplines are shielded from the SBUs which can maintain the traditional IR practices for longer. Similarly, very stable businesses encourage the 'architect' model, if they are large and well managed. Strategic control companies often have a main product range, or a unified structure of control, of which human resource management is a key part. Long-term strategies are followed which favour the 'architect' type. There may be less growth in these companies, and as a consequence, less change, which also encourages the 'architect' model.

I have already commented upon the emerging importance of divisional human resource management roles. The shift towards local management control has raised the status of divisional boards, and it is at the divisional or company level that detailed strategies are typically formulated. In a recent survey, reported by Purcell, the presence of a Personnel Director on the main board was shown to be associated with the strategic involvement of the function (Purcell 1994). He shows that only 30 per cent of companies with two or more employees in the private sector had a director on the board, but in these companies (many of them foreign-owned), the personnel function played an active part in career development and in pay decisions, and in a range of sophisticated activities in such fields as communication policies and equal opportunities.

What is not clear from those results is whether the presence of the Human Resource Director/Personnel Director on the board was the cause or the consequence of the sophisticated human resource policies and strategies pursued. Equally, the Director may not be a personnel specialist, but be undertaking human resource management work along with other duties, or have come to the role from a different function. What the evidence does seem to indicate is that when organisations take human resource management seriously, they ensure that there is someone on the main Board who carries the human resource management portfolio. In the centre versus the divisions debate, Purcell argues that 'the type of personnel management permitted or encouraged at the local level will be found in the Corporate Office.' (p. 26.) Such certainty does not admit the possibility of local company cultures, of devolved responsibilities and of local management autonomy. In companies as diverse as Cadbury-Schweppes, Vickers, BAT, RTZ and Scottish and Newcastle there were considerable differences in approach at local or divisional level, which was seen as a sign of strength rather than weakness by the companies concerned.

CENTRE VERSUS DIVISIONS

The critical issue when discussing the human resource role is what is kept at the centre in personnel strategies and policies, and what is devolved, a question which is reminiscent of Peters' and Waterman's idea of 'Simultaneous tight/loose properties in organisation design'. The human resource policy areas most commonly kept in the centre, according to our survey, were management development, organisation structure design, industrial relations strategy, senior executive pay, and a more general responsibility for 'organisational climate'.

For most organisations in our survey, there was a strong perception that high-potential managers were corporate property who should be developed and maintained by the central HR function, which usually had responsibility for management development activity at the central level. The importance attached to this aspect of the corporate function was demonstrated by chief executive and main board interest. Management or career development committees were found which oversaw the development of the top cadre and those earmarked to enter this élite band. There were several reasons for this. There was a felt need to keep control over the talent which maintained the competitive advantage. There were also technical reasons for controlling management development from the centre: this facilitated movement between divisions, the budget for top talent development could be shared between operating divisions, and the competencies required by senior executives might better be seen from the top down. It is argued that as executives move towards divisional board or main board level the thinking challenge changes and becomes more conceptual, more politically sensitive and outward focused, with a premium on process skills. Finally, there is a connection between management development and the organisational culture: the central head office staff wish to ensure that appropriate cultural values are imparted to high-flying managers and to ensure there are developmental processes which will provide succession and the continuation of the business.

Organisational design is more easily seen as a central role. The strategic reasons include responsibilities of the chairman and the CEO to determine the accountabilities of those reporting to them, and the structural vulnerability for merger or takeover of the business. Perhaps the most important of all is the central need to create an organisational structure which will deliver against the corporate mission. None of these central requirements naturally places organisational design within the purview of the HR function.

From our evidence the staff function for head office senior staff performed by HR directors can give them an entrée to organisational design issues. Who is responsible for what post and who should report in to each person are questions which take in the personalities of the person concerned, the way information will flow throughout the organisation, the complementarity of team skills, and questions about spans of control and the grouping of activities, upon all of which HR specialists should be able to give informed comment. At the broader level, there may also be debates about work organisations (for example 'empowerment', learning organisations and work group autonomy) and organisational cultures which are central to HR philosophies and policies.

It is fair to say that not all the organisations within our study were able to articulate an industrial relations strategy from the centre, nor did they all wish to do so. Where policy areas were concerned which form part of industrial relations, such as communication policies, these were often directives and policy guidelines from the centre. Of course, in some cases employers had taken up what amounted to an ideological position *vis-à-vis* trade unions. In most instances, the objectives from the centre were negative, aimed at restricting industrial relations problems so that there was no adverse impact on any strategies followed by the business. The industrial relations climate was treated as part of the overall climate or 'culture'. At the technical level, the centre sometimes took an interest in the likely impact of settlements on total costs (especially any long-range impact of pay decisions), and generally tried to persuade divisions to avoid taking hostages to fortune.

A related area where the centre was always interested in divisional or SBU HR activity was senior executive pay. Eventually salary scales must interlock, and those who report to the board will be expecting consistency of treatment. The reward structure represents the status structure in the organisation, and the impact of rewards is usually so great that the organisational climate or culture is bound to be affected by reward changes. Incentives and organisational climate are also closely linked together. The values espoused by senior managers at the centre are therefore influences upon reward structures throughout the organisation.

The 'climate' or culture within the various organisations was also of concern to managers at the centre. The question: 'What kind of organisation are you?' has to be answered by all those who wish to influence the City, the shareholders and the general public in a satisfactory fashion. Even if detailed responsibility to answer this question has been devolved, there is still the notion that the Group as a whole should be at ease with itself. This avoidance of obvious dissonance should exclude certain negative possibilities, for example, 'we are not a dishonest organisation, we do not carelessly take risks, we protect shareholder interests', and so on. The ethics of business decision-making are increasingly coming into the public domain through the media, and in the companies surveyed we found ample evidence that minimum standards were set for operating companies from the centre, for example in such fields as equal opportunities. The difficulty comes in policing them without imposing bureaucratic procedures or stifling entrepreneurial effort.

One characteristic feature of senior human resource roles is the dual responsibilities to the board for the values and the almost philosophical aspects of managing the culture, such as management style and communication policies, combined with the entirely prosaic work of day-to-day practical problem-solving.

EFFECTS OF THE RECESSION ON HRM ROLES

Burke and Litwin (1992) argue that two sets of variables are likely to influence organisational performance, which they term transformational and transactional.

- **Transformational variables** are concerned with the boundary between the organisation and its environment. Here we are considering such factors as have been described in the framework earlier as existing at societal level, for example levels of unemployment in specific labour markets, and the broad societal changes initiated by government ideology.

- **Transactional variables**, on the other hand, exist within the organisational level of analysis: these are the sub-systems such as managerial procedures, personnel systems and the motivation of staff.

Burke and Litwin suggest that transformational variables are the more important and long lasting of the two.

If we consider the HRM role, it has moved from being predominantly based on the 'clerk of works' or 'contracts manager' model in the 1970s and early 1980s to being mostly an 'architect' or espoused 'architect' in the mid to late 1980s. This was the period of the boom, sandwiched between the two recessions which began and ended the 1980s. During that time personnel managers used a variety of strategies to improve productivity (for example the Atkinson flexible firm model) and sought to change the nature of the industrial relations climate. These 'transactional' techniques served them so well that they began to adopt new titles in the 'Human Resource Manager' mode. They had become or wished their functions to be defined as the 'architect' model. However, the second recession has produced a different impact. Companies have been going through transformational change, in order to survive. The policies which produced productivity gains in the 1980s, may still be paying off, but the changes required now are more fundamental, being rooted in the organisational design and the approach to contracting, as much as in detailed policies.

The three main influences on HRM from the recession are the changes to planning and corporate strategy creation, the need to operate organisations in a climate of permanent readiness to change, and the devolution of responsibility down to the lowest level possible, to be close to customer demands. These changes have been fostered by macro, societal-level changes to the economy, the uncertainty in the political and economic environment and increased global competition. The accent on change and the organisation-wide scope for change has brought line managers closer to the HR function. Integration between business goals and HR strategies has led to the integration of HR management with the senior line managers responsible for changes.

The move towards more diversification, and hence divisionalisation, has also had the effect of pushing HR managers to divisional level, where they report to senior divisional staff, or the appropriate SBU manager. The constant pressure for change and the need in particular for transformational change has given senior HR managers the opportunity to engage in high-profile work. Hence one outcome from the recession has been the bifurcation in the models adopted. There are clearly demands on companies for senior change-management roles, where there is a programme of interventions to manage. This 'architect' type function may be seen to be acting strategically because the HR staff are in the forefront of managing the changes. By contrast, the 'clerk of works' model persists because there is basic personnel administration to be done, which may be performed by specialists because of the legal aspects to this work. For example, ensuring equal opportunity rules are followed in personnel selection, adopting best practice in communication policies, and the like. From our research we can say that the positioning of each HR function in the organisation does not necessarily follow the logical sequence of the models. Divisional level HR directors may be performing in the architect mode whilst the HR director at head office is following essentially a clerk of works range of activities. The contracts manager model has also survived the recession but operates more in the style of a technical specialist who offers advice, a behind-the-scenes role, perhaps now more closely associated with the clerk of works – an adjunct to senior management, not expected to take the lead as was the case in the 1970s, when the preservation of harmony within the workforce was accepted as a legitimate organisational goal.

The models themselves change and adapt within organisations as changes take place. The 'architect' model has two advanced versions developing, one as change agent, the other as business manager. The change agent is employed to help bring about large-scale organisational change. One unintended piece of evidence from our research was the number of changes which occurred to people in the most senior HR role. Of the 30 companies in our survey, over half had changed their HR director in the three-year period of the research. In a number of cases this was part of a desire to change the people at the top in order to change the organisation. Rather than ask the personnel director who has spent his or her life building up the existing HR infrastructure embodying the old values and priorities, a 'new broom' is brought in to sweep away the old emotional baggage. In any case, such an old retainer would have had difficulty envisioning a new future. The new HR director can remove outmoded policies and concentrate on supporting the new business strategy, even if as a change agent the appointment is on a short-term contract, or as a self-employed consultant.

The new business manager version of the 'architect' model puts the emphasis on integration between human resource strategies and business strategies. The business manager is seeking new opportunities, new ways to improve the utilisation of the people in the business. It is a role which can be and is well performed by people who are not trained as HR specialists. This senior role places a premium on contribution to all elements in the business strategy, whilst interpreting the strategy downwards to HR specialists within the functions in such a way that they can propose programmes to achieve the business objectives. 'Managing' the process becomes like any other senior managerial role: one of setting priorities, organising, agreeing and monitoring budgets, and measuring outcomes. The 'business manager' version has brought two distinct advantages: credibility with senior colleagues, and an orientation to relevance, and value for money. One impact of the recession has been to draw attention to these sensitive areas. The 1990s' recession therefore gave a boost to senior managers taking on the HR portfolio.

STAGES OF ORGANISATIONAL GROWTH

A number of authors have taken the dimension simple–complex as a necessary condition which arises from organisational growth. For Baird and Meshoulam (1988) the argument is that, as organisations grow and change, different integration processes become necessary. They suggest that increasing complexity in HRM takes the function through five stages: 'initiation', 'functional growth', 'controlled growth', 'functional integration' and 'strategic integration'. Similarly, Hendry and Pettigrew (1992) commented on the maturity of the organisation and business complexity as causes of organisational structure complexity and problematic industrial relations. Confirmation that the stage of business development correlates with HRM practices was found by Buller and Napier (1993). Their empirical study was a postal survey of 41 companies in the USA from which a general strategy–HR integration scale was constructed. Their results showed differences between fast growth firms and a random sample of other firms: 'Entrepreneurial, fast-growth firms tended to have more informal and loosely connected HR systems' (p. 85). Rather unsurprisingly, they saw employee selection as a primary need. They also discovered that the overall level of strategic integration was higher in the random sample firms than in fast-growing firms.

One classic framework for examining organisational growth and change was propounded by Greiner (1972). His well-known diagram is shown in Fig. 7, where the potential crises at each stage of growth are supposed to prompt a new direction, which takes the organisation forward.

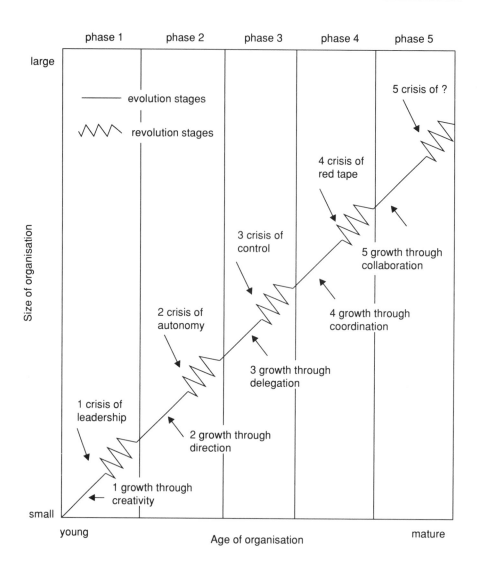

Fig. 7 The five phases of growth
(*Source*: Greiner 1972) Reproduced with the permission of the President and Fellows of Harvard College, from the *Harvard Business Review*, July/August 1972.

Baird and Meshoulam's growth phases of the HR function fit into Greiner's various stages as demonstrated in Table 8, where the links to other research are shown.

Table 8: Comparing research on HR and growth

Greiner	Baird and Meshoulam	Buller and Napier	Hendry and Pettigrew
Stages of growth	*Stages of HR development*	*Integration of HR & BS*	*HR orientation*
Creativity	Initiation	Informal	Personnel administration
Direction	Functional growth		
Delegation	Controlled growth		
Coordination	Functional integation		
Collaboration	Strategic integration	Strategic integration	Strategic integration

small

young

mature

large

The direction stage, according to Greiner, produces a hierarchical departmental structure, with budgeting systems, standards and incentives. This is entirely consistent with Baird and Meshoulam's notion that functional growth occurs at this period. It is also consistent with the idea that in small, entrepreneurial businesses a more informal style has eventually to give way to a more formal, functional structure, as was the case with a company such as Laura Ashley. Often in this phase the strong entrepreneurial founder regrets the passing of the personal involvement which is implied by introducing 'professional' experts in the various management disciplines. One reaction is for the founder, or the family, to keep control over financial decision-making, sometimes to an absurd level of detail. The delegation phase thus is the period when greater responsibility has to be given to managers and the HR emphasis is on control systems. In this way, HR could be seen to be helping to resolve the crises at each stage. The coordination stage, where there are formal planning procedures, strong central services and control over capital expenditure is partly solved by functional integration. The stages of HR development proposed by Baird and Meshoulam could therefore be interpreted as HR growth arising as a consequence of the organisational need to respond to crises at each stage.

The move towards strategic integration is implicitly necessary according to these researchers, as a product of organisational 'maturity', of the product life-cycle and the growth in numbers employed, as well as the complexity of the organisational structure needed to manage the more sophisticated organisation. This conclusion still leaves us with a number of questions. What happens to the development of the HR function in organisations which are already larger and 'mature', and have been so for many years? One might also enquire whether, if managers reduce the organisation's size to simplify the product range, delayer or flatten the organisational structure, there is a regression of the personnel function? The evidence from our research indicates that there is no natural progression from the 'clerk of works' model to the 'architect' model. The changing organisational context determines which model is appropriate and, as the context changes, so ultimately will the model. One effect of the recession has been to force change on organisations, hence the shifting nature of the function. The role of HRM, to represent societal and economic changes, and to reinterpret these at the organisational level, explains why at each stage of growth HRM has to change to resolve the organisational crisis and to reinterpret reality to organisation members by reshaping the function.

THE NEW ORGANISATION DEVELOPMENT

Pettigrew and Whipp (1991) argue that there are five key factors which are taken into account in successful change management: environmental assessment; leading change; linking strategic and operational change; dealing with human resources as assets and liabilities; and managing the coherence of the process. There was ample evidence from our case study companies that these processes were occurring, but not in any neat or easily distinguishable way. The linkage between the strategic and the operational, and the related issue of ensuring coherence were the most significant matters for managers in our study when they looked back on the change processes they had been managing. The degree of change and the different kinds of environmental pressures are producing a new form of organisation development (OD).

Organisations are changing so frequently that it would be correct to say they are reinventing themselves as they shift to respond to societal pressures. Among our study sample, the recently-privatised businesses offer a good example. In each of these organisations the business has been relaunched. British Airways and BT, for example, have made enormous efforts to change management style and to refocus the entire staff on customer needs. At the same time, they have been delayering and taking costs out of the organisation, with a view to becoming more competitive and the need to satisfy their shareholders. The other privatised businesses have been following a similar pattern.

In each case a new OD approach has been created which places the human resource management activity centre-stage in the work on transformational change, typified by changing structures, changing cultures and through management development programmes. New memberships in the top teams, including new HR directors, were also features of new culture creation (as in the cases of British Airways, ScottishPower and BNFL). In addition, the process of strategic planning for these businesses, in a freer atmosphere than previously existed in the public sector, has made managements rethink the way their company should be positioned in the business environment, allowing them to reconsider the question, 'What business should we be in?'

Having begun to reposition their old public sector organisations as new corporations, in different markets, managements then had to move the HR function to the transactional level, in order to change the employee resourcing, development and relations sub-systems to support transformational change. The new OD links transformational change programmes with the work at the micro-organisational level in all the organisations in our survey. Two major problems reported from virtually all the companies in our survey were how to cope with middle and senior managers who either blocked change, or went to the other extreme of becoming addicted to change, and how to avoid inoculating against change the front-line staff, who interact with customers or who make the products. These varying reactions of senior staff seem to arise from the continuous stress induced by constant pressure for change upon change. One reaction is to avoid responsibility and to avoid thinking through the implications of change at a personal level. Another reaction can produce the opposing behaviour of addiction to the pace and to the adrenalin which flows when urgency for change is invoked by top management. Some managers exhibit these symptoms by their desire for endless unproductive meetings, working through weekends, anxiously using the new 'correct' vocabulary (often without understanding what it means) and showing the signs of stress – irritability, irrational behaviour, disturbed sleep and so on. For others, a kind of cynicism combines with resentment, and results in changes only being cosmetic, not accepted or internalised. The 'we've heard it all before' syndrome is common also amongst staff who have been put through so many change programmes that they are enured to them. They will have seen so many glitzy presentations and addresses by the Chairman or CEO (on video or in person), each one explaining the long-term aims and the importance of changing, and hinting at the dire consequences of not changing; have had their jobs retitled; their reporting lines altered; and have met dozens of consultants brought in to report to the board on what is required, that these methods have ceased to be effective.

The 'new OD' has therefore to be based around the reality of the need for change, at the workplace. This entails making the work group semi-autonomous, with responsibility for training, quality, work allocation and sometimes for recruitment into the group and the disciplining of group members. By making the work groups the central unit around which relationships are managed, companies reinforce local-level initiatives in communications and strengthen local-level bargaining. It could be argued that this is not new: OD work, especially as conceived by the Tavistock School, has always seen semi-autonomous work groups as one element in improving the responsiveness of working people to change. However, what does seem to be new is the confluence of so many reinforcing policies, for example total quality management, policies on recognition of employee ideas and increased direct, formal upward-communications. Quality circles, group bonus schemes and briefing groups may not be new, but as tools they can be combined into coherent policies aimed at producing a changed management philosophy.

One objective for such change is to bring the work group close to the customer: to improve the organisation's flexibility in responding to consumer needs (as in the case, for example, of Coats Viyella's production groups); to improve training in high quality; to improve utilisation and to give employees a sense of belonging (as in the case of Rolls-Royce cars, Vickers); and as a way of initiating change and putting pressure on managers to change (as in the case of Glaxo Pharmaceuticals UK). The consequences for organisations of this kind of work group role, together with flatter structures so the groups report to more senior managers, are considerable. While moving companies to this position may seem difficult, there is no going back once the new style and structure are adopted. A move from a hierarchy to a market-driven structure is likely to be inevitable for commercial organisations.

SKILLS AND COMPETENCIES

The changes described in this chapter may seem to put line managers back in the driving seat. Although the kinds of large-scale change required for transforming organisations must be led by top management because such actions fundamentally change the nature of the organisation, the requirement for a range of enabling strategies means HRM is at the heart of the change. One feature of culture change is the centrality of a new 'enabling' climate for new employee relationships to grow, new roles to be accepted and for the structures and systems which deliver output and sales to come to the fore. There is in this respect an urgent need for the sub-systems in all the main HR policy areas to support the changes. The skills required for HR interventions are of a high order, combining the visionary with the practical, with the analytical competencies to judge what is necessary and the political skills to carry change through.

In the last decade, private and public sector organisations have enthusiastically adopted a competency-based approach to delineating the knowledge, skills and understanding required for successful performance. Taking forward ideas originally developed by McBer Consulting in the USA (Boyatzis 1982), there is the notion that one could describe particular skills as behaviours to be researched and recorded as a standard. This has been used to base appraisal systems, performance management systems, succession planning arrangements, development activities and even overall utilisation strategies. This approach has found an institutional champion in the Management Charter Initiative, which has promoted the idea that national standards for management work should be set, to which all management qualifications should be attached. Lead bodies, such as the Institute of Personnel Management (now the Institute of Personnel and Development (IPD)), were asked to produce standards in each specialist area.

From 1992 to 1994 a Personnel Standards Lead Body deliberated and researched, to produce national standards in the human resource management field for Personnel for the Scottish Vocational Qualifications and National Vocational Qualifications. The lead bodies are then being formed into occupational standards councils to monitor and develop the standards. The Lead Body used an extended version of functional analysis which concentrated on the processes by which the elements integrated into organisational needs as well as performing a function for the organisation. This body sponsored a number of research projects which revealed that practitioners valued vocational qualifications, and that sub-specialisms were difficult to distinguish within the HR field. The ratio of specialists to generalists was:

Mainly generalists	34%
Mainly specialists	15%
Mixture of specialists/generalists	51% (McKiddie 1994)

While confirming the constant change to which HR is currently subjected, the surveys also revealed the increasing integration of UK work within line management. Areas which were identified where improvements in competence were required were in communications, development, internal resourcing and identifying potential. The competences which were finally agreed are shown in Table 9.

The criticisms which can be levied against the competency-based approach are the tendency towards bureaucracy and the static nature of the concept. Most competency descriptions remain just that; descriptions which cannot be used analytically because they do not show in what circumstances the competency should be applied, how, when and to what extent. With the refreshing exception of the strategy cluster, the latest list of competences from the Lead Body is remarkably similar to the list produced as a chart by Moxon in 1951. Such lists are influential, as many personnel departments were organised along the functional lines described by Moxon, whose categories were: employment, wages, joint consultation, health and safety, welfare and training.

In our recent research we distinguished three main roles under which there were distinctive competencies required.

Table 9: Competences for Personnel NVQs

Strategy and the organisation
- contribution to organisation strategy
- personnel strategy
- organisation structure and process
- culture and values

Enhanced performance
- performance management
- enhance capability
- long-term individual development
- team development

Resourcing
- resource planning
- recruitment
- internal resourcing
- career resourcing
- release
- sub-contractual
- voluntary staff

Relations with employees
- commitment to change
- communication
- staff welfare
- compliance
- negotiation
- consultation, discipline and grievance
- equality
- health and safety

Compensation and benefits
- reward strategy
- reward criteria
- terms and conditions
- pay
- benefits

(*Source:* McKiddie 1994 and Personnel Standards Lead Body)

HR roles	Competencies required – when and how to:
Strategic	• analyse strategic plans according to people requirements; • integrate HRM strategies within corporate and SBU plans, and how to create coherence between the elements in the HR functional plan; • utilise people as assets and to control labour costs; • develop people as assets; • analyse organisational change needs; • advise on acquisitions and mergers; • identify talent; • work with top teams on team issues.
Tactical	• implement initiatives; • manage relationships with senior line managers; • use policies to achieve the 'right' employee relations climate; • manage change, including 'downsizing'; • manage culture with senior line managers; • market the HR function.

HR roles   **Competencies required – when and how to:**

Operational   ● deliver good quality services;
● negotiate new service agreements with colleagues and other departments;
● firefight – cope with unexpected requirements, crises and emergencies;
● monitor/evaluate policies;
● disseminate information.

Given that organisations grow and change, there is a strong argument for different skills being required at each stage of development. This may explain why HR directors sometimes leave after initiating and carrying out transformational change. The pace of organisational change militates against adopting a similar skill range throughout working life. The really important competencies therefore reside in the analytical ability of the HR specialists – the ability to analyse what is needed at each stage and to seek appropriate solutions. The purpose in seeking a general theory of HRM is to assist the practitioner who needs frameworks and models in order to analyse the situations faced. The internal consultancy skills needed now combine with board membership skills for those at the top, where HR Directors are often the confidant of the Chief Executive, and where the Director is often the staff officer for senior executives.

The erosion of the 'professional' image of HRM as a separate occupation – a profession in the same sense as medical practitioners, lawyers and accountants can claim to be – is of concern to the professional association. Line management responsibility for HR is growing, on the evidence, and there is also the possibility of outsourcing parts of the HR function. The way British managers have become divided into a number of separate 'professional' occupational groups is a peculiarly Anglo-Saxon phenomenon. The 'clubbishness' of this approach may suit the British character, but 'professionalising' as a strategy for organisations of 'professional' practitioners serves two distinct functions. First, by creating a 'qualifying association' they are seeking to restrict entry, in order to improve the standard of work and to enhance the status, knowledge and power of their members (Millerson 1964, Watson 1977, Tyson 1979). Secondly, they are proclaiming a moral status, a set of standards of conduct and an attitude which may set them apart from others or at best will establish standards of conduct based on a shared perception of the moral order (Wilensky 1964). Much of the soul-searching which occurred when the IPM merged with the ITD to become the IPD in 1994 could be attributed to the apparent threat of loss of identity which members suffered and the worry that they would cease to have the same 'professional' status which they believed they had previously enjoyed.

Other European countries do not have the same organisational structure for their specialist occupations. In France the Association Nationale des Directeurs et Chefs de Personnel (ANDCP) has helped to create personnel management programmes in the Technical Universities, as has the Swedish SPF, but neither has sought to offer qualifications in its own right. Similarly the German DGFP provides educational seminars, publishes information and encourages communication between members, as do US associations such as The Society for Human Resource Management. Only the IPD has gone down the route of creating a network of qualifications, almost seeking to instigate a licence to practice.

The need for professional associations in the IPD mould seems to be a function of the educational system and the educational standards. Evidence on the education and training of HR specialists throughout Europe shows that, in the UK, as compared to other countries, a high proportion of graduates in personnel management have arts/humanities degrees and a high proportion of the total have no university degree at all (Tyson and Wikander 1994). One explanation therefore is that the professional association in the UK has had to act as a 'finishing school', educating non-specialists into the specialism and providing a basic management graduate-level education for those without a first degree.

Continuous change for managers prompts a need for continuous professional development (CPD). All European professional personnel associations try to meet these needs, and the IPM has been cited as an example of best practice in this regard (Madden and Mitchell 1993), since it recommends at least 30 days per annum be spent on CPD, and has built CPD into its membership qualifications. All professional managerial groups must learn how to learn and cannot rely on the knowledge gained years ago in their professional training. Schön (1983, 1987) talks of 'artistry' as a feature of any professional expertise, which is gained by 'knowing-in-action' and 'reflection-in-action'. In thinking through and reflecting on what is required, rather than applying routines and knowledge uncritically, managers learn how to use their competencies. Learning through working requires learning ways to understand what is happening in the company, and to be able to put appropriate solutions into place. The knowledge which HR practitioners need thefore, includes learning how to learn and the persistence of certain HR models may derive from the structuring of learning opportunities within the organisation. Transformational change helps to sweep away the old models within organisations and makes it possible for HR managers to learn how to change, and therefore to create new models.

THE NEW HRM

What will be the features of HRM at the start of the next millennium? Will the function have become so much a part of general management in most organisations that to regard personnel management as a separate profession with its own special competencies may appear an anachronism? The changes to organisations discussed in Chapter 6 have brought widescale change to occupational structures. The last recession forced businesses to reduce headquarters staff and to rethink the role of divisions. The need to involve people in managing their own work through autonomous work groups fits neatly into delayered structures, where local management has direct control over labour costs and quality. New information technology has put personnel data on every manager's desk, obviating specialist HR reports and enabling even career management to be handled locally (as in the case of the NatWest Bank).

The outsourcing of HR is already a reality. Consultants have long performed HR specialist roles, introducing job evaluation schemes, performance management systems, headhunting, managing outplacement and helping organisations through change. 'Architect' model HR functions can only survive if they can demonstrate added value to the top team at corporate, divisional or SBU level. This chapter has begun to explore the origins of these trends. From the research described here, HR at the top level is surviving through its role in change management. Transformational change offers the chance to shift the accepted wisdom within the organisation and move the philosophy of management on to new ground: a symbolic as well as an action-oriented role.

BIBLIOGRAPHY

Baird, C. and Meshoulam, I. (1988) 'Managing two fits of strategic human resource management', *Academy of Management Review*, Vol. 13, No. 1, pp. 116–18.

Boyatzis, R. E. (1982) *The Competent Manager. A Model of Effective Performance*, Chichester: John Wiley.

Buller, P. F. and Napier, N. K. (1993) 'Strategy and Human Resource Management integration in fast growth versus other mid-sized firms', *British Journal of Management*, Vol. 4, No. 2, pp. 77–90.

Burke, W. W. and Litwin, G. H. (1992) 'A causal model of organisation performance and change', *Journal of Management*, Vol. 18, No. 3, pp. 525-45.

Greiner, L. E. (1972) 'Evolution and revolution as organisations grow', *Harvard Business Review*, July/August, pp. 37–46.

Hendry, C. and Pettigrew, A. (1992) 'Patterns of Strategic Change in the Development of Human Resource Management', *British Journal of Management*, Vol. 3, No. 3, pp. 137–56.

McKiddie, T. (1994) 'Personnel NVQs: Preparing for Take-Off', *Personnel Management*, February, pp. 30–3.

Madden, C. A. and Mitchell, V. A. (1993) *Professions, standards and competences. A survey of continuing education in the professions*, University of Bristol.

Millerson, G. (1964) *The Qualifying Associations*, London: Routledge & Kegan Paul.

Moxon, G. R. (1951) *The Functions of a Personnel Department*, London: Institute of Personnel Management.

Pettigrew, A. and Whipp, R. (1991) *Managing change for competitive success*, Oxford: Blackwell.

Purcell, J. (1994) 'Personnel earns a place on the board', *Personnel Management*, February, pp. 26–9.

Schön, D. A. (1983) *The Reflective Practitioner*, New York: Basic Books.

Schön, D. A. (1987) *Educating the Reflective Practitioner*, San Francisco: Jossey-Bass.

Tyson, S. (1979) *Specialists in Ambiguity*, unpublished PhD thesis, University of London.

Tyson, S. and Fell, A. (1992) *Evaluating the Personnel Function* (2nd Edition), Cheltenham: Stanley Thornes.

Tyson, S. and Wikander, L. (1994) 'The Education and Training of Human Resource Managers in Europe' in Brewster, C. and Hegewisch, A. *Policy and Practice in European Human Resource Management*, London: Routledge.

Tyson, S. and Witcher, M. (1994) 'Human Resource Strategy: Emerging from the Recession', *Personnel Management*, August.

Watson, T. J. (1977) *The Personnel Managers*, London: Routledge & Kegan Paul.

Wilensky, H. (1964) 'The professionalization of everyone?', *American Journal of Sociology*, Vol. 70, pp. 138–58.

CHAPTER 8

Towards a general theory of human resource management

Alexander the Great died at the age of 33 in Babylon in 323 BC, having during the previous twelve years of his reign, and starting with an army a mere 50 000 strong, conquered Asia Minor, Palestine, Egypt, Mesopotamia, Persia, Central Asia and the Punjab. It is difficult to imagine even our present-day captains of industry with all the modern technology at their command being able to cope with the challenges faced by Alexander and his men. 'Management science', as a reflective rhetoric bounded with many notions, concepts and theories which are not susceptible to proofs, and which are not aimed at practical, testable results, may not seem to be essential to such a task. While academics debate their theories, managers, like Alexander, must move on quickly, to conquer or be conquered.

Those who study management need to remember that management is the object rather than the subject to be studied. Management is a phenomenon, a set of power relationships within and between groups in organisations. Management action is about getting things done; it is a practical set of tasks, which seek to achieve work outcomes. As with any other form of social action, management can be studied from a variety of theoretical perspectives: sociological, psychological, as an economist, or in the context of any other of the social sciences. As Astley (1984) points out, the world of scientific ideas is separated from the world of management practice. Knowledge, he argues, is transmitted to managers by symbolic constructs. Management science is 'a highly subjective enterprise, concerned centrally with the formulation of ideas rather than with the reporting of objective truth' (p. 265).

Management science exists at an ideational level, and influences practising managers through the persuasive use of symbolic constructs, rhetoric and an appeal to intuition, to feelings, as well as to what managers may regard as 'common sense'. In other words, however scientifically rigorous the research presented to managers, unless the results accord with their own sense of realism and of what they regard as normally-occurring activity, such results will not be accepted.

Without a general agreement between researchers and practitioners on what constitutes the proof of a theory, idea or concept as firstly being true, and secondly being of value to the practitioners, the theories produced by researchers are most likely to be ignored by managers. Academic research can, of course, be of interest to other academics. In this case the interest is in impressing one's fellow scholars, achieving recognition and establishing a new 'truth' about some aspect of management. If, however, academics are only to communicate meaningfully with other academics, it would be sensible to see such work as a part of the particular social science discipline on which the research draws, such as industrial sociology, economics or psychology.

Management science still serves a function for practising managers. By helping managers to understand and interpret their everyday reality, and by giving managers a language to describe and explain what is happening to their work and to their lives, management research can influence the way managers think about their managerial work and themselves, their colleagues, bosses and employees. Research and management theories can justify and facilitate action in this way (Cummings 1983). Common sense theories are, after all, theories. If we accept that all people theorise about the world in which they live and attempt to understand it, we can agree with George Kelly that people are 'scientists' in their own right – seeking constantly to discover meaning and to explain reality as they experience it (Kelly 1955, Schutz 1970). The researcher's role may then be seen as to provide insights which will aid the everyday interpretations of reality and give them some meaning.

Alexander the Great was a man of action, but even he needed surveyors, engineers, architects, 'scientists', court officials and historians to accompany his army on their famous conquests. To give meaning to an enterprise requires the translation of one level of reality into another. Alexander's specialist functionaries were needed to make the adventures on which his army was engaged more than a foray into foreign lands. The 'staff' officials of early times performed a number of significant functions: recording events; putting down some kind of communications system; creating monuments, buildings and shrines in order to celebrate and to reinforce victories; to sacrifice to the Gods; and to communicate to those at home that these were the acts of a great leader. The 'staff' performed an important symbolic role: they began by assisting Alexander in creating the legend; and there is evidence that later he came to be regarded as a God, so powerful were the symbols they used (Wallbank 1981).

Theories in management studies seek to explain a reality to managers, and are thus descriptive models. However, to be of practical use theories must be sufficiently analytical of the relationship between phenomena to have some predictive value, as were the Oracles of early times. The appeal to managers of simple truths, well told, is as interpretations; as a way to help individuals to come to understand their work and their own lives. The necessity to convince managers (the objects of study) also serves an academic purpose: theories which managers can understand and which accord with their experience satisfy the criterion of adequacy (Schutz 1970). Briefly, this is one of Schutz's postulates designed to validate an interpretative sociology.

> 'Each term in a scientific model of human action must be constructed in such a way that a human act performed within the life by an individual actor in the way indicated by the typical construct would be understandable for the actor himself as well as for his fellow-men in terms of common-sense interpretations of everyday life.'
>
> (Schutz 1970, p. 279.)

THE CHARACTERISTICS OF A GENERAL THEORY

In his excellent summary of where HRM stands theoretically, Boxall (1992) has set out the two schools of HR theorising: as a 'matching school' which seeks to explain the 'fit' between business and human resource strategy; and the Harvard School which he sees as both prescriptive and analytical. The work of Guest in seeking to explain HRM as a set of policies was a response to the prescriptive aspects of the Harvard theory, whereas Pettigrew has taken the analytical route in his concentration on decision-making and organisational process.

The Harvard model of Beer *et al* (1984) not only takes a unitary frame of reference, but as in Hendry and Pettigrew's (1990) adaptation, there is a systems approach, a closed loop between the organisation and 'society'. Both models imply that situational factors such as the labour market, task technology or product market conditions are the inputs to HR policy choice – that there is then some 'process' within the organisation (which includes employee influence, culture and politics) from which HR policies emerge, which in turn influences the 'outer context' (Hendry and Pettigrew) or stakeholder interests (Beer *et al*). The loop is then closed from these social/stakeholder interests, linking back into the organisation as inputs or situational factors. Whilst this does produce a neat diagram, the thesis is not susceptible to proof. The outer context is so broad, and the situational factors so general, that no linkage between these and policy could be established with precision. It is also difficult to know what one would measure to prove the 'feedback' from an organisational to the societal level.

As Boxall puts it: 'The future academic strength of HRM will depend on how effectively present scholars dedicate themselves to building credible analytical frameworks – primarily at the level of the firm, but with the capability of providing an adequate disciplinary basis for comparative HRM' (p. 75). He goes on to point out that the greatest pay-off theoretically will come from 'explaining the relationship between strategic management and HRM as extensively as possible' (p. 75).

In this book, just such a stance has been taken. The intention throughout has been to set out how we can explain HRM by taking up the question of the contribution made by HRM to the achievement of strategic objectives for the organisation.

In Chapter 2 the need for models of HRM which explain its place in creating the symbolic order and the use of symbols within organisations was discussed. In Chapter 3 we examined the three levels of analysis as a framework for understanding the nature of organisational HR policy responses, and the impact of variables on changing HRM. Chapters 4, 5 and 6 have analysed the empirical evidence on the way HRM is used strategically within organisations, and in Chapter 7 the role of the HR function was described, to see how HRM as a specialist activity operates within the broad framework of variables shown to exist at each level of analysis. It is helpful here to summarise what we may conclude about any general theory of Human Resource Management from the indications of the features found throughout this book.

1 Any general theory of human resource management must explain HRM at the level of analysis where it occurs, which is the organisational level, but must also explain how this level is influenced by actions at the societal level and at the sentient level of organisation members.

2 Any general theory of human resource management must show how symbolic aspects of social action come to represent idea clusters on which organisation members act, and how such members come to believe in the symbols.

3 Any general theory of human resource management must explain why there are variations in HRM between organisations, as well as within organisations over periods of time.

4 Any general theory of human resource management must have sufficiently broad content to be descriptive/analytical of the typical routine or 'common-sense' actions of organisation members who are engaged in what they perceive as human resource management or personnel management activity. Hence such a theory should have some predictive quality.

5 Any general theory of human resource management must comply with the postulate of adequacy.

By bringing together these ideas we can begin to see the shape and direction of a general theory.

THE LEVEL OF ANALYSIS

The framework sketched in Chapter 3 expresses a set of relationships between three levels of analysis. Societal-level variables feed into organisational contingencies. The societal level includes the institutional, legal and governmental influences. These are the outward features shown by a society; they influence all organisations, albeit in different ways. The changes which occur at this level interact within a tension of interrelating pressures at the organisational level of analysis. From these pressures, new strategies flow and new organisational problems emerge. There are also internal pressures from within the organisation, and there are pressures from employee expectations and motivation. As a consequence there are individual or group interpretations of societal pressures.

In this book we have seen how the two recessions and the intervening boom period over the decade from 1980–90 produced a paradigmatic shift in the definition of managerial roles, as witness the shift in HR models and the extensive literature on the move from 'personnel management' to 'human resource management' (Legge 1987, Storey 1992). The powerful impact of societal forces for change have been stressed in the preceding chapters and we know that more often than not organisations do change their strategies in response to societal-level change (Zajac and Shortell 1989). Structural unemployment, changes to government ideologies and institutional changes at European level, for example, have encouraged new labour market strategies within organisations. The 'flexible firm', the issue of how and when to use non-standard hours, and the move from soft towards hard contracting are all examples of these powerful societal effects at the organisational level.

Within organisations, HRM is engaged in reinterpreting these societal changes with the intention to fit them into the organisation's strategic purpose, or to 'work around them'; to find ways to make the best use of trends and laws (Gospel 1992). For example, the secondary labour market, with its ready supply of people seeking work under a variety of contractual conditions, offers a choice of functional strategy. This choice is dependent on the availability, the skill base and cost of the resources, and is conditioned by the legality of the practices adopted.

One example here is the casualisation of work. There is now more weekend working, more part-time working, call-out work for people on zero-hours contracts, night work, temporary relief work and all kinds of 'casual' working arrangements. There has been a substantial increase in the number of women entering the labour market, wanting to work part-time or non-standard hours. Casual work has always existed amongst some occupational groups (for example, in catering, agriculture and the building industries), but a recent feature has been the spread of casual labour higher up the organisation, even to the employment of temporary executives.

HRM is engaged in a balancing act at the organisational level. For, in addition to meeting the demands of senior line managers, the function has at the same time to adjust HR policies in tune with the sentient level, to engage the commitment and the motivation of employees. After all, employees are the 'consumers' of HR policies. If such policies do not have the desired effect on employee behaviour, what is the value of the policy? The differentiation of a 'hard contract' for temporary or casual labour and a 'soft contract' for permanent labour represents the balance struck by the HR function in policy terms, and its attempt to cope with the differing sourcing strategies and the needs and relative power position of the two groups. In addition, the sourcing strategy will seek to appeal to the benefits in casual work – the advantages for those with childcare responsibilities, the benefits of a second income, and the appeal to those engaged in portfolio career-building. The long-term social and economic consequences for casual workers and for society are not an immediate concern for employers, who see advantages in reduced costs and flexibility from casual work. Following the Harvard model, there is a feedback loop here but not one that is beneficial to society: casual workers have no financial security, receive no long-term developmental training from their employers, are unable to save regularly and to obtain mortgages, and live with the anxiety their status brings.

At the organisational level of analysis, the HRM output may be seen in policies, and in HR philosophies, to borrow Schuler's term. However, the process of reinterpretation of economic trends and societal pressures, and the response to perceived strategic needs and issues is an adaptive process. This entails using the ambiguity of the role to gain ground for HRM needs (which may be both functional and/or organisational needs as perceived by specialists and line managers), satisfying interests and balancing decisions (Tyson, 1979 and 1980). The role is not simply reactive, or executive: it operates at the nexus of competing values and stands in the centre of three different levels of analysis – representing and interpreting societal pressures, organisational pressures and employee pressures. HRM is engaged in the task of making work meaningful, but those within the function are conscious that there are different meanings at different levels of analysis. For example, 'work' means different things to managers (the achievement of organisational goals), to employees (a source of pride, of relationships and income) and to Governments (the level of employment, which is one factor in the macro-level management of the economy). The secondary task for HRM is therefore to manage the differences in meaning.

THE SYMBOLIC ORDER

Symbols are used in human resource management for three main reasons. Firstly, to help with the general managerial task in constructing a system of shared meanings and therefore linking the three levels at which HRM must work. Secondly, they are used to convey messages of complex concepts; and thirdly as cultural categories to legitimate management, organisational status systems and legends. Because HRM policies and practices are at the centre of the work relationship, the usage by HR of the symbolic order is critical for its existence as a management function. Taking Pfeffer's point, management is expressive of symbolic action, and there is a connection between the symbolic aspects and the acts themselves. We need to understand both. He argues that analysis should continue in both parts simultaneously: 'One important research issue is the extent and conditions of linkage between symbolic and substantive outcomes in organisations.' (1981 p. 8.)

It is contended here that it is the role of HRM to provide the linkage. If a practical example can be taken the change programmes within organisations in the research reported here were practical acts intended both to change employee behaviour now and to influence behaviour in the future through attitudinal restructuring. But they were also intended to symbolise a new management philosophy, a signal to shareholders, customers, suppliers, trade unions and employees. These programmes had a strong symbolic value. It was evident from our research that those involved in the process were aware of these roles. This may be true of external consultants also.

Brown (1992) suggests that OD consultants should consciously play symbolic roles – as symbols of change to come, of changing norms and values, of power redistribution, of fate or the inexorable movement of time, and of organisational empowerment – these last two roles being part of the consultant's exit strategy.

Change management has been described throughout this book as essential for the HR role, and the symbolic aspects of these change programmes derive from the way changes to structures and jobs come to represent wider change. This is how the HR function can bridge the symbolic and instrumental realities, and operate on two aspects of consciousness, leveraging the demand for change in employees' minds off each reality.

HRM deals in abstract concepts such as 'jobs', 'responsibilities' and 'competencies'. These terms are shorthand expressions for complex variables, each of which makes assumptions about the realities it represents. The terms are used symbolically, partly to avoid the problems of having to explain what these terms might mean. HR people then trade in these concepts. The activities of HR belong to the symbolic order. For example, although there is no such physical entity as a 'job' or a 'training need' as we have already discussed, these concepts nevertheless are necessary if managerial work is to proceed. The concepts are a kind of managerial mathematics, a set of symbols which can be manipulated as ideas in order for managers to make decisions under pressure, in a variety of circumstances, when there is little time available.

'Symbols are not only more economical and more abstract than words; they can also be made to conform to rules which allow no irregularities.'

(Firth 1973, p. 55.)

For HR managers, there is the problem that the manipulation of these symbols results in moving the discussion to ever higher levels of abstraction. Symbols of symbols such as job evaluation schemes may come to be studied as sciences in their own right. It is usually at this stage that HRM loses touch with the reality faced by its employees, who are, after all, the end-users of HR policies. This aspect of HRM can be destructive to relationships with line manager colleagues and to employees. The antidote to this problem is to ensure there is a connection between the business strategy and the HR policy followed.

Symbols derive their power from the images generated in the mind. They are representational to a degree and therefore convey special messages to the listener. Symbols are much used in magic and in ritualistic ceremonies because of this power to conjure up deeply emotional ideas. Symbols which attach to the status of the person therefore carry a heavy message beyond the obvious meaning. They are used to sustain the status structure and to legitimate power in an organisation. Reward systems are good examples of how some symbols carry messages about people, and are therefore of particular significance. Such mundane matters as the company car scheme, job titles, office size, numbers of direct reports and even humble pieces of modern technology such as the mobile phone carry symbolic value – they represent somehow the importance and the recognition accorded to an individual.

Because HR managers have a central responsibility for maintaining the organisation's social structure, they are involved in the conscious use of symbols to that end. The removal of status symbols is itself symbolic. This is one reason why redundancy has such a powerful impact on the individual. The act, and the meaning of the act therefore have to be considered. For example, single status agreements are deliberate acts of policy aimed at changing perceptions about the self and also the perceptions of work colleagues. The symbolic order is directly manipulated by HR functions in order to create, maintain or change organisational culture in this way. This may well be a way to attach people to the organisation, for example by manipulating notions of reciprocity.

VARIATIONS IN HRM BETWEEN AND WITHIN ORGANISATIONS

That there is not one best practice in HRM is self-evident now to academics. Since *Evaluating the Personnel Function* was published it has been accepted that there are different models of the function. The data contained in the research reported here confirms this original finding.

The variations between the functions in different case study companies were explicable by reference to a number of factors. Diversification strategies produce highly devolved structures, with strong divisions. The changes to organisational structure prompted by the recession and by the 'new OD' have also brought HRM into different positions within the structure. The extent to which there is a powerful central organisational culture, expressed through values and controls, was also a factor. Related to these last two factors, the corporate governance structure, as represented by the Goold and Campbell framework, explained variation in the models adopted between companies. In summary, the structural relationship which places the HR function close to the main decision-making caucus for that particular business is the most influential in deciding the HR model for the business.

Variations in the models within organisations over periods of time may be understood in terms of the changes to the business. For example, there are the processes of growth and renewal as businesses move through the product life-cycle, and also as businesses change and grow for other reasons. The 'relaunch' of companies, which is also a process of renewal, calls for a new-look HR function. 'Greenfield sites' can be in the minds of senior management as much as in reality. The desire for a fresh start implies new employment relationships. Examples drawn from the recently-privatised businesses were found in this study.

Changes over time in the HR function are also occasioned by the changing top team. HR directors are as likely to be casualties of reshuffled teams as other functional directors. Unlike some other areas, such as finance, it is less disruptive to change the HR function: for example, to manage without an HR director for a period, as was the case with British Airways. It is also possible, with the retirement or removal of the HR champion on the Board, to push down HR to reporting into lower level managers in the organisation. Another option is outsourcing HR activities, which means the work may still be performed, but in a rather different way. Temporary reorganisation can always be changed back if there is perceived to be a major need. Increasingly, organisations may be seen as temporary delivery mechanisms, to be set up or reorganised or closed as markets change. Societal-level variables, as has already been argued, are likely to have a determining effect on change. The labour market has a large impact and changes here, resulting for example in less militant industrial relations and easier recruitment, produces a demand for a rather different HR function.

Variations in all the factors listed above in themselves produce a different set of priorities in the researcher's perceptions. The dynamics of a modern society produce variations on the researcher's categories. Changes to the 'architect' model can be seen, as it shifts closer to the business, or to become more consultancy-oriented. However, our own perceptions of what it means to be 'closer to the business', for example, are subject to societal pressures, as the ideological ground of academic discourse is moved to the right.

HRM ACTIVITIES

It can be difficult for those in HRM to give a description of their work to others outside the field.

What are the disciplines on which HRM is based? The answer in the 1960s and 1970s would probably have been 'the social sciences', especially industrial sociology, industrial or occupational psychology, labour economics and employment law. For the 1980s, the attempt to escape from the restrictions of an administrative, paper-pushing range of activities succeeded in shifting most HR functions towards the architect model, and towards implementing the business plan, therefore giving HR a strong managerial orientation. The move towards the 'new OD' as a central feature is the sign of the applied nature of HRM. The activities of HR managers, while encapsulating the range of competencies familiar to Moxon and to the modern Personnel Lead Body, are fragmented and not necessarily concentrated on one area at a time.

> 'The manager typically switches every few minutes from one subject or person to another, rarely completing one task before being involved in another. There are few opportunities for uninterrupted work for half an hour or longer. This hectic pattern is, in part, a demand of most managerial jobs because the manager must respond to a variety of people and problems. It can also be, in part, a choice as observational studies have shown.'
>
> (Stewart 1984, p. 326).

In spite of the fragmented nature of all managerial jobs, HR specialists have a distinctive role which is to analyse organisational needs and to work to reconcile these needs with the pressures from the societal and the sentient levels. HRM has an organisation-wide span of activities. Although using the basic disciplines to work in the traditional areas of employee resourcing, employee development and employee relations, HRM is more concerned now with analytical skills. These are the skills needed to understand the model of HR required, at the moment for the particular organisation, and then the skills to set up processes and systems to serve its various client groups. Service agreements between HR and its main client groupings are now more common, which set down costs or prices and the performance standards to be met. Sensitivity and interpersonal skills have to be mixed with judgemental and analytical ability in a combination with which most senior managers would be familiar. This is one dilemma for HR specialists. There are interesting technical jobs, such as designing assessment centres, but these do not occur all the time, and as such are vulnerable to outsourcing with consultants. The other interesting area is work at the top, where the business skills mingle with the specialist knowledge, so that HR becomes very applied and has a clear direct relevance to business objectives. Change management programmes have been evidenced as characteristic of this kind of work.

The response to the question: 'What do you do?' should perhaps be couched in terms of the work which is obviously relevant to the business. For example, at Rolls-Royce cars (Vickers) one response could be: 'We have been creating highly-motivated teams who are ready to launch our new model'; or at Scottish and Newcastle, 'We are working to integrate our acquisition of Chef and Brewer restaurants into the company and dealing with the organisational standards and cultural issues this implies'; or at Kingfisher plc, 'We have been strengthening senior management capability so we can work in a decentralised, non-bureaucratic way, with a lean staff of high calibre.' These sorts of response show the reality of HRM programmes – driven by direct business needs, and using systems and the symbolic order to achieve them. The typicality of HRM, i.e. the extent to which the work can be performed through applying general theories, may be seen at the skills level, where the analytical and process skills are significant. It can also be seen in the HRM subjects used in programmes, the programmes of work themselves being dependent on the organisational context. The subjects remain those of the social sciences. While it is true that many managers rely on their own common-sense theorising, the present felt need for 'benchmarking' is indicative that this is not enough. The social sciences, although they operate with different standards of proof, may be imperfect, but the theories we have from them are the only bodies of knowledge we possess. They are our best chance to produce ideas which are predictive of behaviour and which can analyse the causes and likely consequences of social action.

THE POSTULATE OF ADEQUACY

In Chapter 2, it was argued that human resource management has to work at both the mediate and the empirical level, because the task is to translate the organisation's symbolic order into actions and this is accomplished by managing the meanings of the symbols. Schopenhauer's 'mediate' knowing is similar to Schön's 'reflection in action' – it is the analytical, reflective work which HR management must undertake. However, managerial work is such that it is all applied, and therefore empirical knowing or 'knowing in action' is just as important to managers, because they have to learn to apply knowledge as much as possessing abstract knowledge itself.

The postulate of adequacy ties in a form of proof with a way of knowing. One way we understand or 'know that we know' is by applying knowledge and seeing it produce the effect we anticipated. For example, it is one thing to be able to believe that a particular kind of OD intervention might be successful; it is another to experience its success, and to know which behaviours and processes produced success in that particular organisation. This latter form of knowing can only take place if managers have acknowledged the validity of their own common-sense theorising; that is, they have seen the possibility that a particular action might be successful. In this sense, tactics can be taught to managers, whereas strategy cannot. The models of HRM created from a limited data set by Alan Fell and the author (Tyson and Fell 1986) were only popularly acknowledged because personnel specialists recognised at least some of the elements in each model as being within their own experience. As Weberian 'ideal types' these models served an heuristic purpose: they had enough verisimilitude for managers to compare the models with their own experience and to point to the differences, and therefore to explain to themselves and to others, by using the language of the models, what changes were occurring.

The use of symbols to bring together the two types of knowing is one way to characterise the HRM role. By dealing in symbolic concepts which have an acceptance to employees as being adequate for their experience, or within their own province of meaning, HRM is able to bring into play ideas which have meanings within different realities, and therefore to translate one reality into another. For example, in our survey of companies, the notion of 'empowerment' was being used by managers and by their employees. The HR function was usually the guardian of this notion, which symbolised the new way employees were to be managed. Only if HR were able to pass ownership of the concept both to line managers and to employees was the concept of any value. Although these two groups may have attributed some different qualities to the idea of 'empowerment', for any action to occur there had to be sufficient agreement between them on the meaning.

Typical constructs are themselves often symbols. They are common-sense understandings, things which are 'known in action', part of the empirical knowledge of the world, and may indeed be symbols such as 'jobs', 'rewards' or 'industrial relations'. The postulate of adequacy requires that these 'typical constructs' are traded within the organisation consistently. They are the currency of management speech and reports. It is a task of all senior managers, and especially of the HR function, to maintain the value of this currency and to ensure employees as well as managers trade in the same terms. For example, 'the competencies' which so many companies now use as a basis for appraisal, development and reward are phrases used to describe particular skills, but these words (such as 'flexibility') come to be endowed with a special meaning because they have a value in so many

HR systems. Given the HR role to interpret the societal and the sentient levels into the organisational level, the symbolic order with its 'tradeable' currency of symbolic words is the powerful medium used to make the connections between levels.

EVALUATING HRM

This book has been concerned with the way the human resource is used within organisations to achieve business objectives. The tacit assumption has been made throughout that one may evaluate the function by testing its contribution to the achievement of objectives. This has been seen within the planning process itself, in the strategic levers pulled to help the organisation adjust to new strategic directions, and in the new emphasis on organisation development. In particular, we have looked at how HRM is concerned to adapt the organisation to new societal conditions and to reinterpret organisational objectives through the symbolic order.

Our sample of companies was chosen, in part, for their financial performance. Even if we accept that such performance measures as described in Chapter 4 are transitory, average long-term performance must be considered as one significant indicator of business success. In Appendix 2 there is a further discussion of the ratios used. There are considerable methodological problems in discovering the relationship between particular policy choices and financial performance. Some of the reasons for this are the time-lag, the impact of other variables on company performance and the way accounting conventions distort actual performance. Most of the companies in our survey were large and highly divisionalised. Not only were there different policies frequently being pursued in different divisions, but there were often no publicly available accounts of financial performance for separate divisions.

The test applied therefore seems the only reasonable course of action. This was to take overall good performances in each industry sector, taking into account their survival capabilities; include recently-privatised businesses which were also good performers; and were going through major strategic change; and to ensure that long-run survivors or industry leaders, such as British Aerospace, were included when short-run performance changes were due to the recession. This approach also accommodates the theoretical assumption that there are different models of personnel or human resource management, and that it is therefore impossible and very unproductive to evaluate HRM· by examining HR practice within companies and then to draw conclusions from comparison between the reality and a theoretical model of HRM.

A recent paper by Fernie *et al* (1994) illustrates this point. This paper asks: 'Does HRM Boost Employment–Management Relations?' and reports an analysis of the third (1990) Workplace Industrial Relations Survey, which is a nationally representative sample of around 2000 workplaces. It looks at the association between what is described as 'the climate of employee–management relations' and a set of characteristics which are said to be those most typically found in human resource management. The six features of HRM taken as being most typically found are the 'nature of the personnel function', employee involvement, forms of payment systems, single status, organisational flexibility and the extent of formal procedures. The conclusions drawn are surprising: 'Having a personnel specialist in the workplace and/or a director responsible for HRM on the board is no guarantee of good relations. If anything the reverse is true.' (p. 19.) They go on to state that relations are worse when there is a board member responsible for personnel than when there is no board member. This conclusion drew an angry response from the Institute of Personnel and Development, since it was given considerable publicity.

The results in this secondary analysis of data from the beginning of the recession are open to a number of different interpretations. First, there are some questions concerning the statistical methodologies used, since the analysis seems to concentrate on the minor differences in rating the employee relations climate on a seven-point scale, where in fact 93 per cent of personnel managers responding had rated the climate good to very good. Second, the notion that there is a causal relationship is nonsense, even if the correlations are acceptable. The causes of the appointment of HR specialists and of a climate that is less than satisfactory could be other factors, for example the need to reorganise employee relationships, to downsize, or to bring about change. Similarly, employee relations experts are surely most likely to be appointed when there are problems with the employee relations climate. Finally, the authors have set up a definition of HRM and suggested that these practices are a standard model to which all should conform. By failing to understand the importance of different models, the researchers have merely demonstrated that there are different models, not that one is better than another.

We have dealt with this research report from respected authors at the LSE in some detail because it demonstrates the difficulty of evaluating the HR function. In particular, it shows the significance of different models, and the dangers of survey techniques which do not take account of organisational variations and of the organisational context. By contrast the research design adopted in the Cranfield study, which concentrated on evaluating HRM by assessing its contribution to the business strategy, is shown to be the appropriate methodology. The Fernie *et al* study is really unable to show what HRM has contributed to the business, yet HRM only exists for that purpose. It is to advance the cause of the business that HR functions are created – and the functions can only be evaluated in relation to that objective.

THE FUTURE FOR HUMAN RESOURCE MANAGEMENT

Human resource management may be perceived as a branch of learning; a phenomenon for exploration by sociologists, psychologists and the other social sciences. To explain what has happened in HRM is to explain the social context of economic relationships in a given society. The societal changes we are now experiencing will have long-term effects on the HR function, and thus have consequences which will influence the theoretical stance taken by those who study it. Practitioner and academic interests will therefore come together.

The cycle of change seems to start with international safety needs, the very least of these being the avoidance of a nuclear war, and is closely followed by scientific and technological advance. Economic mechanisms for exploiting technological innovation produce an imbalance in wealth, and social issues then come to the fore, arising from wealth distribution inequalities. There are trends and issues which help to shape change in our society: demographic changes, new social security policies, European economic and social convergence, changes to social values brought about by disillusionment with national politics, and the ever-pressing problems of the Third World. HRM is linked closely into these societal trends and, whatever the company context, is not isolated from broad societal change. A direct impact is made by moves to make companies more accountable to their shareholders; the institutional changes to increase worker involvement through joint consultation; changes to minimum standards brought in by European Community law; and similar trends.

Commentators are starting to say now that fundamental change is necessary, if we are to survive intact as a society: for example, in the face of permanently high levels of unemployment, the economic supremacy of the countries on the Pacific Rim, and the shift away from manufacturing in Western Europe towards a service economy. Some are extremely pessimistic about the problems, even if optimistic in forecasting the future response.

'Management and control are breaking down everywhere. The new world order looks very likely to end in disorder. We can't make things happen the way we want them to at home, at work or in government, certainly not in the world as a whole. There are, it is now clear, limits to management. We thought that capitalism was the answer, but some of the hungry and homeless are not so sure.'

(Handy 1994, p. 16.)

It is the author's view that human resource management will become more important as a functional activity in the solution of some of this societal-level disorder. However, the author believes this will be achieved through HRM's integration with line management. Because social change has become such a feature of everyday life, managers of all kinds need to be involved in handling that change. It is in this way that men and women of action will become men and women of reflection, that the mediate and the empirical will merge, and those who go out like Alexander to conquer new markets, to build new organisations and to place their mark on their industry will do so through their strategic use of the human resource.

BIBLIOGRAPHY

Astley, W. G. (1984) 'Subjectivity, sophistry and symbolism in management science', *Journal of Management Studies.*

Beer, M., Spencer, B., Lawrence, P. R., Quinn Mills, D. and Walton, R. E. (1984) *Managing Human Assets*, New York: Free Press.

Boxall, P. (1992) 'Strategic Human Resource Management. Beginnings of a new theoretical sophistication', *Human Resource Management Journal*, Vol. 2, No. 3.

Brown, M. L. (1992) *The Symbolic Roles of the Organization Development Consultant*, Working Paper 18, November, Faculty of Administrative Studies, York University, Ontario, Canada.

Cummings, L. L. (1983) 'The logics of management', *Academy of Management Review* 8, pp. 582–8.

Fernie, S., Metcalf, D. and Woodland, S. (1994) 'Does HRM Boost Employee–Management Relations?', *LSE Working Papers* 548.

Firth, R. (1973) *Symbols, Public and Private*, London: George Allen & Unwin.

Gospel, H. F. (1992) *Markets, Firms and the Management of Labour in Modern Britain*, Cambridge: Cambridge University Press.

Handy, C. (1994) *The Empty Raincoat*, London: Hutchinson.

Hendry, C. and Pettigrew, A. (1990) 'Human Resource Management. An Agenda for the 1990's', *International Journal of Human Resource Management*, Vol. 1, No. 1, pp. 17–43.

Kelly, G. (1955) *The Psychology of Personal Constructs*, Vol. I and II, New York: Norton.

Legge, K. (1989) 'Human Resource Management: a critical analysis' in Storey, J. (Ed) *New Perspectives on Human Resource Management*, London: Routledge.

Pfeffer, J. (1981) 'Management as symbolic action: the creation and maintenance of organizational paradigms', *Research in Organizational Behaviour*, Vol. 3, pp.1–52.

Schutz, A. (Wagner, H. (Ed)) (1970) *On Phenomenology and Social Relations*, Chicago: University of Chicago Press.

Stewart, R. (1984) 'The Nature of Management? A Problem for Management Education', *Journal of Management Studies* 21.3, pp. 323–30.

Storey, J. (1992) *Developments in the Management of Human Resources*, Oxford: Blackwell.

Tyson, S. (1979) *Specialists in Ambiguity*, unpublished PhD thesis, London: University of London.

Tyson, S. (1980) 'Taking advantage of ambiguity', *Personnel Management*, February, p. 45.

Tyson, S. and Fell, A. (1986) *Evaluating the Personnel Function*, London: Hutchinson.

Wallbank, F. W. (1981) *The Hellenistic World*, London: Fontana.

Zajac, E. J. and Shortell, S. M. (1989) 'Changing generic strategies: Likelihood, directions and performance implications', *Strategic Management Journal*, Vol. 10, pp. 413–30.

Research methods adopted

METHOD OF DATA COLLECTION

We arranged to interview the HR director or equivalent, and often other senior managers in divisions or other parts of the business. We had decided that where (as was often the case) we were dealing with a conglomerate, or a highly divisionalised business, we would seek to interview an appropriate person at divisional or company level within the corporate group. In these situations we asked at corporate level to be directed to the division or company which either contributed most to the corporation and/or which could be taken as most representative of the corporation as a whole.

We used a common semi-structured interview schedule, details of which are in this appendix. We also gathered background information about the company from financial reports, publicity documents and a search of newspaper/journal databases, as well as from the IV Consultants database (*see* Appendix 2).

In addition, we were able to gain access to particular local-level information in many companies through our existing work at Cranfield (for example, management development programmes we were running for participating companies, MBA student projects within companies, and in some cases the involvement of the companies in other research projects with Cranfield School of Management). We were aware that this sort of data was not systematically collected from all our respondents. We therefore only used such data as background, or sometimes as divisional-level data, to illustrate issues which arose in the main survey. The very nature of a case study approach does mean that data from a number of sources may be available, and it is the qualitative richness of such data which makes the case study method so valuable.

RESEARCH TEAM

The research team was:

Professor Shaun Tyson, Cranfield School of Management

Mr Michael Witcher, Witcher/Stronge (formerly of P–E International).
Ms Noeleen Doherty, Senior Research Officer, HRRC, Cranfield School
of Management.
Mr Dennis Henry, VI Consultants (formerly of P–E International).

We were also assisted in data collection by John Barnard of P–E
International, and by five MBA students and by two junior consultants
from P–E International. However, the bulk of the interviews were
conducted by the research team.

DEFINITION OF TERMS

We used a common set of definitions in each case, drawn from the
literature.

Definitions

Strategy	The expressed intentions of how managers expect to achieve particular business results over a stated period of time.
Mission	The purpose for which the business exists – the markets, standards and long-term aims adopted.
Corporate strategy	Overall strategy of the corporation, including the rationale for the portfolio of businesses.
Business strategy	Strategy of individual business unit/company.
HR strategy	The intentions of the corporation, both explicit and covert, towards the management of its employees, expressed through philosophies, policies and practices.
HRM 'fit'	The relationship of the HR strategy to the business or corporate strategy.
Manpower strategy	The analysis of the company's Human Resource needs; anticipating changes/monitoring responses.

Organisation development	The application of specialist HR knowledge to the processes of managing organisational changes (e.g. job design, changes in organisation structure).
Employee/management development	Career development/succession planning/individual training and development/skills enhancement.
Rewards	The reward system/job evaluation/ performance measurement/incentives/ benefits.
Performance management	Appraisal/performance evaluation/ productivity/attendance/discipline.
Employee relations	The formal set of relationships between the company and its employees.
Industrial relations	The institutional framework of relationships between trade unions and the employer.

INTERVIEWER BRIEF

Background information

Individuals should gather as much background information about the company as possible, including the most recent accounts, organisational charts, publicity documents, etc, so that the interview can be approached from an 'informed position'. This should include any information that can be obtained directly from the company in advance (request information at first telephone contact).

This should be supplemented with the current static and dynamic information on individual companies, taken from the database.

The interviewer should use the short bullet-point schedule as the working document during the interview. Also obtain any documentation in support of the interview areas at the time of the interview (e.g. mission statements, strategy statements, HR strategy statements).

The expanded interview schedule should be used as the working document for writing up the results of the interview for analysis.

EXPANDED INTERVIEW SCHEDULE FRAMEWORK FOR WRITE-UP

The information obtained at the interviews should be written-up within the following framework.

Corporate/business strategy

1 Brief outline of recent changes.
2 To what is present performance status attributed:

financial
people
performance management
market share
others

3 Major differences between the company and major competitors.
4 Mission/vision for the business.
5 How has this particular vision/culture evolved?
6 How does this shape/influence business strategy?
7 What is the business strategy?
8 What is the process through which the business strategy is derived?
9 Who is involved in determining/creating the business strategy. Who coordinates the process?
10 What is the time-frame of the business strategy – how frequently does it change/how does it change?
11 Differentiation between corporate and business strategy.

HRM strategy

1 Is there a defined coherent HR strategy?
2 How does the HR strategy emerge from the business strategy?
3 How does the HR strategy contribute to (fit) the business strategy?
4 What processes are used to formulate the HR strategy?
5 What are the key characteristics of the HR strategy?
6 Which of these key characteristics is most influential in achieving the business strategy?
7 Is there an HR director? Where does he/she fit in the organisation?
8 What is the position of the HR function in the organisation?
9 What involvement does the HR function have in the development of the business strategy?
10 Is there a consistent HR strategy which is followed over all divisions?

11 If not, in what way is the HR strategy implemented differently between divisions?

12 How much autonomy is granted to subsidiary companies/divisions in the implementation of the HR strategy?

13 Which company is the best performer in the group?

14 How is the utilisation of human resources planned?

15 What is the time-frame for the operation of the HR strategy?

16 What quality (defined) considerations are included in the HR strategy?

17 How responsive to change is the HR strategy?

18 How quickly does the HR strategy change to bring it on line with the business strategy (examples of how things have been dealt with in the past)?

19 How is change to the HR strategy managed?

20 To what extent are changes to the business anticipated, in terms of the HR strategy?

21 How has the HR function developed/changed recently?

22 What is the extent of the influence of external factors on the HR strategy?

23 How is the HR strategy monitored and reviewed?

24 How is information fed into the policy-making decision process?

25 Where does the HR information come from?

26 Are there regular meetings of senior management about strategic policy-making?

Operation of the HR strategy

1 Is there a system of feedback on the operation of the HR policies in practice?

2 Are HR specialists used in setting up HR policies?

3 Are HR specialists or line management more involved in the implementation of HR policies?

4 Is there a written HR strategy document (copy)?

5 How is the contribution of the HR strategy to the business strategy assessed?

6 Give examples of practical applications of HR strategy which contribute to the achievement of the business strategy.

7 Specific aspects of the following HR policies which have contributed to the success of the business strategy over the past five years are:

manpower strategy
organisational development
recruitment and selection

employee/management development (self-development)
rewards
performance management
employee relations
industrial relations

8   Evaluation of policies (examples, frequency, content of surveys, etc).
9   Are HR reports presented at board meetings – is something done regularly?

Database companies

The database is run by J Dennis Henry of VI Consultants, Glasgow, who has provided the following description.

THE DATABASES

The databases are updated daily as annual accounts become available. The UK database is also updated from interim and preliminary statements. They are, therefore, dynamic and as up-to-date as is possible.

The database contains data on the companies which are largest, by turnover, in the industrial and commercial sectors. The finance, property and energy sectors are not included as their ratios are incompatible.

The European database includes the largest UK companies from the UK database and many of the largest companies from the rest of Western Europe. Their combined turnover was just under £21 000 billion and they employed about 12 million people world-wide (as at 1991).

One of the uses to which this data is put is to produce profiles which compare a company's performance to that of the database companies. A company's performance on each of the ratios is compared to the median and the spread of all the database companies.

PROFILE

The ratios for each company are compared with those for the companies in the database, and their distribution from the median is shown visually. A median performance scores 50, i.e. the centre line, with the quartiles at 25 and 75 and the deciles at 10 and 90.

The profile compares the ratios from a company's latest accounts with the most up-to-date ratios from the total database. The ratio for margin is updated from interim accounts to give the margin for the latest 12 months if the latest information is for the interim period, i.e. the latest six months plus the second half figures for the previous year. Ratios which require the balance sheet cannot be updated in the same manner as only a few companies issue balance sheets at the interim stage. Companies are ranked on three criteria to produce an overall ranking. The three criteria used are:

Profit margin
Return on total assets
Added value/pay

By having a reference base, it is easy and accurate to position and 'score' the performance on each ratio against the total database:

Very good	1–50
Good	51–100
Average	101–150
Poor	151–200
Danger	201–250

Definitions for performance profiles

Profitability:	Return on total assets; this is profit before tax expressed as a percentage of the total assets, i.e. fixed plus current assets.
Profit margin:	Profit before tax expressed as a percentage of sales.
Asset utilisation:	Sales expressed as a percentage of total assets.
Return on capital employed:	Profit before tax expressed as a percentage of capital employed, i.e. total assets less total liabilities, short-term and long-term.
Sales/employee:	Sales divided by the number of full-time equivalent employees.
Capital employed/employee:	Capital employed divided by the number of full-time equivalent employees.
AV/pay:	The added value divided by the total remuneration cost, i.e. including pension, social security, etc.

COMPANY RANKING IN EACH INDUSTRY SECTOR

The columns are:

A Latest margin

This is profit before tax/sales per cent. A fundamental business ratio, as without a positive result there is no long-term business. The latest margin is derived from the PBT for the most recent 12 months divided by the sales for that period. The latest figures are those for the most recent trading year, if the latest announcements are for the full fiscal year for the company. If the most recent announcement is the interim statement, then the latest figures are derived from taking those for the first half of the current year, and then adding them to those for the last six months of the previous year. This provides the latest information and avoids any distortion from seasonal business.

B Return on total assets (ROTA)

This ratio shows how well a company is using its financial and physical assets to generate profit. Total assets are used rather than the capital employed, which is more easily affected by liabilities and by creative accountancy techniques. It also shows how well the management is using its own assets rather than those of its suppliers. The ROTA ratio has been seen to give better statistical correlations.

The ratio is derived from the PBT divided by the sum of the fixed and current assets, with no reduction for any liabilities.

C Added value pay

Detailed analyses of several thousand companies has shown that this is the single most sensitive business performance ratio. Added value is sales less bought-in materials and services and pay. It is the total cost of employment for everyone in the business from the Chairman down and includes social security and pension costs.

This ratio has the advantage that it compensates for different levels of sub-contracting or factoring. A company which sub-contracts much of its work will therefore have a smaller Added Value but it should have a lower payroll and so the ratio should be stabilised.

The combined use of the ROTA (B) and added value/pay (C) ratios has the advantage of enabling companies to be compared across sectors as well as within sectors. One which is capital intensive should, by definition, have a low labour intensity; and vice versa. This capital intensive-company is likely to have a low ROTA because the denominator, total assets, is high. However, because it should have a low payroll, having a low labour intensity, the added value/pay ratio should be high. Another company with the opposite characteristics, even within the same sector, can then be compared with the first one.

Correlation analyses have shown, as would be expected, that companies which are low in both ratios are certain to be amongst the bottom performers in their sector and, of course, the opposite is equally true. The winners are those which use *all* of their assets, financial, physical and human, effectively; and of these, the human one has the most significance.

To produce the ranked tables on pp. 178–94, the procedure is:

1   Each company is ranked on each of these three factors and given a rank number, with 1 being the best, and the highest number going to the poorest performer. The ratio for each factor is shown under the heading 'Values'.

2   The rank positions for each factor are shown for all companies under the heading 'Ranks'. Equal weighting is given to the three factors.

3   Then the sums of the ranks are obtained, which enables an overall ranking to be produced. The sums of the rankings are shown under 'Total – rank by weight' and the final figure is the 'Overall rank' position.

J Dennis Henry

	Values			Ranks			Total	
	Latest Margin	AV/Pay		Weightings:			Rank	Overall
	Ret on Total Ass.(ROTA)			1	1	1	by	Rank
	A	B	C	A	B	C	Weight	
GLAXO HOLDINGS	34.14	22.46	2.47	3	2	2	7	1
ISOTRON	41.52	16.63	2.79	1	9	1	11	2
MEDEVA	22.99	18.83	1.95	5	5	3	13	3
SMITHKLINE BEECHAM	19.79	22.43	1.85	7	3	4	14	4
WELLCOME	33.51	26.79	1.75	4	1	11	16	5
QUALITY CARE HOMES	34.62	11.51	1.81	2	13	7	22	6
SETON HEALTHCARE	16.62	17.04	1.81	10	8	6	24	7
SMITH & NEPHEW	17.98	17.44	1.76	8	7	10	25	8
BESPAK	14.35	18.24	1.76	12	6	9	27	9
ZENECA	14.46	12.94	1.77	11	11	8	30	10
INTERCARE	11.05	21.35	1.66	15	4	12	31	11
LIFE SCIENCES INT'L	17.83	15.76	1.61	9	10	14	33	12
UNICHEM	3.18	10.26	1.83	21	15	5	41	13
TAKARE	20.50	6.34	1.48	6	21	19	46	14
SCHOLL	9.71	9.90	1.53	17	16	18	51	15
COMMUNITY HOSPITALS	13.28	5.17	1.54	13	23	16	52	16
ASSOCIATED NURSING SERV'S	10.23	3.93	1.64	16	24	13	53	17
GRAMPIAN HOLDINGS	4.11	10.32	1.45	19	14	20	53	17
NESTOR-BNA	4.09	11.72	1.44	20	12	21	53	17
AMERSHAM	11.22	9.80	1.38	14	17	23	54	20
AAH HOLDINGS	2.60	8.34	1.58	22	18	15	55	21
LONDON INTERNATIONAL	1.72	6.85	1.54	23	20	17	60	22
HUNTINGDON INT HOLD'S	5.10	6.06	1.30	18	22	24	64	23
FISONS	0.08	7.90	1.44	24	19	22	65	24
ML LABORATORIES	(55.16)	(1.95)	0.02	25	25	26	76	25
BIOCURE	(67.83)	(21.66)	0.09	26	27	25	78	26
BRITISH BIO-TECHNOLOGY	(189.14)	(18.54)	(0.97)	27	26	28	81	27
HAEMOCELL	(189.32)	(32.05)	(0.58)	28	28	27	83	28
PROTEUS INTERNATIONAL	(24,152.38)	(32.07)	(1.70)	30	29	29	88	29
TEPNEL DIAGNOSTICS	(4,454.84)	(33.31)	(3.84)	29	30	30	89	30

	STATIC Rankings As at 07-04-94					
Printed: 07-04-94						Page 1
	Retailers, Multi Dept.					

	Values			Ranks			Total Rank by Weight	Overall Rank
	Latest Margin	AV/Pay		Weightings:				
	Ret on Total Ass.(ROTA)			1	1	1		
	A	B	C	A	B	C		
BETTERWARE	24.46	33.72	2.71	1	1	2	4	1
MARKS & SPENCER	12.74	15.70	2.28	5	2	3	10	2
GREAT UNIVERSAL ST'S	16.72	11.13	2.12	2	5	5	12	3
BROWN, N	11.62	13.95	2.20	6	3	4	13	4
ARGOS	7.52	10.09	3.45	8	7	1	16	5
ASPREY	13.16	10.06	2.07	3	8	6	17	6
BEATTIE, JAMES	8.26	13.31	1.47	7	4	9	20	7
KINGFISHER	6.90	9.18	1.51	9	9	8	26	8
ROSEBYS	5.76	10.31	1.40	10	6	11	27	9
CHRISTIES	12.87	2.40	1.25	4	13	15	32	10
STOREHOUSE	2.35	2.60	1.55	13	12	7	32	10
LIBERTY	4.32	7.23	1.28	11	10	13	34	12
LEWIS, JOHN PARTN'P	3.86	3.33	1.28	12	11	14	37	13
BURTON GROUP	0.98	1.24	1.43	14	14	10	38	14
SEARS		(2.51)	1.38	15	16	12	43	15
BENTALLS	(0.48)	(1.01)	1.12	16	15	16	47	16

Printed: 07-04-94			**STATIC Rankings As at 07-04-94**						Page 1
			Engin'g, Divers' & Aero						

	Values			Ranks			Total	
	Latest Margin	AV/Pay		Weightings:			Rank	Overall
	Ret on Total Ass.(ROTA)			1	1	1	by	Rank
	A	B	C	A	B	C	Weight	
HALMA	17.99	24.31	1.67	1	1	2	4	1
CHEMRING	14.47	16.61	1.61	3	2	3	8	2
IPECO HOLDINGS	16.52	13.91	1.51	2	4	6	12	3
SMITHS INDUSTRIES	14.41	16.54	1.53	4	3	5	12	3
JONES STROUD	9.19	13.46	1.47	9	5	8	22	5
BAYNES, CHARLES	8.99	11.08	2.13	12	11	1	24	6
FR GROUP	12.32	9.84	1.43	6	14	9	29	7
SIEBE	11.33	8.64	1.57	7	19	4	30	8
VSEL	13.27	9.29	1.41	5	16	12	33	9
TRANSTEC	7.72	11.63	1.48	18	9	7	34	10
VOSPER THORNYCROFT	9.00	11.76	1.38	11	8	15	34	10
CARCLO ENGINEERING	9.39	10.20	1.39	8	13	14	35	12
CONCENTRIC	8.04	12.02	1.37	16	7	16	39	13
MCKECHNIE	7.80	9.38	1.43	17	15	10	42	14
MORGAN CRUCIBLE	8.36	8.20	1.41	14	21	11	46	15
AIM GROUP	8.83	9.24	1.37	13	17	17	47	16
WEIR	8.35	12.17	1.29	15	6	26	47	16
PROSPECT INDUSTRIES	6.85	11.15	1.26	19	10	31	60	18
TI GROUP	9.01	6.25	1.32	10	28	23	61	19
BROMSGROVE	5.91	7.69	1.37	25	23	18	66	20
WESTLAND	6.81	7.13	1.35	20	27	20	67	21
IMI	6.62	7.54	1.34	22	24	22	68	22
WAGON INDUSTRIAL	5.53	8.62	1.32	26	20	24	70	23
EIS	6.79	8.13	1.25	21	22	32	75	24
MEGGITT	6.47	9.12	1.25	23	18	34	75	24
GLYNWED INTERNAT'AL	4.71	5.94	1.35	29	29	19	77	26
HAMPSON INDUSTRIES	5.21	10.72	1.21	28	12	37	77	26
HUNTING	3.52	7.21	1.34	33	26	21	80	28
DICKIE, JAMES	4.11	7.28	1.31	32	25	25	82	29
FKI	5.40	5.85	1.27	27	30	29	86	30
SENIOR ENGINEERING	6.21	2.74	1.28	24	34	28	86	30
BULLOUGH	2.87	4.43	1.26	34	31	30	95	32
RANSOMES	(5.37)	0.63	1.41	44	39	13	96	33
JOHNSON & FIRTH BROWN	2.36	2.81	1.25	36	33	33	102	34
AYRSHIRE METAL PRODUCTS	4.12	1.24	1.25	31	37	35	103	35
APV	1.48	3.62	1.18	38	32	39	109	36
BRITISH AEROSPACE	(2.20)	(2.31)	1.28	42	41	27	110	37
AEROSPACE ENGINEERING	1.07	1.00	1.22	40	38	36	114	38
HOPKINSONS	1.40	2.40	1.18	39	35	40	114	38
VICKERS	4.68	(4.23)	1.16	30	43	41	114	38
CLYDE BLOWERS	2.77	1.84	0.96	35	36	45	116	41
ROLLS ROYCE	2.16	(6.03)	1.19	37	44	38	119	42
BRAY TECHNOLOGIES	0.25	0.34	1.12	41	40	42	123	43
600 GROUP	(4.10)	(2.44)	1.03	43	42	44	129	44
ML HOLDINGS	(8.64)	(18.74)	1.05	45	45	43	133	45

	Values — Latest Margin / AV/Pay / Ret on Total Ass.(ROTA)			Ranks — Weightings:			Total Rank by Weight	Overall Rank
	A	B	C	1 A	1 B	1 C		
BLICK	28.66	25.53	2.12	1	1	3	5	1
CML MICROSYSTEMS	24.97	18.11	1.66	2	9	4	15	2
BOWTHORPE	15.30	19.74	1.59	6	4	6	16	3
FAIREY	16.74	20.92	1.56	5	3	8	16	3
MTL INSTRUMENTS	18.35	18.47	1.63	3	8	5	16	3
DRUCK HOLDINGS	16.79	16.39	1.57	4	10	7	21	6
TUNSTALL	14.43	18.87	1.52	8	5	9	22	7
TELEMETRIX	13.06	18.56	1.50	9	7	11	27	8
EUROTHERM	12.66	18.74	1.46	10	6	12	28	9
CRAY ELECTRONICS	8.15	22.08	1.45	14	2	14	30	10
ALBA	4.62	11.19	2.22	19	15	2	36	11
GEC	14.89	14.21	1.40	7	12	17	36	11
DOMINO PRINTING SCIENCES	11.10	11.79	1.44	11	13	15	39	13
CONTROL TECHNIQUES	8.68	9.78	1.45	12	17	13	42	14
LINX PRINTING TECH'Y	2.63	16.02	1.52	22	11	10	43	15
INDUSTRIAL CON'L SERV'S	7.84	11.40	1.42	15	14	16	45	16
AMSTRAD	(9.63)	(6.45)	2.23	23	22	1	46	17
PEEK	7.67	9.81	1.32	16	16	19	51	18
GRASEBY	8.42	1.29	1.26	13	21	21	55	19
RACAL ELECTRONICS	4.38	7.20	1.33	20	18	18	56	20
INSTEM	5.28	7.05	1.23	17	19	22	58	21
UNITECH	4.77	3.52	1.31	18	20	20	58	21
PRESTWICK HOLDINGS	(11.02)	(15.66)	1.11	24	24	23	71	23
TADPOLE TECHNOLOGY	3.27	(26.63)	0.80	21	25	25	71	23
FERRANTI	(15.53)	(9.44)	1.09	25	23	24	72	25

	Values — Latest Margin / AV/Pay — Ret on Total Ass.(ROTA)			Ranks — Weightings:			Total Rank by Weight	Overall Rank
	A	B	C	A (1)	B (1)	C (1)		
VODAFONE	45.87	37.09	8.27	1	1	1	3	1
CABLE & WIRELESS	23.76	14.12	2.85	2	3	2	7	2
BRITISH TELECOM	18.13	9.29	2.12	3	4	3	10	3
SECURICOR	9.88	15.26	1.15	4	2	4	10	3

	Values			Ranks			Total	
	Latest Margin	AV/Pay		Weightings:			Rank	Overall
	Ret on Total Ass.(ROTA)			1	1	1	by	Rank
	A	B	C	A	B	C	Weight	
SCOTTISH POWER	20.93	19.80	3.00	1	1	4	6	1
SOUTH WALES ELECTRICITY	16.94	17.18	2.35	3	2	8	13	2
SCOTTISH HYDRO-ELEC	19.91	12.99	3.76	2	14	3	19	3
LONDON ELECTRICITY	14.52	14.55	2.34	6	5	9	20	4
SOUTHERN ELECTRICITY	14.50	14.30	2.48	7	8	5	20	4
NATIONAL POWER	15.97	12.68	3.80	4	16	2	22	6
POWERGEN	13.82	13.22	4.29	9	13	1	23	7
MIDLANDS ELECTRICITY	14.87	14.41	2.24	5	7	12	24	8
MANWEB ELECTRICITY	13.60	14.07	2.43	10	9	7	26	9
NORTHERN ELECTRICITY	13.11	16.79	2.17	11	3	14	28	10
NORWEB ELECTRICITY	12.77	15.91	2.26	13	4	11	28	10
EASTERN ELECTRICITY	12.45	13.90	2.48	14	10	6	30	12
YORKSHIRE ELECTRICITY	14.21	12.80	2.33	8	15	10	33	13
SEEBOARD ELECTRICITY	11.31	14.49	2.08	16	6	16	38	14
EAST MIDLANDS ELECTRICITY	12.15	13.75	2.19	15	11	13	39	15
SOUTH WESTERN ELECTRICITY	12.91	13.35	2.11	12	12	15	39	15

	Values			Ranks			Total	
	Latest Margin	AV/Pay		Weightings:			Rank	Overall
	Ret on Total Ass.(ROTA)			1	1	1	by	Rank
	A	B	C	A	B	C	Weight	
NICHOLS J N (VIMTO)	17.47	26.88	3.00	2	1	1	4	1
DEVRO	19.07	9.99	2.03	1	13	2	16	2
CADBURY SCHWEPPES	11.11	11.23	1.84	3	8	6	17	3
ASSOC BRITISH FOODS	7.71	11.47	1.65	4	6	10	20	4
NORTHERN FOODS	7.63	16.29	1.54	5	2	14	21	5
UNILEVER	6.95	12.65	1.65	6	5	11	22	6
ACATOS & HUTCHESON	4.57	14.36	1.93	16	3	4	23	7
PERKINS FOODS	5.13	13.91	1.89	14	4	5	23	7
TATE & LYLE	6.02	9.14	1.96	8	14	3	25	9
HAZELWOOD FOODS	6.69	11.35	1.63	7	7	12	26	10
JLI GROUP	4.41	10.94	1.72	17	10	9	36	11
EVEREST FOODS	5.71	8.23	1.78	12	18	7	37	12
FINLAY, JAMES	5.96	4.18	1.73	9	25	8	42	13
DALGETY	2.34	11.05	1.56	24	9	13	46	14
MATTHEWS, BERNARD	5.78	8.84	1.47	11	15	20	46	14
UNIGATE	5.58	10.65	1.42	13	11	23	47	16
LINTON PARK	5.93	6.18	1.48	10	22	18	50	17
BARR, A G	4.63	8.26	1.48	15	17	19	51	18
DALEPAK FOODS	1.60	10.48	1.52	25	12	15	52	19
BOOKER	2.43	8.09	1.50	23	19	16	58	20
UNITED BISCUITS	3.38	8.34	1.43	20	16	22	58	20
ALBERT FISHER GROUP	2.45	6.07	1.49	22	23	17	62	22
HILLSDOWN HOLDINGS	3.53	6.70	1.38	19	20	25	64	23
UNION INTERNATIONAL	3.25	6.18	1.40	21	21	24	66	24
BORTHWICKS	4.06	5.17	1.34	18	24	26	68	25
SIMS FOOD GROUP	(1.38)	(0.62)	1.44	26	26	21	73	26

STATIC Rankings As at 08-04-94

346-Household requisites

	Values			Ranks			Total	
	Latest Margin	AV/Pay		Weightings:			Rank	Overall
	Ret on Total Ass.(ROTA)			1	1	1	by	Rank
	A	B	C	A	B	C	Weight	
MAYBORN GROUP	10.64	20.28	2.62	3	1	1	5	1
RECKITT & COLMAN	12.38	10.66	2.04	1	3	2	6	2
PATERSON ZOCHONIS	12.31	8.72	1.58	2	4	3	9	3
BLACK, PETER	8.47	12.62	1.48	4	2	4	10	4
JEYES GROUP	4.29	7.89	1.40	5	5	5	15	5

	Latest Margin (A)	AV/Pay (B)	Ret on Total Ass.(ROTA) (C)	Rank A (Wt 1)	Rank B (Wt 1)	Rank C (Wt 1)	Total Rank by Weight	Overall Rank
HARDYS & HANSONS	22.33	13.99	2.27	2	1	3	6	1
MORLAND	17.43	6.35	2.45	3	9	1	13	2
HOLT, JOSEPH	26.84	13.56	1.91	1	2	11	14	3
DEVENISH, T/O BY GREENALL	16.73	6.50	2.18	5	8	5	18	4
BODDINGTON	17.00	7.81	1.89	4	4	12	20	5
MARSTON THOMPSON & EVER'D	15.95	7.32	2.13	7	6	7	20	5
GREENE KING	14.81	5.93	2.39	8	11	2	21	7
WOLVERHAMPTON & DUDLEY BR	16.35	7.27	2.07	6	7	8	21	7
SCOTTISH & NEWC'E BR	11.98	7.63	2.06	10	5	9	24	9
BASS	11.41	8.33	1.96	12	3	10	25	10
WETHERSPOON JD	13.89	5.49	2.16	9	13	6	28	11
MANSFIELD BREWERY	11.41	5.37	2.21	13	14	4	31	12
GREENALLS GROUP	11.46	5.14	1.85	11	15	14	40	13
FULLER SMITH & TURNER	10.08	6.09	1.70	15	10	16	41	14
VAUX	11.34	4.60	1.88	14	16	13	43	15
WHITBREAD	7.20	5.70	1.68	17	12	17	46	16
BURTONWOOD BREWERY	6.80	3.65	1.78	18	17	15	50	17
YOUNG & CO'S BREWERY	7.40	3.17	1.55	16	18	18	52	18

	Values — Latest Margin, AV/Pay, Ret on Total Ass.(ROTA)			Ranks — Weightings:			Total Rank by Weight	Overall Rank
	A	B	C	1 A	1 B	1 C		
FORTH PORTS	29.00	14.49	2.15	1	2	5	8	1
MERSEY DOCKS & HARBOUR	21.20	8.02	1.72	3	6	6	15	2
ASSOC BRITISH PORTS	27.37	5.62	2.73	2	10	4	16	3
NATIONAL EXPRESS	6.69	18.79	1.51	7	1	8	16	3
BAA	(0.90)	8.66	2.92	13	5	3	21	5
STAGECOACH	8.39	10.53	1.31	5	3	13	21	5
DAWSONGROUP	1.49	5.85	4.01	12	9	2	23	7
P & O	9.11	4.43	1.44	4	11	10	25	8
NFC	5.52	10.37	1.31	8	4	14	26	9
TIBBETT & BRITTEN	6.72	8.01	1.22	6	7	15	28	10
TRANSPORT DEVEL'T GP	4.89	6.78	1.42	9	8	11	28	10
TIPHOOK	(76.62)	(1.44)	5.95	15	14	1	30	12
BRITISH AIRWAYS	3.23	2.91	1.47	11	12	9	32	13
OCEAN GROUP	4.57	2.33	1.38	10	13	12	35	14
GOODE DURRANT	(9.13)	(12.37)	1.52	14	15	7	36	15

	Values			Ranks			Total Rank by Weight	Overall Rank
	Latest Margin	AV/Pay		Weightings:				
	Ret on Total Ass.(ROTA)			1	1	1		
	A	B	C	A	B	C		
EUROCAMP	11.03	19.94	2.94	6	1	1	8	1
VARDON	26.37	12.19	2.09	1	5	4	10	2
FIRST LEISURE	26.11	10.09	2.72	2	9	2	13	3
MANCHESTER UNITED	20.57	11.56	2.06	3	8	5	16	4
CITY CENTRE REST'TS	13.24	13.40	1.60	4	3	13	20	5
GRANADA	10.90	12.06	1.90	7	6	7	20	5
AIRTOURS	7.40	12.50	1.98	12	4	6	22	7
SINCLAIR, WILLIAM	9.84	11.68	1.81	8	7	8	23	8
RANK ORGANISATION	13.13	9.32	1.70	5	11	11	27	9
COMPASS	8.35	15.50	1.28	10	2	20	32	10
THORN EMI	6.29	9.10	1.78	15	12	9	36	11
PIZZAEXPRESS	9.02	9.55	1.35	9	10	18	37	12
STAKIS	7.44	2.58	1.63	11	18	12	41	13
ALLIED LEISURE	(58.84)	4.45	2.14	23	16	3	42	14
STANLEY LEISURE ORG	4.10	5.78	1.53	16	14	14	44	15
BOOSEY & HAWKES	6.74	7.00	1.30	14	13	19	46	16
BARR & WAL' ARNOLD	1.89	5.09	1.46	17	15	16	48	17
LADBROKE GROUP	1.44	0.87	1.73	18	20	10	48	17
FORTE	7.19	3.63	1.27	13	17	21	51	19
WEMBLEY	(6.77)	(3.10)	1.50	22	22	15	59	20
OWNERS ABROAD	0.81	1.84	1.27	19	19	22	60	21
SAVOY HOTEL	(1.84)	(1.23)	1.19	20	21	23	64	22
QUEENS MOAT HOUSES	(429.33)	(83.57)	1.41	24	24	17	65	23
HI-TEC SPORTS	(3.90)	(11.93)	0.93	21	23	24	68	24
RESORT HOTELS	(462.09)	(105.59)	(3.31)	25	25	25	75	25

	Values			Ranks			Total	Overall
	Latest Margin	AV/Pay		Weightings:			Rank	Rank
	Ret on Total Ass.(ROTA)			1	1	1	by	
	A	B	C	A	B	C	Weight	
LEEDS GROUP	15.35	18.01	1.57	2	1	1	4	1
READICUT INTERNAT'L	33.35	12.28	1.43	1	2	3	6	2
ALLIED TEXTILES	10.74	11.49	1.47	3	4	2	9	3
HICKING PENTECOST	9.34	11.93	1.37	4	3	5	12	4
LAMONT HOLDINGS	6.35	5.81	1.39	5	7	4	16	5
COURTAULDS TEXTILES	4.20	7.09	1.31	7	5	6	18	6
COATS VIYELLA	6.16	6.46	1.29	6	6	7	19	7
RICHARDS	(0.10)	(0.29)	1.14	8	8	9	25	8
MARLING INDUSTRIES	(13.41)	(16.28)	1.26	9	9	8	26	9

	Values			Ranks			Total Rank by Weight	Overall Rank
	Latest Margin	AV/Pay		Weightings:				
	Ret on Total Ass.(ROTA)			1	1	1		
	A	B	C	A	B	C		
ROTHMANS INTERNAT'L	21.19	14.96	2.16	2	3	2	7	1
WILLIAMS HOLDINGS	12.66	16.06	1.77	6	2	4	12	2
CHARTER CONSOLIDATED	31.93	30.87	1.42	1	1	12	14	3
BTR	13.10	12.01	1.72	5	5	5	15	4
SUTER	20.44	11.00	1.64	3	7	6	16	5
BAT INDUSTRIES	15.34	5.03	2.21	4	15	1	20	6
WASSALL	9.95	12.48	1.54	8	4	8	20	6
HANSON	10.41	4.22	1.84	7	16	3	26	8
TT GROUP	6.68	11.15	1.47	12	6	10	28	9
LONRHO	8.64	6.77	1.44	9	11	11	31	10
ADWEST	7.39	7.83	1.42	10	10	13	33	11
COOKSON	6.64	6.67	1.49	13	12	9	34	12
TOMKINS	7.22	9.21	1.41	11	9	14	34	12
HARRISONS & CROSF'LD	4.43	6.52	1.57	15	13	7	35	14
STAVELEY INDUSTRIES	6.42	9.97	1.31	14	8	16	38	15
POWELL DUFFRYN	3.53	5.77	1.33	16	14	15	45	16
BIBBY (J) & SONS	0.89	1.48	1.28	17	17	17	51	17
PORTER CHADBURN	0.17	(4.39)	1.25	18	18	18	54	18
SCOTTISH HERITABLE	(23.58)	(9.15)	0.95	20	19	20	59	19
TRAFALGAR HOUSE	(8.95)	(12.71)	0.79	19	20	21	60	20
WHITECROFT	(34.43)	(47.27)	1.11	21	21	19	61	21

	Values			Ranks			Total Rank by Weight	Overall Rank
	Latest Margin	AV/Pay		Weightings:				
	Ret on Total Ass.(ROTA)			1	1	1		
	A	B	C	A	B	C		
POLYPIPE	13.75	17.23	2.15	4	3	2	9	1
HALSTEAD, JAMES	14.75	16.82	1.81	3	4	4	11	2
ALUMASC	17.08	20.68	1.66	2	2	8	12	3
ANGLIAN GROUP	12.62	38.50	1.80	5	1	6	12	3
MB-CARADON	17.60	15.07	1.64	1	5	9	15	5
EPWIN GROUP	9.19	14.58	1.55	8	6	12	26	6
REDLAND	11.30	6.46	1.76	6	14	7	27	7
RUGBY GROUP	8.45	10.52	1.60	11	8	10	29	8
HEPWORTH	8.90	8.99	1.60	10	10	11	31	9
BAGGERIDGE BRICK	6.78	4.09	1.81	13	16	3	32	10
MARSHALLS	9.08	6.98	1.49	9	12	17	38	11
SPRING RAM CORP'N	(15.20)	11.03	1.81	28	7	5	40	12
LILLIESHALL	6.45	9.51	1.45	14	9	18	41	13
RMC GROUP	5.03	7.47	1.54	17	11	13	41	13
RUSSELL, ALEXANDER	4.68	(2.88)	2.17	18	24	1	43	15
BLUE CIRCLE INDUST'S	6.85	4.00	1.51	12	17	15	44	16
BPB INDUSTRIES	6.41	4.24	1.52	15	15	14	44	16
HEYWOOD WILLIAMS GROUP	9.63	2.57	1.21	7	19	24	50	18
NEWMAN TONKS	6.13	6.74	1.28	16	13	22	51	19
MARLEY	(0.18)	1.61	1.39	21	20	19	60	20
PILKINGTON	2.02	1.32	1.28	19	21	21	61	21
NORCROS	(9.92)	2.95	1.37	26	18	20	64	22
EXPAMET	0.01	0.03	1.21	20	22	23	65	23
CRAIG & ROSE	(5.45)	(0.74)	1.05	24	23	27	74	24
ASHLEY GROUP	(1.12)	(5.40)	1.02	22	26	28	76	25
STARMIN	(83.23)	(34.83)	1.51	30	30	16	76	25
BERISFORD INTERNATIONAL	(6.92)	(4.00)	0.53	25	25	30	80	27
HAVELOCK EUROPA	(3.26)	(18.71)	0.95	23	29	29	81	28
IBSTOCK JOHNSEN	(16.99)	(6.77)	1.18	29	27	25	81	28
TARMAC	(11.57)	(13.02)	1.11	27	28	26	81	28

	Values			Ranks			Total	
	Latest Margin	AV/Pay		Weightings:			Rank	Overall
	Ret on Total Ass.(ROTA)			1	1	1	by	Rank
	A	B	C	A	B	C	Weight	
REUTERS	23.53	25.03	2.15	4	2	3	9	1
BARBOUR INDEX	24.01	23.13	2.14	3	4	4	11	2
INT'L BUSINESS COMM'S	71.22	354.45	1.61	1	1	10	12	3
HAYNES PUBLISHING GROUP	18.92	23.31	1.88	7	3	5	15	4
MIRROR GROUP NEWSP'S	27.70	11.68	2.34	2	13	1	16	5
REED ELSEVIER	19.10	12.71	1.87	6	10	6	22	6
NEWS INTERNATIONAL	22.77	1.74	2.27	5	19	2	26	7
UNITED NEWSPAPERS	15.16	15.43	1.64	10	8	9	27	8
METAL BULLETIN	16.52	20.98	1.51	8	6	14	28	9
EMAP	12.94	15.65	1.59	13	7	11	31	10
JOHNSTON PRESS	14.48	22.98	1.50	12	5	15	32	11
HODDER HEADLINE	5.09	14.33	1.83	18	9	7	34	12
TRINITY INT'L HOLD'S	14.85	12.06	1.41	11	11	16	38	13
DORLING KINDERSLEY		11.91	1.71	19	12	8	39	14
STERLING PUBLICATIONS	12.65	10.88	1.56	14	14	13	41	15
DAILY MAIL & GEN' T'ST	9.75	7.28	1.59	15	16	12	43	16
PEARSON	16.30	7.02	1.29	9	17	19	45	17
PORTSMOUTH & SUND'D NEWS'	6.05	9.32	1.32	17	15	18	50	18
BRISTOL EVENING POST	7.25	6.56	1.35	16	18	17	51	19

	Values			Ranks			Total	
	Latest Margin	AV/Pay		Weightings:			Rank	Overall
	Ret on Total Ass.(ROTA)			1	1	1	by	Rank
	A	B	C	A	B	C	Weight	
QS HOLDINGS	12.01	29.69	2.20	4	1	2	7	1
BODY SHOP	12.66	14.09	1.92	2	7	3	12	2
FINE ART DEVELOPM'TS	11.40	14.64	1.85	5	3	5	13	3
BOOTS	9.56	14.49	1.66	6	5	8	19	4
NEXT	13.51	12.26	1.58	1	9	11	21	5
TIE RACK	7.60	14.61	1.63	8	4	9	21	5
LLOYDS CHEMISTS	6.14	14.30	1.69	10	6	6	22	7
WYEVALE GARDEN CENTRES	12.16	6.31	1.66	3	14	7	24	8
FROST GROUP	4.32	12.02	4.91	16	10	1	27	9
COUNTRY CASUALS	6.27	13.51	1.51	9	8	13	30	10
COURTS	5.00	4.75	1.89	12	16	4	32	11
ETAM	5.45	10.65	1.57	11	12	12	35	12
SMITH, W H & SON	4.97	10.60	1.61	13	13	10	36	13
T&S STORES	3.57	19.91	1.43	18	2	16	36	13
MFI FURNITURE GROUP	7.63	4.47	1.33	7	17	19	43	15
MENZIES, JOHN	2.75	10.72	1.41	19	11	18	48	16
MOSS BROS	4.49	5.20	1.28	14	15	20	49	17
CHURCH & CO	4.32	2.96	1.20	15	18	21	54	18
DIXONS	(9.51)	2.68	1.46	24	19	15	58	19
STYLO	2.19	(0.55)	1.41	20	22	17	59	20
WEW GROUP	(1.97)	(4.03)	1.46	22	23	14	59	20
AUSTIN REED	3.67	1.92	1.07	17	20	25	62	22
ASHLEY, LAURA	0.51	0.97	1.15	21	21	24	66	23
SIGNET	(3.77)	(4.32)	1.19	23	24	23	70	24
ALEXON GROUP	(10.81)	(20.39)	1.19	25	25	22	72	25

| | Printed: 08-04-94 | | | STATIC Rankings As at 08-04-94 | | | | Page 1 |
| | | | | Chemicals | | | | |

	Values			Ranks			Total Rank by Weight	Overall Rank
	Latest Margin	AV/Pay		Weightings:				
	Ret on Total Ass.(ROTA)			1	1	1		
	A	B	C	A	B	C		
ALLIED COLLOIDS	12.87	17.65	1.99	3	1	1	5	1
KALON	13.20	15.78	1.72	1	2	6	9	2
LAPORTE	12.25	12.32	1.80	4	5	3	12	3
YORKSHIRE CHEMICALS	11.62	11.54	1.83	6	7	2	15	4
BTP	9.74	11.82	1.68	8	6	7	21	5
PORVAIR	11.64	10.36	1.64	5	10	8	23	6
BOC GROUP	11.01	8.92	1.75	7	13	4	24	7
COURTAULDS	9.55	13.00	1.60	9	4	12	25	8
SCAPA GROUP	13.03	10.36	1.58	2	11	13	26	9
CRODA INTERNATIONAL	9.28	10.43	1.63	10	9	9	28	10
YULE CATTO	8.97	14.99	1.55	13	3	14	30	11
MANDERS	9.18	6.61	1.75	11	17	5	33	12
WOLSTENHOLME RINK	7.72	9.91	1.60	14	12	11	37	13
WARDLE STOREYS	9.12	10.87	1.31	12	8	19	39	14
HICKSON INTERNATI'AL	6.00	6.88	1.60	15	15	10	40	15
BRENT INTERNATIONAL	5.76	7.57	1.26	17	14	21	52	16
BRITISH VITA	4.46	6.76	1.32	18	16	18	52	16
CANNING	2.02	5.73	1.36	20	18	16	54	18
ICI	3.52	4.05	1.44	19	20	15	54	18
MCLEOD RUSSEL HOLD'S	5.83	5.48	1.31	16	19	20	55	20
MTM	(22.39)	(38.16)	1.35	21	21	17	59	21

BIBLIOGRAPHY

Abegglen, J. C. and Stalk, G. (1985) *Kaissha, The Japanese Corporation*, New York: Basic Books.

Ackermann, K-F. (1986) 'A contingency model of HRM strategy. Empirical research findings reconsidered', *Management Forum*, Band 6, pp. 65–83.

Ansoff, H. I. 'Managing Strategic Surprise by response weak signals', *California Management Review*, Vol. XVIII, No. 2, Winter, pp. 21–33.

Armstrong, M. (1992) *Human Resource Management. Strategy and Action*, London: Kogan Page.

Astley, W. G. (1984) 'Subjectivity, sophistry and symbolism in management science', *Journal of Management Studies*.

Atkinson, J. (1985) 'Flexibility: Planning for an uncertain future', *Manpower Policy and Practice* 1, Summer, pp. 25–30.

Bailey, A. and Johnson, G. (1992) 'How strategies develop in organisations' in Faulkner, D. and Johnson, G. (Eds) *The Challenge of Strategic Management*, pp. 147–78, London: Kogan Page.

Baird, C. and Meshoulam, I. (1988) 'Managing two fits of strategic human resource management', *Academy of Management Review*, Vol. 13, No. 1, pp. 116–18.

Bassett, P. (1986) *Strike Free*, London: Macmillan.

Beer, M., Spencer, B., Lawrence, P. R., Quinn Mills, D. and Walton, R. E. (1984) *Managing Human Assets*, New York: Free Press.

Bell, M. (1993) 'Manpower Planning in the TSB Group' in *Human Resource Planning in the Banking Sector Conference Book*, Commission of the European Communities, pp. 109–26.

Berger, P. (1966) *Invitation to Sociology*, London: Penguin.

Berle, A. A. (1954) *The Twentieth Century Capitalist Revolution*, New York: Harcourt Brace.

Berry, J. (1983) 'Review of In Search of Excellence', *Human Resource Management* 22(3), pp. 329–33.

Blauner, R. (1964) *Alienation and Freedom: The factory worker and his industry*, Chicago: University of Chicago Press.

Bowey, A. (1973) *A Guide to Manpower Planning*, London: Macmillan.

Bowman, C. (1992) 'Interpreting Competitive Strategy' in Faulkner, D. and Johnson, G. (Eds) *The Challenge of Strategic Management*, pp. 64–78, London: Kogan Page.

Boxall, P. (1992) 'Strategic Human Resource Management. Beginnings of a new theoretical sophistication', *Human Resource Management Journal*, Vol. 2, No. 3.

Boyatzis, R. E. (1982) *The Competent Manager. A Model of Effective Performance*, Chichester: John Wiley.

Brewster, C. and Bournois, F. (1991) 'Human Resource Management: A European Perspective', *Personnel Review*, Vol. 20, No.6, pp. 4–13.

Brewster, C. and Connock, S. (1987) *Industrial Relations: cost-effective strategies*, London: Hutchinson.

Brewster, C., Gill, C. G. and Richbell, S. (1983) 'Industrial Relations Policy. A Framework for Analysis' in Thurley, K. and Wood, S. (Eds) *Industrial Relations and Management Strategy*, pp. 62–72, Cambridge: Cambridge University Press.

Brödner, P. (1990) 'Technocentric-anthropocentric approaches towards skill-based manufacturing, p. 101, in Warner, M., Wobbe, W. and Brödner, P. (Eds) *New Technology and Manufacturing Management*, Chichester: John Wiley.

Brown, M. L. (1992) *The Symbolic Roles of the Organization Development Consultant*, Working Paper 18, November, Faculty of Administrative Studies, York University, Ontario, Canada.

Bühler, K. (1986) 'The Key Principle: the sign character of language' in Innis, R. (Ed) *Semiotics*, London: Hutchinson.

Buller, P. F. and Napier, N. K. (1993) 'Strategy and Human Resource Management integration in fast growth versus other mid-sized firms', *British Journal of Management*, Vol. 4, No. 2, pp. 77–90.

Bullinger, H. J. (1990) 'Integrated Technical Concepts. Towards the Fully Automated Factory' in Warner, M., Wobbe, W. and Brödner, P. *op. cit.*

Burawoy, M. (1979) *Manufacturing Consent*, Chicago: University of Chicago Press.

Burke, W. W. and Litwin, G. H. (1992) 'A causal model of organisation performance and change', *Journal of Management*, Vol. 18, No. 3, pp. 525–45.

Burnham, J. (1960) *The Managerial Revolution*, Bloomington, Indiana: Indiana University Press.

Burns, T. and Stalker, G. M. (1961) *The Management of Innovation*, London: Tavistock.

Chandler, A. D. Jr. (1962) *Strategy and Structure: Chapters in the History of the Industrial Enterprise*, Cambridge. Mass: MIT Press.

Child, J. (1974) 'Quaker Employers and Industrial Relations', *Sociological Review*, November.

Clark, J. (1993) (Ed) *Human Resource Management and Technical Change*, London: Sage.

Clegg, S. (1990) *Modern organisations: organisation studies in the post-modern world*, London: Sage.

Connock, S. (1991) 'H R Vision', *Managing a Quality Workforce*, London: IPM.

Cresap/BIM (1987) *The Effective Head Office*, report published jointly.

Crichton, A. (1968) *Personnel Management in Context*, London: Batsford.

Crofts, P. (1992) 'New direction for London Underground', *Personnel Management Plus*, Vol. 3, No. 8, August.

Crozier, M. (1964) *The Bureaucratic Phenomenon*, Chicago: University of Chicago Press.

Cummings, L. L. (1983) 'The logics of management', *Academy of Management Review* 8, pp. 582–8.

Cyert, R. M. and March, J. G. (1963) *A Behavioural Theory of the Firm*, New York: Wiley.

Dahrendorf, R. (1959) *Class and Class Conflict in Industrial Society*, London: Routledge & Kegan Paul.

Deal, T. E. and Kennedy, A. A. (1982) *Corporate Cultures*, Reading, Mass.: Addison-Wesley.

Department of Employment (1968) 'Company Manpower Planning', *Manpower Papers*, No.1, HMSO.

Di Maggio, P. J. and Powell, W. W. (1983) 'The iron cage revisited: Institutional isomorphisms and collective rationality in organizational fields', *American Sociological Review* 48, pp. 147–60.

Doherty, N. and Tyson, S. (1993) *Executive Redundancy and Outplacement*, London: Kogan Page.

Doherty, N. and Viney, C. (1993) *Organisational Perspectives on Outplacement*, Human Resource Research Centre, Cranfield University.

Faulkner, D. and Johnson, G. (Eds) (1992) *The Challenge of Strategic Management*, London: Kogan Page.

Fernie, S., Metcalf, D. and Woodland, S. (1994) 'Does HRM Boost Employee–Management, Relations?', *LSE Working Papers* 548.

Firth, R. (1973) *Symbols, Public and Private*, London: George Allen & Unwin.

Fombrun, C. J., Tichy, N. M. and Devanna, M. A. (1984) *Strategic Human Resource Management*, New York: Wiley.

Fox, A. (1974) *Beyond Contract: Work, Power and Trust Relations*, London: Faber.

Goldthorpe, J. H., Lockwood, D., Bechhofer, F. and Platt, J. (1968) *The Affluent Worker: Industrial Attitudes and Behaviour*, Cambridge: Cambridge University Press.

Goold, M. and Campbell, A. (1986) *Strategies and Styles: The Role of the Centre in Managing Diversified Corporations*, Oxford: Blackwell.

Gospel, H. F. (1992) *Markets, Firms and the Management of Labour in Modern Britain*, Cambridge: Cambridge University Press.

Gowler, D. and Legge, K. (1982) 'Status, effort and reward' in Bowey, A. (Ed) *Managing Salary and Wage Systems*, Aldershot: Gower.

Grahl, J. and Teague, P. (1991) 'Industrial Relations Trajectories and European Human Resource Management' in Brewster, C. and Tyson, S. (Eds) *International Comparisons in Human Resource Management*, London: Pitman Publishing.

Gramsci, A. (1971) *Selections from the Prison Notebooks*, London: Lawrence & Wishart.

Greiner, L. E. (1972) 'Evolution and revolution as organisations grow', *Harvard Business Review*, July/August, pp. 37–46.

Grundstein, N. D. (1981) *The Managerial Kant*, Weatherhead School of Management: Case Western Reserve University.

Grundy, T. (1992) *Corporate Strategy and Financial Decisions*, London: Kogan Page.

Guest, D. (1987) 'Human Resource Management and Industrial Relations', *Journal of Management Studies*, Vol. 24, No. 5, September, pp. 503–21.

Guest, D. (1989) 'Personnel and HRM: can you tell the difference?', *Personnel Management*, January.

Guest, D. (1992) 'Right enough to be dangerously wrong: an analysis of the In Search of Excellence phenomenon' in Salaman, G. (Ed) *Human Resource Strategies*, Open University and Sage: London.

Guest, D. and Hoque, K. (1993) 'The Mystery of the Missing Human Resource Manager', *Personnel Management*, June, pp. 40–41.

Habermas, J. (1982) 'A reply to my critics' in Thompson, J. B. and Held, D. (Eds) *Habermas. Critical Debates*, London: Macmillan.

Hamilton, K. (1992), 'RHM bakes a new cake to fight bid', *Sunday Times*, 18 October, p. 5.

Hampden-Turner, C. (1990) *Charting the Corporate Mind*, New York/London: The Free Press/Collier Macmillan.

Handy, C. (1978) *The Gods of Management*, London: Penguin.

Handy, C. (1989) *The Age of Unreason*, Boston: Harvard Business School Press.

Handy, C. (1994) *The Empty Raincoat*, London: Hutchinson.

Harrison, R. (1972) 'How to describe your organization', *Harvard Business Review*.

Hendry, C. (1993) 'Personnel Leadership in Technical and Human Resource Change' in Clark, J., (Ed) *Human Resource Management and Technical Change*, London: Sage.

Hendry, C. (1994) *Human Resource Strategies for International Growth*, London: Routledge.

Hendry, C. and Pettigrew, A. (1990) 'Human Resource Management. An Agenda for the 1990's', *International Journal of Human Resource Management*, Vol. 1, No. 1, pp. 17–43.

Hendry, C. and Pettigrew, A. (1992) 'Patterns of Strategic Change in the Development of Human Resource Management', *British Journal of Management*, Vol. 3, No. 3, September, pp. 137–56.

Hennart, J. F. (1993) 'Control in Multinational Firms: The role of price and hierarchy in organization theory and multinational corporations' in Ghoshal, S. and Westney, D. E. (Eds) *Organizational Theory and the Multinational Corporation*, London: Macmillan.

Herzberg, F., Mausner, B. and Snyderman, B. (1959) *The Motivation to Work*, New York: Wiley.

Hobsbawm, E. J. (1964) *Labouring Men*, London: Weidenfeld & Nicolson.

Hofer, C. and Schendel, D. (1978) *Strategy Formulation: Analytical Concepts*, St. Paul: West Publishing.

Homans, G. C. (1954) 'Industrial Harmony as a goal' in Kornhauser, A., Dubin, R. and Ross, A. M. (Eds) *Industrial Conflict*, New York: McGraw-Hill.

Hudson, R. (1989) 'Labour market changes and new forms of work in old industrial regions', *Environment and Planning Society and Space* 7, pp. 5–30.

Inkson, K. and Coe, T. (1993) *Are career ladders disappearing?*, London: Institute of Management.

Jackson, S. E., Schuler, R. S. and Rivero, J. C. (1989) 'Organizational characteristics as predictors of personnel practices', *Personnel Psychology* 42, pp. 727–86.

Jaques, E. (1976) *A General Theory of Bureaucracy*, London: Heinemann.

Johnson, G. (1987) *Strategic Change and the Management Process*, Oxford: Basil Blackwell.

Kakabadse, A. (1983) *The Politics of Management*, Aldershot: Gower.

Kakabadse, A. (1991) *The Wealth Creators*, London: Kogan Page.

Kanter, R. M. (1983) *The Change Masters*, New York: Simon & Schuster; (1983) London: Allen & Unwin.

Kelly, G. (1955) *The Psychology of Personal Constructs*, Vol. I and II, New York: Norton.

Lash, S. (1988) 'Post-modernism as a regime of signification', *Theory, Culture and Society* 5 (2–3), pp. 311–36.

Lawrence, P. R. and Lorsch, J. W. (1967) *Organization and Environment: Managing Differentiation and Integration*, Boston: Harvard University Press.

Legge, K. (1978) *Power, Innovation and Problem-solving in Personnel Management*, London: McGraw-Hill.

Legge, K. (1988) 'Personnel Management in Recession and Recovery: a comparative analysis of what the surveys say', *Personnel Review*, Vol. 17, November.

Legge, K. (1989) 'Human Resource Management: a critical analysis' in Storey, J. (Ed) *New Perspectives on Human Resource Management*, London: Routledge.

Legge, K. (1993) 'The Role of Personnel Specialists: centrality or marginalization' in Clark, J. (Ed) *Human Resource Management and Technical Change*, London: Sage.

Lengnick-Hall, C. A. and Lengnick-Hall, M. L. (1988) 'A perspective on business strategy and human resource strategy interdependence', *Academy of Management Review*, Vol. 13, No. 3, pp. 454–70.

Likert, R. (1959) 'A motivational approach to a modified theory of organization and management' in Haire, M. (Ed) *Modern Organization Theory*, New York: Wiley.

McGregor, D. (1960) *The Human Side of Enterprise*, New York: McGraw-Hill.

McGregor, D. (1966) *Leadership and Motivation*, Cambridge, Mass.: MIT Press.

McKiddie, T. (1994) 'Personnel NVQs: Preparing for Take-Off', *Personnel Management*, February, pp. 30–3.

Madden, C. A. and Mitchell, V. A. (1993) *Professions, standards and competences. A survey of continuing education in the professions*, University of Bristol.

Miles, R. E. and Snow, C. C. (1978) *Organizational Strategy, structure and process*, New York: McGraw-Hill.

Miles, R. E. and Snow, C. C. (1984) 'Designing Strategic Human Resource Systems', *Organizational Dynamics*, pp. 36–52.

Miller, D. and Friesen, P. H. (1986) 'Porter's (1980) Generic Strategies and Performance: An Empirical Examination with American Data. Part 1 Testing Porter', *Organizational Studies*, Vol. 7, No. 1, pp. 37–55, and 'Part 2 Performance implications', *Organizational Studies*, Vol. 7, No. 3, pp. 255–61.

Miller, E. J. and Rice, A. K. (1967) *Systems of Organisation: The Control of Task and Sentient Boundaries*, London: Tavistock.

Millerson, G. (1964) *The Qualifying Associations*, London: Routledge & Kegan Paul.

Mintzberg, H. (1987) 'Patterns in Strategy Formation', *Management Science*, May, pp. 934–48.

Mitchell, T. (1985) 'In Search of Excellence versus the 100 Best Companies to work for in America: a question of perspectives and value', *Academy of Management Review*, 10(2), pp. 350–5.

Monks, K. (1993) 'Models of Personnel Management: A means of understanding the diversity of personnel practices', *Human Resource Management Journal*, Vol. 3, No. 2, pp. 29–41.

Morgan, G. (1986) *Images of Organization*, London: Sage.

Morgan, G. (1993) *Imaginization*, London: Sage.

Moxon, G. R. (1951) *The Functions of a Personnel Department*, London: Institute of Personnel Management.

Murray, A. I. (1988) 'A contingency view of Porter's Generic Strategies', *Academy of Management Review*, Vol. 13, No. 3, pp. 390–400.

Nichols, T. (1969) *Ownership Control and Ideology*, London: George Allen & Unwin.

Niven, M. (1967) *Personnel Management 1913–1963*, London: IPM.

Norburn, D. and Birley, S. (1988) 'Top Management Teams and Corporate Performance', *Strategic Management Journal* 9, pp. 225–37.

Offe, C. (1985) *Disorganized Capitalism*, Cambridge: Polity Press in association with Basil Blackwell.

O'Toole, J. (1985) 'Employee practices at the best managed companies', *California Management Review*, Vol. XXVIII, No. 1, pp. 35–66.

Peters, T. (1987) *Thriving in Chaos: Handbook for a Management Revolution*, New York: Knopf.

Peters, T. and Waterman, R. (1982) *In Search of Excellence*, New York: Harper & Row.

Pettigrew, A. and Whipp, R. (1991) *Managing change for competitive success*, Oxford: Blackwell.

Pfeffer, J. (1981) 'Management as symbolic action: the creation and maintenance of organizational paradigms', *Research in Organizational Behaviour*, Vol. 3, pp. 1–52.

Pickard, J. (1992) 'We've had the bottle to change, says Calor Gas', *Personnel Management Plus*, Vol. 3, No. 9, September.

Porter, M. (1980) *Competitive Strategy*, New York: The Free Press/Macmillan.

Pugh, D. S., Hickson, D. J. and Hinings, C. R. (1969) 'The context of organisation structures', *Administrative Science Quarterly*, Vol.14, March, pp. 91–114.

Purcell, J. (1989) 'The impact of corporate strategy on human resource management' in Storey, J. (Ed) *New Perspectives on Human Resource Management*, London: Routledge.

Purcell, J. (1994) 'Personnel earns a place on the board', *Personnel Management*, February, pp. 26–9.

Radcliffe-Brown, A. R. (1952) *Structure and Function in Primitive Society*, London: Cohen and West.

Reader, W. J. (1975) *Imperial Chemical Industries*, Oxford: Oxford University Press.

Ritzer, G. and Trice, H. M. (1969) *An occupation in conflict. A study of the personnel manager*, Cornell: Cornell University.

Saunders, J., Brown, M. and Lavernick, S. (1992) 'Research notes on the Best British Companies: A Peer Evaluation of Britain's Leading Firms', *British Journal of Management*, Vol. 3, Issue 4, pp. 181–95.

Schön, D. A. (1983) *The Reflective Practitioner*, New York: Basic Books.

Schön, D. A. (1987) *Educating the Reflective Practitioner*, San Francisco: Jossey-Bass.

Schuler, R. S. (1987) 'Personnel and human resource management choices and organizational strategy', *Human Resources Planning*, Vol. 10, pp. 1–17.

Schuler, R. S. and Jackson, S. E. (1987) 'Linking competitive strategies with human resource management practices', *Academy of Management Executive* 1.3.

Schuler, R. S. and Jackson, S. E. (1987) 'Organizational strategy and organizational level as determinants of HRM practice', *Human Resource Planning*, Vol. 10, No. 3, pp. 125–41.

Schumacher, E. F. (1973) *Small is Beautiful*, London: Blond and Briggs.

Schutz, A. (Wagner, H. (Ed)) (1970) *On Phenomenology and Social Relations*, Chicago: University of Chicago Press.

Senge, P. (1990) *The Fifth Discipline*, London: Century Business.

Sharma, S., Netermeyer, R. and Majajan, V. (1990) 'In Search of Excellence Revisited: An Empirical Evaluation of Peters' and Waterman's Attributes of Excellence', *Proceedings of the American Marketing Association Education Conference*, Chicago, Vol. 1, pp. 322–7.

Silverman, D. (1970) *The Theory of Organisations*, London: Heinemann.

Smith, A. R. (Ed) (1976) 'Manpower Planning in the Civil Service', *Civil Service Studies 3*, London: HMSO.

Starkey, K. and McKinlay, A. (1993) *Strategy and the Human Resource*, Oxford: Blackwell.

Stewart, R. (1984) 'The Nature of Management? A Problem for Management Education', *Journal of Management Studies* 21.3, pp. 323–30.

Storey, J. (Ed) (1989) *New Perspectives on Human Resource Management*, London: Routledge.

Storey, J. (1992) *Developments in the Management of Human Resources*, Oxford: Blackwell.

Thompson, J. D. (1967) *Organizations in Action*, New York: McGraw-Hill.

Thurley, K. (1983) 'How transferable is the Japanese industrial relations system? Some implications of a study of industrial relations and personnel policies of Japanese firms in Western Europe', *Paper at the 6th World Congress of International Industrial Relations Association*, Kyoto, 28–31 March.

Thurley, K. and Wood, S. (Eds) (1983) *Industrial Relations and Management Strategy*, Cambridge: Cambridge University Press.

Tofler, A. (1980) *The Third Wave*, London: Pan Books.

Tonnies, F. (1955) *Community and Association*, London: Routledge & Kegan Paul.

Trist, E. L. *et al.* (1963) *Organisational Choice*, London: Tavistock.

Tyson, S. (1979) *Specialists in Ambiguity*, unpublished PhD thesis, University of London.

Tyson, S. (1980) 'Taking advantage of ambiguity', *Personnel Management*, February, p. 45.

Tyson, S. (1983) 'Personnel Management in its organisational context' in Thurley, K. and Wood, S. (Eds) *Industrial Relations and Management Strategy*, Cambridge: Cambridge University Press.

Tyson, S. (1987) 'The Management of the Personnel Function', *Journal of Management Studies*, Vol. 24, No. 5, September, pp. 523–32.

Tyson, S. (1988) 'The dilemmas of Civil Service Personnel Management', *Personnel Management*, September, pp. 49–53.

Tyson, S., Ackermann, K-F., Domsch, M. and Joynt, P. (1988) *Appraising and Exploring Organisations*, Beckenham: Croom Helm.

Tyson, S. and Fell, A. (1986) *Evaluating the Personnel Function*, London: Hutchinson.

Tyson, S. and Fell, A. (1992) *Evaluating the Personnel Function* (2nd Edition), Cheltenham: Stanley Thornes.

Tyson, S. and Jackson, T. (1992) *The Essence of Organisational Behaviour*, Hemel Hempstead: Prentice Hall.

Tyson, S. and Kakabadse, A. (Eds) (1987) *Cases in Human Resource Management*, London: Heinemann.

Tyson, S., Lawrence, P., Poirson, P., Manzoline, L. and Vicente, C. S. (Eds) (1993) *Human Resource Management in Europe*, London: Kogan Page.

Tyson, S. and Wikander, L. (1994) 'The Education and Training of Human Resource Managers in Europe' in Brewster, C. and Hegewisch, A. (Eds) *Policy and Practice in European Human Resource Management*, London: Routledge.

Tyson, S. and Witcher, M. (1994) 'Human Resource Strategy: Emerging from the Recession', *Personnel Management*, August.

Tyson, S. and York, A. (1982) *Personnel Management*, Oxford: Heinemann.

van Houten, G. (1989) 'The implications of globalism: New management realities in Philips' in Evans, P., Doz, Y. and Laurent, A. (Eds) *Human Resource Management in International Firms*, London: Macmillan.

von Clausewitz, C. (1949) *On War*, Vol. III, London: Routledge & Kegan Paul.

Wächter, H. (1973) *Grundlagen der Langfristigen Personalplanning*, Berlin: Herne.

Walker, C. J. and Guest, R. H. (1952) *The Man on the Assembly Line*, Cambridge: Harvard.

Walker, J. W. (1977) 'Linking Human Resources Planning and Strategic Planning', a paper presented at XIII International Meeting of the Institute of Management Sciences, Athens, August.

Wallbank, F. W. (1981) *The Hellenistic World*, London: Fontana.

Watkins, J., Drury, L. and Preddy, D. (1992) 'From Evolution to Revolution. The pressures in professional life in the 1990s', Bristol: University of Bristol.

Watson, T. J. (1977) *The Personnel Managers*, London: Routledge & Kegan Paul.

Weber, M. (1947) *The Theory of Social and Economic Organisations*, New York: The Free Press.

Westney, D. E. (1993) 'Institutionalization Theory and the Multinational Corporation' in Ghosal, S. and Westney, D. E. (Eds) *Organization Theory and the Multinational Corporation*, London: Macmillan.

Whitaker, A. (1992) 'The Transformation in Work. Post-Fordism revisited' in Reed, M. and Hughes, M. (Eds) *Rethinking Organizations*, London: Sage.

Wickens, P. (1987) *The Road to Nissan. Flexibility, Quality, Teamwork*, London: Macmillan.

Wilensky, H. (1964) 'The professionalization of everyone?', *American Journal of Sociology*, Vol. 70, pp. 138–58.

Williamson, O. E. (1973) 'Markets and hierarchies: some elementary considerations', *American Economic Review* LXIII, pp. 316–25.

Williamson, O. E. and Ouchi, W. G. (1983) 'The markets and hierarchies programme of research: origins, implications and prospects' in Francis, A., Turk, J. and Willman, P. (Eds) *Power, Efficiency and Institutions*, London: Hcinemann.

Winter, G. (1966) *Elements for a Social Ethic*, New York: Macmillan.

Wood, S. (1989) (Ed) *The Transformation of Work*, London: Unwin.

Woodward, J. (1958) *Management and Technology*, London: HMSO.

Woodward, J. (1965) *Industrial Organization Theory and Practice*, Oxford: Oxford University Press.

Zajac, E. J. and Shortell, S. M. (1989) 'Changing generic strategies: Likelihood, directions and performance implications', *Strategic Management Journal*, Vol. 10, pp. 413–30.

Zucker, L. G. (1987) 'Institutional Theories of Organization', *Annual Review of Sociology* 13, pp. 443–64.

INDEX